See Bloody Mary recipe

D0820464

THE INDEPENDENT COOK

JEREMY ROUND

THE INDEPENDENT COOK

Strategies for seasonal cooking

ILLUSTRATIONS BY MICHAEL DALEY

BARRIE & JENKINS

LONDON

First published in Great Britain in 1988 by
Barrie & Jenkins Ltd
289 Westbourne Grove, London W11 2QA

British Library Cataloguing in Publication Data

Round, Jeremy
The independent cook: strategies for
seasonal cooking.
1. Food – Recipes
I. Title
641.5

ISBN 0 7126 2195 4

Typeset by SX Composing Ltd, Rayleigh, Essex
Printed and bound in
Great Britain at the
University Printing House, Oxford

DEDICATED TO MY MOTHER AND FATHER,
COOK AND EATER

Contents

ACKNOWLEDGEMENTS

Material for this book has been gathered from many sources. The author is particularly grateful for the assistance of Michael Day and the staffs of the British Food Information Service of Food From Britain and the Fresh Fruit and Vegetable Information Service. Special thanks are due to Hilly Janes, Henrietta Green, illustrator Michael Daley, editor Vicky Hayward for her hard work and clear thinking and, above all, Jeremy Trevathan for his constant support.

INTRODUCTION

Seasonal strategies

SHOPPING SEASONALLY

This book grew out of a series of articles, originally called 'The Month in the Kitchen', which I wrote in an attempt to discover when and why fresh foods were at their best – by which I mean most delicious.

Many people would argue that such a seasonal approach to food has become outdated. Developments in the retail scene have had an extraordinary effect on food shopping over the last couple of decades: half the market is now controlled by the five biggest supermarket chains, whose massive buying power has altered patterns of British production and food imports out of all recognition. Their professed aim is to offer ever wider choice and better quality.

Likewise, ask top chefs about seasonal foods and, putting aside a few obvious examples of some soft fruits, shellfish and game, most will tell you that fast, international supply lines and modern storage techniques mean that they can obtain almost anything throughout the year. Nowadays, fresh raspberries adorn hot soufflés in January as well as ice-creams in July; scallops and asparagus pop up together in late summer mille-feuilles as often as they do separately in their different official seasons.

To a certain extent, the chefs have a point because they often have access to specialist suppliers who make sure they are getting the best of what's coming into the country or being grown in special conditions here. Their white currants in December may be better than the ones the rest of us can buy in the height of the season from our local greengrocer, if we can buy them at all. And to a certain extent, yearning for the 'good old days' of the six-week pea season is more a comment on the whimsy of eighties' nostalgia than a realistic alternative to modern market forces.

But the fact remains that fresh produce, as sold to the domestic consumer, changes seasonally – even from week to week – to a remarkable degree, despite the stated intentions of the largest retailers to regularise supplies and destroy seasonality. This was brought home to me again and again during the year in which I wrote the articles.

Take fruit as an example. Strawberries are now offered for ten months of the year from more than half a dozen different countries. But, for flavour, nothing comes close to the English outdoor-grown strawberries that can only be found for perhaps ten weeks. And seasonality applies equally to new exotica. Flagship branches of supermarkets are often keen to offer tamarillos, loquats and the like, but apply little real care in selecting them. So the adventurous customer can end up buying a nasty, sour, unripe specimen, hating it, thinking this is what the fruit is like – and never buying another.

This is the crunch. Most food exporters, producers and retailers care very little about an item's eating quality as against it's 'eye-appeal' and ability to keep. Many characterful and tasty varieties never see the neon light of supermarket-shelf day because they aren't particularly glamorous to look at and start to go off in a day or two, or cannot be produced in large or consistent enough quantities. So, for example, you have little chance of coming across sorrel or medlars unless you grow or gather them yourselves.

Underlying this attitude is an assumption that taste is subjective and that there is no point in assessing products for their eating quality. Astonishingly, this affects the whole food business – from gigantic national concerns, such as the citrus trade in Israel or the tomato trade in the Netherlands, to the buyers for individual supermarket chains. This is why it is so important that we learn to make judgements about eating quality ourselves.

Knowing when things are in their best season is the first step. Added bonuses to products being at their best are that they tend to be more plentiful, readily available and reasonably priced. This can apply as much to sharon fruit from Israel or mangoes from Venezuela as to broad beans or new potatoes from our own back yards.

This naturally leads on to knowing where to find good produce. In some cases it can be bought from local chain supermarkets. But in many fields, the supermarkets are in fact limiting choice by enforcing standards that are to do more with shelf-life, regular size and colour than, for example, flavour. Yes, you can get apples for 365 days a year, but these days the choice is usually red or green – the 600 or so traditional varieties of English apple that had distinct tastes and perfumes make rarer and rarer appearances.

Curiously, British-run delicatessens and health stores are not much help. With rare and notable exceptions, they concentrate on dried, canned and otherwise preserved items marketed with, in the case of delicatessens, a post-war attitude to non-staple food as 'gourmet fancy goods', and, in that of health food stores, a more-holistic-than-thou zeal to ignore flavour and pleasure for the betterment of the soul. Foreign-run delis suffer no such inhibitions on the whole – especially those in the hands of Italians, French or Spaniards, which often also offer delicious ranges of freshly pre-pared dishes to take-out and eat at home.

The first places to try are the traditional, specialist small retailers – greengrocers, fishmongers, butchers and the like. Until recently, it seemed that town-centre rates, lack of convenient parking, short-age of resources to train staff and the customer's love of one-stop shopping were tolling the death knell for them. But in the last few years, the tide has begun to turn. It seems that the British consumer is beginning to look for quality and service rather than cheapness.

There are other sources to search out too: specialist shops serving specific ethnic communities, which often offer real choice in their sometimes unfamiliar ranges of produce; farm-gate sales direct from producers themselves, especially those who concentrate on a specialist range of, for example, fresh herbs or stone-ground flour; local markets, including the excellent Women's Institute markets all over the country; finally, mail-order suppliers, particularly use-ful for cheeses and smoked products. There are now several guides to these 'alternative' suppliers available in most bookshops.

COOKING SEASONALLY

If there is any one over-riding strategy that I would like you to take away from this book, it is hardly to plan meals in advance at all. Good eating is based on good shopping. If you decide what you are going to cook before you go shopping, you may just be lucky in finding that every shop you visit has exactly what you need in prime condition. But more often, you will find yourself having to put up with at least a degree of second or third-best in order to fit your plan. Instead, go out to shop with a clear idea of good produce you can expect to find, using the monthly shopping lists as a guide, and have one or two flexible schemes floating around in your head, then adjust them to fit the very best of what is available.

The recipes here simply offer a starting point, an extra round or two of ammunition for your own assault on each day's market. Some of the recipes within a chapter can be juggled to make complete meals, occasionally along a particular theme, but this is not how the book is supposed to be used. I reckon following one recipe is quite enough for any meal.

Most of the recipes given are seasonal in that their main characteristic ingredients are available in good condition during the month in which the recipes appear. These can obviously be prepared with equal success during any other time of the year when the same range of prime produce is around. I have also tried as far as possible to match the moods of dishes and seasons: for example, richer, stodgier food for colder, dark, wintery months.

Accepting that hardly anyone ever comes up with a totally new recipe, I claim no great originality for the ones I give here. The cookery books I like best are anthologies collating recipes from people, meals eaten in various circumstances, current books, culinary trends and so on; in other words, tried and trusted favourites. In this sense, the book is a personal approach to ingredients and styles of cooking that I like rather than any kind of reference work. The inherent cast of my particular appetites means that it boils down to something like a collection of comfort foods, with a perhaps disproportionate emphasis on some of my favourite ingredients, such as potatoes, garlic, pork and offal.

About a third of the recipes have been gathered on travels in various countries, particularly Turkey, where I lived for a while; a smaller third are collected from chefs and books, sometimes heavily adapted and sometimes not; the final third I would in some way consider my own. Of course, this is always a tricky area; the problem with good recipes is that once you've cooked them with a few personal twists and liked them, they tend to get absorbed into your repertoire and so you come to assume some sense of proprietorship over them. (American home-cooks are the worst at this, always anxious to be begged for details of their buttermilk biscuits or smirking slyly about the secret ingredient in their butterscotch frosting.) But in any case, the recipes are not supposed to be definitive; they are intended as much to jog your own ideas.

Less than a quarter of the recipes require you to like red meat and almost half are for vegetarians, including twenty-five or so for vegans. The balance is in poultry, game and fish.

ENTERTAINING SEASONALLY

Unless you are a real cookery fiend, the business of preparing special food for six to eight people can take away much of the joy of seeing them. Of the many solutions to this problem, eschew any that rely on the culinary shorts cuts, convenience substitutes and other such kitchen indolence fostered by books entitled *Elegant Dinner Parties in Seconds*, *Budgetwise Microwave Entertaining* or the like. Do not be misled. The real answer to the problem, strategically sneaky without being mean, is to arrange all the dinners you might want to give in the year in tight little seasonal clusters just a few days apart. Late spring/early summer and mid-autumn are particularly good times for exciting seasonal produce. This has the following advantages:

1. All the rearranged furniture, flowers, extra glasses and so on can stay out for the whole period of each group of dinners, thereby causing much less palaver than digging out everything afresh at extended intervals.

2. More or less the same menu can be served at the dinners within each cluster. That way, you really get on top of the minutiae of putting the thing together, as in performing a play night after night. Timing the vegetables and so on becomes second nature and you hone each recipe until you understand it fully and get it exactly as you want it. Less perishable items, such as the robuster elements of the cheese board, can be recycled; as decent selections of cheese can come expensive, this means the range of cheeses and number of whole specimens can be more lavish. More obviously, serving the same, or very similar, menus also cuts down on the number of shopping expeditions, although all fresh ingredients must be bought on the day of each party to show at their best.

3. Items such as elaborate salad dressings, home-made chocolate

truffles and so on can be made up in one big initial batch to serve for all the dinners.

To produce a really handsome dinner without too much effort, spend as much as you can on the quality of peripheral courses and main ingredients, but only plan one of the courses to require cooking on the night.

For larger 'duty' parties, the kind given reluctantly under peer pressure in, for example, the peak season Christmas burst of hospitality, there are a few basic cynic's rules to ensure that guests depart after no more than a couple of hours.

1. Give them at odd times such as 11am, 5pm or after the cinema.

2. Ensure that there are at least twice as many guests as there are chairs or floor-space.

3. Never give any choice of food. The dish you serve should be slightly difficult to eat and rather rich. Energy and appetite will soon flag (see December for four ideas matching food and drink in this way).

4. The only choice of drinks should be between a relatively numbing and sticky alcoholic concoction for non-drivers and a non-alcoholic version of the same thing (or as close as you can get) for all other guests. Prepare roughly equivalent quantities of each, then juggle the jugs if the alcoholic is disappearing too quickly.

5. Present all the food and drink together as the party starts. Then you will be free to join in and, as the food cools and the drink warms, a natural end to the proceedings will declare itself. If people want more, you can always suggest they reserve a table for you all in half an hour's time at the local Indian.

The Store Cupboard

While it may be obvious that the excellence of fresh ingredients can transform a dish, it is worth restating that quality is also an important factor when choosing dried, canned, frozen or otherwise preserved items. The difference between ordinary supermarket canned sardines in unspecified vegetable oil and a fine French, Portuguese or Italian brand in olive oil can be immense. Even when using packet goods as a relatively minor component of a dish, significant advantage is often to be gained from not merely making do with inferior "economy" labels.

The other important point is that preserved goods may have a longer shelf-life than fresh produce, but this is hardly ever indefinite. Oils go rancid, tinned vegetables eventually ferment, flour loses its virtue, frozen items leach flavour, dried pulses, legumes, pasta, rice and other cereals go stale. Having these things in store tends to mean that we forget how old they are. Keep an eye out for signs of tiredness and anguish. Replace items regularly rather than risk ruining a dish.

Here is a list of essentials, useful standbys and a few extra treats, such as the smoked oysters.

Anchovies. Tins of fillets in oil for ordinary use; packed in dry salt (always rinse well) for best flavour.

Angostura Bitters. For pink gins, stews, braises and marinades.

Artichoke Hearts. Frozen or canned stand-by. Use in casseroles, pizzas, paellas and so on.

Asparagus. Canned for secret snacks.

Baking Powder. Cream of tartar, bicarbonate of soda, baking powder.

Beans. Dried red kidney, white haricot, butter and flageolets; canned borlotti, cannellini and flageolets.

Beer and Cider. For carbonnades and instead of wine in northern European and some American dishes.

Broad Beans. Frozen stand-by.

Broccoli. Frozen stand-by.

Capers. Jars in brine for ordinary use; packed in dry salt for specially fresh and intense flavour (always rinse well before use).

Chickpeas. Dried and canned.

Chilli Oil. Oriental flavoured oil; use to jazz up stir-fries and the like or, particularly good, mix with sesame oil and groundnut oil for dribbling over steamed fish.

Cocoa Powder. To drink and for cakes etc.

Cooking Chocolate. Bitter. To add richness and depth to some savoury sauces (especially Latin American), as well as for dessert use.

Couscous. Pre-cooked (most sorts available here are, even if the packet doesn't say so).

Cracked Wheat. called variously bulgar, boulghoul and many variations – a good alternative to rice.

Dried Fruit. Prunes, apricots, pears, apples, figs, dates and so on. Apart from soaking to reconstitute and eat straight, also useful chopped in cake and bread mixes and as a constituent of savoury dishes, especially braises and stuffings.

Flour. Plain white, strong white for bread, chappati flour (fine, semi-whole meal), maize flour (corn meal), cornflour.

Fruit in Alcohol. Especially prunes in Armagnac. A great stand-by instant pudding (served with thick cream and delicate biscuits).

Golden Syrup. Or corn syrup, for making pecan pie.

Harissa. Fiery North African paste. Dilute with stock or water to use as a condiment with cous cous and for marinades etc.

Herbs. Dried bay, mint, oregano, rosemary, sage and thyme. Generally useful only for very savoury dishes which are cooked long and slow, marinades and so on.

Honey. Clear, runny, delicate acacia or herby Hymetus. For marinades, meat glazes and used sparingly as a flavouring in salad dressings and other savoury dishes. Also for cakes and puddings, the easiest being thick Greek yoghurt, chilled, dribbled with honey and sprinkled with toasted almonds.

Horseradish Sauce. Not cream. Apart from its usual role as the essential condiment with roast beef and hearty smoked fish, this is the secret to the success of a really good Bloody Mary. Posh store cupboards also keep a tube of green Japanese *Wasabi* horseradish (or the dry powder mix) to eat with sashimi.

Lentils. Green, brown, orange and the best tasting, *lentilles du Puy*.

Lime Pickle. Hot Indian condiment, addictive to those with a taste for sour, salty, spicy-hot things.

Mange-Tout Peas. Frozen stand-by.

Mango Chutney. Indian condiment, useful for sweetening savoury sauces when necessary.

Mustard. Dry English, jars of Dijon.

Nut Oils. Groundnut (peanut) as the best multi-purpose bland cooking and salad oil, useful when other ingredients are delicate or you don't want to cloud a particular flavour combination; hazelnut and walnut used sparingly in distinctively dressed salads, often in combination with a bland filler such as groundnut (both go rancid quite quickly after opening, so buy in small bottles and keep in the fridge).

Nuts and Seeds. Pine kernels (or pine nuts) for grinding to thicken Middle Eastern sauces, adding to stuffings and salads, or garnishing dishes; almonds for thickening, flavouring and garnishes; hazelnuts for toasting and grinding to use in cakes, meringues and the like; sesame seeds for flavouring, sprinkling on to baked items before cooking and garnishes. All these develop an especially good flavour when toasted. Toasted sesame, ground and mixed with a quarter or fifth the volume of salt, makes an excellent everyday condiment.

Okra. Dried (brought back from Middle Eastern holidays); good in stews. Available in some Turkish shops here.

Olive Oil. Pure, for cooking and bland salad dressings; best quality, fruity; cold-pressed extra-virgin for seasoning and more assertive salads; keep unpalatably harsh, 'hot', throat-grasping virgin or extra-virgin olive oil (the different grades refer to the degree of acidity) to use sparingly in cooked dishes, especially braises and bakes, or for rubbing roasts before cooking.

Olives. Vacuum-packed Greek black; jars of the tiny, sweet Niçoise black in brine; tins of Spanish olives stuffed with anchovy; jars of cocktail olives stuffed with pimentos for martinis; jars of green Spanish manzanilla in brine (after opening, float a slice of lemon on top and keep in the fridge for up to two months). Drained olives marinated in olive oil with fresh herbs, garlic and perhaps a splash of wine, make a good nibble with drinks.

Pasta. Italian brands such as de Cecco and Barilla.

Peanut Butter. Crunchy. High-energy snack, especially when eaten in a sliced white bread sandwich also spread thickly with jam.

Peas. Dried yellow split, frozen petits pois and bottled French petits pois.

Peppercorns. Black, for grinding freshly into almost everything and as an everyday condiment; white, which is hotter but less aromatic, essential to the balance of flavouring in some dishes and also used for grinding freshly into dishes the appearance of which would be spoiled by black flecks; canned green in tins for sauces; mixed peppercorns, usually including black, white, green, red *baie rose* and allspice (or Jamaican peppercorns), great for stocks, sauces, marinades and grinding on to steaks before or after grilling.

Phyllo Pastry. Frozen.

Pickles. Cucumber (dill pickle), gherkins, samphire, walnuts.

Pimentos. Cans of red, roasted or unroasted, for braises and pizzas.

Rice. Long-grain, short-grain, Italian risotto (arborio), Spanish paella, basmati, whole-grain and wild (not really a rice at all).

Rice Wine. For pepping up stir-fries; substitute dry sherry in Chinese and other oriental dishes if you don't have it.

Salt. Maldon sea salt, for cooking and as an everyday condiment; crumble it on with your fingers or use it in the right sort of mill (the wrong sort, designed for hard crystals, will clog if used with Maldon).

Salt Cod. From Iberian, Italian, Greek or West Indian shops.

Sardines. In olive oil, the more expensive the better.

Sauerkraut. canned or jarred.

Sesame Oil. Used sparingly to season oriental-ish dishes such as stir-fries just before serving; not good for cooking.

Smoked Oysters and Mussels. Canned in hideous oil, which needs draining off very thoroughly. Good on hot toast.

Soy Sauce. Light and dark.

Spices. The ideal is to buy whole in small quantities as required and then grind, if necessary, just before use. I also keep allspice (whole and ground), caraway (whole), cardamom pods, chilli powder (various proprietary mixtures, mostly for making chilli con carne), whole chilli peppers (various sorts, dried whole and powdered, including cayenne), cinnamon (sticks and powdered), cloves (whole), coriander (whole, the ground too rapidly becomes flavourless), cumin (whole and ground), fennel (whole), five-spice powder (for Chinese cooking), ginger (powdered for cakes and baking), juniper berries, nigella (black onion seed for sprinkling over breads before baking), nutmegs (whole, in their own mill-grater), paprika (whole dried Spanish varieties and various powdered sorts), poppy seed (for sprinkling over breads before baking, and cooking in some Indian dishes), saffron (authenticated, expensive Spanish in tiny phials), star anise (whole for Chinese cooking), turmeric (powdered).

Spinach. Frozen stand-by, the whole leaf not the chopped.

Spirits. Eaux de vie, such as *vielle prune*, *poire william* and *framboise*, good for scenting custards, frangipanes and cakes; useful liqueurs which add a distinctive flavour to fruit dishes and puddings include Amaretto, Benedictine, Calvados, Cointreau, Grand Marnier and kirsch.

Sugar. Caster, granulated and demerara.

Tabasco Sauce. To add bite to almost everything.

Tomatoes. Sun-dried and packed in jars with olive oil.

Tomato Ketchup. For chips and non-purist toasted bacon sandwiches. Also used secretly in tiny amounts to give kick and colour to some sauces. The most delicious use is mixed to taste with horseradish, Worcester, Tabasco, lemon juice, black pepper and olive oil as the authentic New Orleans-style dip for raw oysters.

Tomato Purée. For sparing use in some dishes to underpin the flavour rather than act by itself; without care, it can be crudely overwhelming.

Treacle. Black.

Tuna. In olive or soya oil, the more expensive the better.

Turkish Delight. Rose-scented and pistachio. The best, from Haci Bekir in Istanbul, is now available in this country. Stores well. Great chewed with strong black coffee after a meal.

Vanilla Essence. Not the cheaper vanilla flavouring.

Vinegar. Old sherry, red wine, white wine, balsamic, cider and tarragon for salads, marinades, sauces and so on; spirit for pickling; speciality vinegars such as raspberry, garlic, champagne, etc, always look nice in the shop, but I find that I use them very rarely.

Water Chestnuts. Canned, for chopping and adding crunch to stuffings; especially good whole, when threaded on to skewers with chunks of chicken liver wrapped in smoked bacon and grilled.

Wild Funghi. Especially dried or bottled porcini (ceps or boletus) and morels, and jars of Spanish black truffles in their own juice.

Wine. As long as you boil off the alcohol, wine improves many savoury sauces, stews, braises and so on. Also useful in marinades and instead of vinegar in salad dressings.

Worcestershire Sauce. Rescues almost anything savoury from blandness. (Vegetarians should beware its inclusion in apparently nonmeat dishes as most brands contain anchovies.)

Yeast. Dried.

Utensils

The best policy is to buy as expensive as you can afford, slowly building a small *batterie* of indispensable items as you experiment with new recipes and extend your repertoire of techniques. Making do with cheap utensils is as false an economy in kitchenware as it is in shoes.

The first 21 headings below cover the most essential basic items; the rest are listed in order of usefulness (a personal view, of course).

ESSENTIAL BASIC ITEMS

Knife. Large, well balanced, sharpenable, stainless-steel cook's knife with at least a 7in-9in blade. The blade metal should be fully washable (not wooden). For safety and ease of use, this should be kept razor sharp.

Steel. To sharpen the knife every time you use it. The shop assistant or your butcher should show you how; there is no mystique, just an easily acquired knack.

Chopping board. Large, heavy wooden, or professional white plastic board, which can be scrubbed and dried.

Stirrer. Perhaps the item you will use most. Some people like a flexible, heat-resistant spatula, others a slotted spoon, wooden spatula or one of many variations. The most convenient are ones that can be used for frying as well as mixing and stirring boiling liquids. Mine is a horrible plastic-handled flexible slotted-spoon coated with non-stick material. Other types retain the flavour of what was last stirred more readily, even after washing, so you may want to keep at least two on the go, with one reserved only for delicate dishes such as custards and sweet sauces.

Pans. A non-stick milk saucepan for milk, sauces and small quantities; a medium-sized to large medium-weight aluminium or stainless-steel saucepan with lid for boiling vegetables and heating larger quantities of liquid; a heavy, enamelled cast-iron medium-sized to large saucepan with lid and ovenproof handle for frying, browning, sautéeing, stewing, braising, sweating, simmering and so on.

Casserole. Large, heavy, lidded, flameproof, preferably enamelled cast-iron round or oval casserole for everything from frying and pot-roasting to stewing and braising.

Frying Pan. Large, heavy, preferably non-stick cast-iron with lid and high enough sides for sautéing chicken joints and the like.

Grill Pan. With rack.

Roasting Tin. With rack, the more substantial the better.

Baking Sheet. The more substantial the better.

Mixing Bowls. Large, medium-sized and small heat-proof glass or white-ware. The large one doubles as a salad bowl.

Colander. Stainless steel is best.

Sieves. Fine nylon for sifting, coarser metal for draining and sieving.

Wooden Spoons. For mixing.

Swivel-Headed Vegetable Peeler. For carrots, potatoes and so on.

Kitchen Scales. Any sort you like.

Measuring Jug. Preferably heat-proofed glass.

Spoons. Teaspoon and tablespoon for measuring.

Oven Gloves.

Corskscrew.

Can Opener. With bottle-opener in handle.

Salt and Pepper Mills. Also mills for coriander, sesame salt, nutmeg, mixed peppercorns, white pepper and so on, if you use enough.

Heat Diffuser Mat. To maintain low even temperatures if you have an electric hob.

Steamers. Preferably substantial, lidded, stainless-steel, the right size to fit snugly on the rim of one of your saucepans. Tiered sets are the ultimate. Also Chinese rattan steamer baskets.

Wire Balloon Whisks. For beating the maximum amount of air into cream, egg whites and so on.

Salad Spinner. Plastic and easy to wash.

Pestle and Mortar. Heavy, fine, white stone ware.

Small Vegetable Knife.

Gratin Dishes. Preferably flame-proof, enamelled cast-iron.

Wok. Only if you have a good gas hob.

Food Processor and Liquidiser. You need both: the former is more adaptable and makes brilliant pastry, the latter gives purées and soups a smoother texture.

Flan Rings, Cake Tins, Tart Tins and Pie Dishes.

Griddle. Heavy cast-iron plate for placing over a gas ring to convert it into a surface suitable for griddling steaks, fish, vegetables and so on.

Serrated Fruit Knife. Stainless steel. Good for peeling oranges easily in one go – inner membrane and all.

Grater. Preferably square and stainless-steel.

Lemon Squeezer.

Kitchen Scissors. For opening packets and snipping herbs.

Fish Slice. For carefully picking up fried eggs, poached fish fillets and so on.

Slotted Spoon. For removing solid bits from their stock or sauce and draining things as you serve them.

Carving Fork. With finger-guard.

Carving Knife.

Bread Knife.

Ramekins and Soufflé Dishes.

Paella Pan.

Filleting Knife. With thin flexible blade.

Poultry Shears. For snipping through bones and joints.

Rubber Spatula. For cleaning out mixing bowls.

Pastry Brush.

Gravy Jug. With two spouts, one from the top and one from the bottom, useful for pouring the fat off meat juices.

Mincer. For grinding meat and stuffings.

Omelette Pan.

Apple Corer.

Citrus Fruit Zester.

Garlic Press. Useful for extracting small quantities of juice from diced raw onions or ginger (to use in marinades etc) as well as for mincing garlic, although the fag of washing them up means that I now generally just smash the cloves up with the flat of a large knife blade.

How to Use this Book

Seasonal Notes
At the beginning of each chapter on a particular month in the kitchen, you will find background seasonal information, some ideas for preparation and a shopping list. There are two categories for the items on the lists: British grown or import season best, given in heavy type; available and of good quality, in lighter type. Some of the shopping lists are followed by a paragraph pointing out some of the less commonly available imports and rare British produce in season, with some again picked out in bold.

Recipes
Every recipe must be read through completely before starting to cook. In the methods I have mostly assumed that ovens and grills will be pre-heated, except in one or two cases when it is particularly important and I have laboured the point. The £ symbol at the head of each recipe – from £ to £££££ – suggests a comparative ingredient cost per portion for the dish. At the time of writing each £ symbol is equivalent to around 50p a serving. So ££ = around £1, and £££££ = around £2.50 a head or more.

To clarify ambiguous cooking terminology, 'simmer' here means cook at a very low boil, with only the odd bubble breaking the surface; 'coarsely chopped' means roughly hacked about a bit; 'cubed' means cut quite evenly into usually small-bite-sized cubes a little bigger than a sugar cube; 'diced' means quite carefully chopped into little, squarish pieces the size of a small pea; 'chopped' means quite carefully chopped into regular, small fragments about the size of dry rice grains; 'finely chopped' means carefully chopped into regular tiny pieces as fine as granulated sugar. 'Minced garlic' is the peeled clove squashed flat with the flat of a large knife blade, then chopped finely until it is little more than pulp (or use a garlic press).

Ingredients
Preparation notes preceding the hyphen are tied in with measurement; preparation notes following the hyphen should be carried out after measurement (e.g. for '2 tablespoons chopped parsley',

you have to chop the parsley before you can measure 2 table-spoons; for '2 oz parsley, washed, dried thoroughly, trimmed and finely chopped', you take 2 oz parsley, and prepare it. Obviously, you are not necessarily left with 2 oz.)

All recipes were tested with imperial measures, which I use almost without exception. Converting a recipe to metric measures does not work systematically; you have to nudge everything up or down for them to stay in the same proportion. I would rather that this was done by readers who like cooking and thinking metrically than risk giving my own untested conversions, possibly with errors; so I refer them to the conversion tables below. All spoon measures are slightly rounded, unless specified heaped or level.

Where it is important, I have stated whether to use salted or unsalted butter, granulated or caster sugar, and so on. Where a particular type is not specified, you can use more or less what you like. In these cases, I would use slightly salted butter; size 3 free range eggs; white plain flour; pure French olive oil; freshly ground black pepper; white caster sugar and white bread made from a properly fermented dough (available only from some master bakers). Chickens are always roasters. 'Best' olive oil means as good as you've got, preferably mild, fruity, cold-pressed virgin or extra virgin.

Glossaries

These are not comprehensive, just a personal selection, giving information on seasonality and sources as well as some basic preparation techniques where these have not been covered elsewhere in the book. They also cross-refer to more detailed preparation techniques, eating and recipe suggestions elsewhere in the book.

Metrication Tables

Ounces and Fluid Ounces (oz/fl oz)		Grammes and Millilitres (g/ml)
1/8	=	4
1/4	=	7
1/2	=	15

Ounces and Fluid Ounces (oz/fl oz)		Grammes and Millilitres (g/ml)
3/4	=	25
1	=	30
1 1/2	=	45
2	=	60
2 1/2	=	75
3	=	90
3 1/2	=	100
4	=	120
5	=	150
6	=	175
7	=	200
8	=	250
9	=	275
10	=	300
11	=	340
12	=	375
13	=	400
14	=	430
15	=	460
16	=	500
17	=	525
18	=	550
19	=	575
20	=	600

Imperial Pounds (lbs)		Grammes and Kilos (g and kg)
1	=	500g
1 1/4	=	600
1 1/2	=	750
1 3/4	=	850
2	=	1kg
2 1/4	=	1.1
2 1/2	=	1.25
2 3/4	=	1.4
3	=	1.5
3 1/4	=	1.6
3 1/2	=	1.75
3 3/4	=	1.9
4	=	2

Imperial Pints (pints)		Millilitres and Litres (ml and l)
¹/₄	=	150ml
¹/₂	=	300
³/₄	=	450
1	=	600
1¹/₄	=	750
1¹/₂	=	900
1³/₄	=	1l
2	=	1.2
2¹/₄	=	1.3
2¹/₂	=	1.5
2³/₄	=	1.6
3	=	1.8
3¹/₄	=	1.9
3¹/₂	=	2

THE
MONTHS
IN THE
KITCHEN

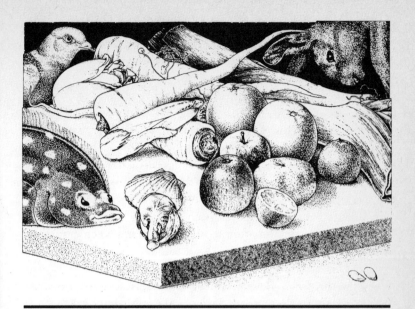

JANUARY

Too much is made of the gluttony associated with Christmas. The media and retail business patronise us with images of consumerism they'd like us to ape and January's supposed belt-tightening after the feast becomes laboured. 'Suffering from one mince pie too many? Lose those extra pounds'. This is a pity because January, far from offering a bleak prospect of ravaged shelves, is one of the year's best months for fresh produce. The highlights are British-grown vegetables, fish and shellfish from home waters, imported exotic and citrus fruits.

VEGETABLES

Root vegetables are the season's glory. Quality and abundance depend heavily on the weather, but, without too much rain or severe frosts to interfere with digging, storage and distribution, there should be plenty of most varieties about – both young, small specimens for light steaming, boiling or sautéeing whole, and

This is also the middle of the season for native oysters, mussels

No winter should pass without Jansson's Temptation for supper one night – just very thinly sliced potatoes and onions layered with black pepper, double cream and fillets of tinned anchovy in a gratin dish. Brush the top with melted butter and bake in a hot oven for an hour – 30 minutes covered with foil, 30 minutes open to brown.

Be careful when buying native greens after periods of sharp frost. Even if produce leaves the fields in good condition, it can still be nipped badly in storage with the wholesaler or retailer. Tell-tale signs are dark, waxy-looking areas with a spongy or slimy texture to the touch; check especially at the bottom of the leaves around the root end of larger vegetables such as Savoy cabbages. Frost-damaged root vegetables often show dark blotches when cut open.

Shopping list

Avocados, **beetroot**, **Belgian chicory**, **Brussels sprouts**, **Brussels tops**, cabbages (including **red**, **Savoy**, **white** and **winter green** varieties), **carrots**, cauliflowers, **celeriac**, celery, chilli peppers, cucumbers, **curly kale**, **fennel**, **garlic**, green beans (French), greens, herbs (parsley), **Jerusalem artichokes**, **kohlrabi**, **leeks**, lettuce and some salad leaves, mooli, mushrooms (cultivated), **okra**, **onions**, **parsnips**, **potatoes**, pumpkins (imported), **salsify**, **scorzonera**, **shallots**, **swedes**, sweetcorn, **sweet potatoes**, **turnips**, watercress.

As well as these seasonal staples, imports in good condition this month should include calabrese and courgettes from Spain and Italy, Spanish mange-touts, Chinese leaves from Israel, very early new potatoes from North Africa, Kenyan dudi and American **butternut squash**. At the height of their season but difficult to find in this country, are **arrowhead**, **bamboo shoots**, cardoon, **chard**, Chinese artichokes (crosnes), **fresh black truffles**, horse-radish, **seakale** and **water chestnuts**. Keep an eye out for them in specialist outlets.

FRUIT AND NUTS

This is the last really good month for fruit until the summer, with still-toothsome domestic-grown apples and pears and a full range of nuts and imported easy-peel citrus varieties as well as the exotica.

Shavings of fresh coconut make a good snack, sprinkled loosely over a baking tray and toasted in the oven before being sprinkled with salt. For a taste of the Middle Ages, make a soup by thickening well flavoured home-made meat, poultry or vegetable stock with ground almonds. Almond paste makes a good stuffing for baked apples.

The end of the month sees the most important date in the home-preserver's calendar – the start of the brief Seville orange season.

Shopping list
Almonds, **apples** (UK – Cox and Bramley; import – North American reds), **Asian pears** (nashi), bananas, **Brazil nuts**, **chestnuts**, **clementines**, coconuts, cranberries, grapefruit, **kumquats**, lemons, limes, **lychees**, mangoes, **mineolas**, oranges (Shamouti and Navel), **ortaniques**, **pears** (UK – Conference and Comice), persimmons, **pineapples**, **pomegranates**, **pomelos**, **rhubarb** (forced), **satsumas**, **Seville oranges**, **sharon fruit**, **ugli fruit**, **walnuts**

Although the seedless, sweet sharon fruit is taking over the affection previously reserved for less user-friendly parent, the persimmon, this, too, is now in season and available from specialist shops. Look also for **physalis** (Chinese gooseberry) with its papery lanterns concealing a tart, orange berry. Many stores have fruit such as **apricots**, **figs**, **dates** and **prunes** dried in the autumn and still in prime condition (often the best are sold loose).

FISH

The holidays at the beginning of the month disrupt the fish trade more noticeably than other food supply lines and bad weather can easily halt landings at this time of year, seriously affecting prices and availability. But as far as quality is concerned, January is a good month for many Atlantic and North Sea fish, which seem firmer and brighter the colder the waters they are fished from. At the same time, the processing plants which grab all the fish they can before Christmas have now loosened their grip on the market.

As a rule, the fresher and finer the fish, the less you need to do to them in order to enjoy them at their best. Most good medium-sized whole fish eat well after just a few minutes under a hot grill. If you like, brush them with olive oil or just season them before cooking. They are done when the meat lifts easily off the bone.

and scallops, although crustacea such as crabs and lobsters are at their scarcest and poorest.

Bony fish and seafood stews seem to fit a January mood. For a basic version, add chunks of potato, garlic and herbs to a large pan in which you have already browned some chopped onions. Cover well with water and boil until the potatoes are almost ready, then add a selection of whole small or cut-up large fish. Boil gently for another 5 to 10 minutes until they are cooked. The fun is in experimenting with mixtures of fish, balancing textures and flavours from different groups of fish (oily, white, flat and so on). Try mackerel, gurnard and whiting to start, or coley, skate, crayfish and mussels.

Shopping list

Brill, clams, cockles, **cod, coley, conger eel**, dab, **Dover sole**, eel, **flounder, grey mullet, gurnard, haddock, hake, halibut, herring, huss, John Dory**, langoustines (scampi or Dublin Bay prawns), **lemon sole, ling, mackerel**, monkfish, **mussels, oysters (native and** Pacific), **plaice, scallops**, sea bass, **skate, smelt, sprats (fresh and smoked)**, tuna, **turbot, whiting**, winkles, **witch**

Israel exports quantities of farmed **carp** at this time of year and, in some British stores, exotica from further afield, Senegal and the Seychelles, might include sardines, tilepia, saupe, red grouper, vara vara, job jeune and red emperor.

MEAT

The meat trade generally has to acknowledge a steep post-Christmas plummet. There is an understandable lack of interest in poultry while red meat – especially beef – becomes almost reasonable in price through the fall in demand.

Game birds still in season are in their last, old tough months, with the exception of pigeon, so mixed game casseroles and pies are a good way to see them out. Or make a thick game stew and bake it, either almost covered by a piped ring of raw choux paste to make an elegant *gougère*, or topped with flour and butter rubbed together with salt, spices and crushed, toasted hazelnuts for a savoury crumble.

Shopping list

beef, **chicken**, duck (farmed), **goose**, **guinea-fowl**, **hare**, lamb (mature), mallard, partridge, pheasant, **pigeon**, **pork**, **rabbit**, snipe, teal, **turkey**, veal, **venison**, woodcock

As well as home-reared lamb, now relatively mature, some suppliers fly in chilled (not frozen) younger carcasses from New Zealand.

CHEESE

This month sees the last of the previous year's soft British cheeses, such as Bonchester and Sharpham, and late-summer vintages of hard English cheeses such as Appleby Cheshire are eating well with four or five months maturation behind them. Some Stiltons are now in better condition than they would have been before Christmas. French varieties to look out for include Boudard de Neufchâtel, Bresse Bleu, Cantal, Chaource, Explorateur, Pont l'Evêque, Roquefort and Vâcherin Mont d'Or.

Toasted Chickpeas

serves 4-6 as nibbles with drinks £

Home-spiced nuts hit the domestic party circuit a few years ago. Elizabeth Lambert Ortiz records the moreish Mexican equivalent in her *Book of Latin American Cooking*. Here is an adaptation.

8 oz chickpeas, soaked overnight, or 1 15 oz can chickpeas
3 tablespoons pure olive oil (not virgin or extra-virgin)
1 clove garlic, peeled and finely minced

big pinch cayenne pepper
big pinch ground cumin
salt and freshly ground black pepper

If using soaked chickpeas, simmer in fresh water until tender, drain and leave to cool. If using canned chickpeas, drain and rinse well.

Heat olive oil in a frying pan, preferably non-stick, until shimmering. Dry chickpeas thoroughly on a clean cloth or kitchen paper. Toss into the oil. Stir around for a few seconds to coat, then add the garlic.

Sauté over medium heat, stirring and tossing from time to time, until the skins are golden brown and have taken on the appearance of a tough jacket around the pea. This can take 20 minutes or more. The peas will pop and jump a little – if they get out of hand, turn the heat down slightly or cover the pan. To achieve the final golden colour more quickly, turn the heat up and cover the pan tightly.

When ready, tip the peas on to clean cloths or multiple thicknesses of kitchen paper and pat well to remove as much oil as possible. Then, while the peas are still hot, toss them in the cayenne pepper, cumin, salt and black pepper.

Serve warm, to eat like nuts. Good alongside olives and radishes or other crudités.

Tapenade

serves 8-10 £

More than just a gutsy Provençal dip. This dark, piquant paste can be eaten spread on hard-boiled eggs (quail if you're feeling flash), with strips of raw vegetable, hunks of French bread and so on as a starter. It can be made hours beforehand and keeps for days in the fridge, so goes well before main courses which require last minute fuss.

Recipes vary wildly. My first introduction was the version from Irene Canning, chef/proprietor of Gibson's restaurant in Cardiff, published in *The Good Food Guide's Second Dinner Party Book*. She uses equal quantities of black and green olives for a mild effect.

Elizabeth David's recipe in *French Provincial Cooking* keeps the full force of the original, including a squeeze of lemon juice and optional extras of mustard and a few drops of 'Cognac or other spirit'. Others leave out the tuna or include garlic, freshly ground black pepper and a leaf or two of fresh herbs such as basil, bay, thyme, mint or flat-leaf parsley. I have found fino sherry a happy, although completely unauthentic, addition.

A common snack-time elaboration is to mash some finished

tapenade with the yolks from halved hard-boiled eggs, then pile the mixture back into the whites.

It is relevant here to restate the importance of the quality of ingredients even if none of them are fresh. There is a truly remarkable difference between a good tapenade – made from tiny sweet Niçoise or lushest Greek olives, dry salted rather than brine-packed capers, best extra-virgin olive oil, good Italian canned tuna and bottled anchovies available from specialist delicatessens – and a corner-cutting version made from cheap supermarket substitutes.

5-7 oz stoned black olives (stoned weight) – roughly chopped
6 anchovy fillets tinned in oil – chopped
3 oz tuna tinned in oil (drained weight)

2 tablespoons capers (drained if in brine, thoroughly rinsed if in dry salt)
4 fl oz olive oil
2 teaspoons fino sherry

Pound the first four ingredients in an enormous pestle and mortar (difficult) or whizz up in a food processor or liquidiser (easy). Work in the olive oil, drop by drop at first, as if for a mayonnaise, to prevent curdling. Stir in the sherry. Spoon into serving bowl.

Salt Cod with Leeks and Truffles

serves 4 as a starter ££££

Humble rustic ingredients often make the most spectacular foil for extravagant luxuries – potato for caviar, turnip for foie gras, boiled white beans for lobster. The silky tang of salt cod and mild sweetness of sautéed leeks marry perfectly with the fascinatingly unwholesome whiff of truffle. The idea is from Rowley Leigh of the restaurant Kensington Place in Notting Hill Gate.

8 oz salt cod
1 lb leeks – trimmed, cleaned thoroughly, dried and sliced finely
1 oz unsalted butter

1 tablespoon finely chopped black truffles
2 tablespoons double cream
freshly ground black pepper

If the cod is very tough and dry, soak in plenty of cold water for

12-24 hours, changing the water once or twice; you may need to extend this up to 36 hours, depending on the quality and cut of the cod. If it's relatively tender, you can pour boiling water over, leave for an hour, then repeat as necessary. Before cooking, check that the soaked cod is not still corrosively salty. Flake the fish and put aside.

Sauté the leek in the foaming butter for a few minutes. Add the truffle, then continue cooking – stirring from time to time – until the leeks are just beginning to colour.

Stir in the cream, pepper and flaked fish. Heat through very gently.

Belgian Chicory and Ham Gratin
serves 2 as a main course, 4 as a starter £

This chicory and ham gratin with a glossy cheese sauce makes either a good winter lunch or supper with lots of crusty white bread to mop up the sauce, or a robust starter for a grander meal.

Many vegetables easily carry a starring role in simple gratins: quartered fennel bulbs braised in butter and baked in a medium-hot oven under a generous coat of grated Parmesan; cauliflower or broccoli florets freshly cooked *al dente* – then sprinkled with home-made breadcrumbs, dotted with butter and crisped up at the top of a hot oven; boiled salsify blanketed in creamy white sauce and finished off under the grill.

White sauces thickened with a butter and flour roux – both the basic béchamel (milk based) and velouté (stock based), plus all their off-spring flavoured variously with cheese, capers, tomato purée, tarragon and so on – deserve a comeback. One of the sorrows of *nouvelle cuisine* has been that it has turned the mass-market gourmet off such delicious pillars of *cuisine ancienne*. Sometimes for absurd reasons.

Flour sauces have suffered as much as anything. Supposedly they're bad for your health – but the truth is not half as much as the little slice of brioche on your side plate. Wholefood cookery has not helped either: the depths are plumbed in books which replace white flour with wholemeal to turn a good white sauce into a milky porridge. But if made properly – with butter and other flavourings – a good white sauce is the making of many dishes.

As with all grilled gratins, and indeed most grilled dishes, it is essential to pre-heat the grill by putting it on full at least 5 minutes before use.

4 heads Belgian chicory	1 oz flour
3 oz butter	½ pint milk
3 tablespoons lemon juice	2 oz grated Gruyère
salt	freshly ground black pepper
4 slices good cooked ham	cayenne pepper
Dijon mustard	freshly grated nutmeg

Cut cones out of the bitter stem-end of the chicory heads and remove any brown edges from outside leaves. Melt 2 oz of the butter in a heavy saucepan, add lemon juice, a big pinch of salt and the chicory. Cook, partly covered over a low flame, turning from time to time, until a skewer passes through with only a little resistance in the middle. This should take around 30 minutes. It doesn't matter if the outsides of the chicory brown slightly.

Spread each slice of ham with Dijon mustard then wrap around a chicory head. Arrange in a heated gratin dish with the overlapping ham flaps underneath.

Meanwhile, melt the other 1 oz butter in a saucepan. Stir in flour and cook together for a couple of minutes until a very pale straw colour. Bring milk almost to the boil in a separate pan. Take flour and butter roux off heat and pour in the hot milk all at once, beating with a wire whisk. Put the sauce back on a low flame and bring to the boil, stirring all the time. When thick, smooth and bubbling, leave to simmer for a minute or so. Take off heat and stir in the cheese, peppers and nutmeg.

Pour steaming sauce over the still-hot chicory, then place the whole dish under pre-heated grill until the surface is well coloured.

Scallop and Jerusalem Artichoke Salad

serves 4-5 ££

The brilliant idea of putting Jerusalem artichokes and scallops together was first given popular airing by Margaret Costa with a soup
in her classic *Four Seasons Cookery Book*. For a simpler version, just
heat through the finely diced shellfish from raw in a well seasoned
slop of cooked artichokes puréed with home-made chicken stock,
then grate a little orange zest over.

The recipe below, a good-looking warm salad, is a simple adaptation of one served by John Burton Race at his restaurant, L'Ortolan
in Berkshire. As a starter, it goes well before a rich meat or game
braise. It is open to infinite variation. Jane Grigson, in her *Vegetable
Book*, waxes lyrical about the sweetness of prawns with Jerusalem
artichoke. Or try slices of monkfish. Equally, you can substitute
olive for hazelnut oil, in which case use 2-3 tablespoons olive to 3-4
of the bland groundnut oil, to prevent the delicate flavours of the
main ingredients getting swamped. Old sherry vinegar is mellow
with a sweet edge. Balsamic vinegar makes a powerful substitute,
perhaps lightened with a little Seville orange juice or experiment
with a mixture of Seville orange juice, lemon juice, red wine vinegar and sugar.

As an extra garnish, you could throw a few coarsely crushed
roasted hazelnuts and/or some freshly cut julienne strips of apple
over the salad before the corals.

½ teaspoon grated orange zest
½ teaspoon grated lemon zest
5 tablespoons groundnut oil
1 tablespoon hazelnut oil
6-8 large fresh scallops (queens
   and frozen will not do)
1 clove garlic – peeled and minced
1 tablespoon old sherry vinegar
salt and freshly ground black
   pepper

lemon juice and/or sugar to
   correct dressing
1 lb Jerusalem artichokes (as
   smooth and unknobbly as
   possible)
1-2 shallots – peeled and very
   finely chopped
4 oz mixed delicate salad leaves –
   washed and dried thoroughly

Put citrus zests together in a fine-meshed tea-strainer and run half a
kettle of boiling water through. Leave to drain. Mix oils together.
   Cut off scallop corals (the orange 'beaks') and cut off and discard

the hard white knot from the edge of the main body. Slice each coral in half lengthways and wash out any dark strands. Put aside for the final garnish.

Slice each scallop, across the whole muscle, into three or four rounds – there should be enough altogether to give five or six slices for each portion. Lay these slices in a bowl and sprinkle with the blanched zests, 2 tablespoons of the mixed oils and a tiny scrape of the garlic. Turn so that all the surfaces are covered and leave to marinate in the fridge for at least an hour.

Make a vinaigrette with the rest of the mixed oils, the vinegar and rest of the garlic. Season well. Taste and add a little lemon juice and/or sugar until you like the balance.

Peel artichokes (cutting off the fiddlier knobs) and put straight into lightly salted water acidulated with a little lemon juice. Bring to boil then cook very gently for around 15 minutes until a skewer glides in smoothly; watch out – like potatoes, they are equally unpleasant under-cooked and crunchy or over-cooked and pappy. Drain. Slice into rounds of comparable size and shape to the scallop slices. While still hot, put in a single layer on an oven-proof plate, sprinkle with enough of the vinaigrette to coat both sides plus the shallots and some generous extra twists of black pepper.

Everything will now wait around for up to 4 hours. Go on to the next stage about 10 minutes before serving.

Tear the salad leaves fairly small, toss in the rest of the dressing and arrange in a neat pile to one side of each of four or five medium-sized plates.

Heat a dry, preferably non-stick cast-iron frying pan or griddle until very hot. Sear the scallops in this for up to 30 seconds on each side until the edges are an attractive golden brown. Do not have more slices in the pan at one time than you can cope with.

Flash the plate of artichokes under a very hot grill to heat through.

Arrange a row of overlapping, alternate slices of scallop and artichoke to the side of each pile of salad. At the very last minute, fling the corals into the frying pan and throw some on top of each pile of leaves.

Celeriac Dauphinoise

serves 4 £

An elegant but comforting vegetable accompaniment to roast or grilled meats, intended originally to go with the pigeon recipe below, but also good enough to eat by itself with green salad as a lunch or supper dish. There are other baked gratins, listed in the index.

1 lb celeriac – peeled and very finely sliced	7 fl oz double cream
lemon juice	¼ teaspoon freshly grated nutmeg
1 lb floury potatoes – peeled and very finely sliced	2 cloves garlic – peeled and minced
butter	salt and freshly ground black pepper

Blanch celeriac as soon as you've sliced it, by plunging it into a large pan of boiling water acidulated with a little lemon juice and bringing the water back to the boil. Drain.

Layer celeriac and potato alternately in a small, buttered, ovenproof dish, spooning cream all over each layer and sprinkling the nutmeg, garlic and seasonings conservatively between.

Bake, uncovered, at Gas 3/160°C/325°F for 2 hours, perhaps turning the heat up a little towards the end to brown the top. Serve hot, warm or at room temperature.

Pigeon with Gravy

serves 2-4 (depending on size of pigeons) £

An inexpensive, sophisticated main course, easy to prepare with the added advantage that it leaves a little time for other things while the stock simmers. Good served with a swadge of the Celeriac Dauphinoise above, or another starchy accompaniment such as mashed parsnips, plus a pile of watercress alongside.

The basic method is translatable to any prime cut of poultry, game (especially hare) or red meat with sufficient related bones. Experiment with different gravy vegetables, spices and alcohol.

The satisfying integrity of saucing meat (or fish) with juice derived from its own skeleton is, in terms of flavour, a development of the old idea that things are sweeter cooked on the bone. But in this case, the cook has taken the work out of eating the dish.

2 wood pigeons
marinade:
4 fl oz red wine
2 tablespoons olive oil
2 oz onion – peeled and very finely chopped
freshy ground black pepper
gravy:
1 oz butter
4 oz leek – trimmed and roughly chopped
4 oz carrot – peeled and roughly chopped

4 oz celery – trimmed and roughly chopped
2 oz smoked bacon – de-rinded and cut into thin strips
1 bay leaf
1 clove garlic – peeled and crushed
1 teaspoon mixed peppercorns (red bay berries and allspice both add savour to this dish)
2 tablespoons brandy
3 pints water
½-1 teaspoon rowan, red currant or white currant jelly
salt

Cut breasts off the birds as close to the bone as possible. Put in a glass, pottery or stainless steel dish with all the marinade ingredients. Leave covered in a cool place.

Brown rest of pigeon carcasses in butter in a heavy, lidded casserole. Throw in the leek, carrot, celery, bacon, bay leaf, garlic and peppercorns. Cook and stir until the vegetables begin to colour. Pour in brandy; light, shaking the pan to make sure it all flames. Add the water, bring to the boil, turn down the heat, cover and let bubble away for at least 2 hours.

Strain the stock into a saucepan, pressing out as much juice as possible from the debris. Add marinade strained off breasts, then, with the lid off, start to boil this mixture hard. The aim is to reduce the liquid in quantity to ¼ pint, when it will be rich and thick. Towards the end of the process, add the fruit jelly and seasoning.

Wipe breasts of excess moisture and onion bits. Heat a dry griddle-plate or cast-iron frying pan until very hot. Sprinkle the surface with ½ teaspoon salt, then fling in the breasts. A minute on each side should turn the outsides a healthy brown while leaving the insides rare. Continue flipping for medium rare or more, although after about 3 minutes on each side the breast is in danger of becoming tough and dry.

Serve cut in thick slices with the gravy poured over.

Kars Salad

serves 6 £

Try this bracing little winter salad from Kars, near the Soviet border – a sort of ur-gazpacho. Carrot and mooli are firmly established partners in many Asian salads. The cold water crisps it up, as with the shredded mooli or daikon, which garnishes Japanese presentations of raw fish.

10 oz mooli (large white radish) – peeled and grated
10 oz carrot – peeled and grated
2 cloves garlic – peeled and minced

1-2 teaspoons salt
juice of 1-2 large lemons
8 fl oz ice-cold water

Mix everything together. Adjust quantities of salt and lemon juice to taste. The consistency should be very wet, almost soupy. Serve chilled in bowls with warm, white pitta bread as part of a *meze* (hors d'oeuvre) selection.

Cooking with Stilton

Remnants of Christmas Stilton can be rescued before they get too high and dry with one of these ideas culled from London professionals, of the generation that has grown up making confident use of British ingredients, which formerly took second place to anything French.

John King of the Ritz Club, Piccadilly, deep-fries ½in cubes of Stilton in a light batter and serves them on fresh salad leaves with a dribble of sweet cranberry purée over the top. Kevin Kennedy of Boulestin bundles finely diced Stilton mixed with chopped and sautéed chanterelles into small pouches of buttered phyllo pastry, brushes them with egg-wash and bakes them for 15 minutes in a hot oven.

Another idea, suggested by both John Lounton from the Dorchester Hotel and Ian McAndrew, who established his name at Restaurant Seventy Four in Canterbury before setting up in London, is a main course made by topping medallions of panseared meat with a little mound of cheesy mousse. Lounton tops each with a half walnut; McAndrew serves his with a rosemary sauce.

Steak with Stilton Mousse

serves 4 £££

4 oz raw chicken breast – well chilled	freshly ground black pepper
	1 oz Stilton
dash of sherry (dry, medium or sweet)	4×5 oz medallions fillet steak or veal
4 fl oz double cream – well chilled	

Whizz chicken breast in a food processor until it forms a smooth paste. Stir in sherry, cream, pepper and crumble in the cheese. Keep chilled until you are ready to go on to the last stage.

Quickly brown the outsides of the medallions on a very hot griddle or in a pre-heated, preferably heavy non-stick, frying pan. Take out of the pan. Divide the mousse between the four pieces of meat, smoothing it over the whole top surface of each medallion.

Bake for 5 minutes in an oven pre-heated as high as it will go.

Warm Stilton and Port Sauce

serves 2 £

Peter Kromberg of the Inter-Continental Hotel on Hyde Park Corner prepares this simple port and Stilton sauce to serve with savoury soufflés of celery, fresh pear and walnut. It also works well with plainly grilled steaks, veal chops, chicken joints, straight omelettes, cooked vegetables such as celeriac or mushrooms, or even – God save us – slices of left-over turkey. I like it best over softly poached eggs on fried bread.

2 fl oz port	grated lemon rind to taste
4 oz Stilton – crumbled	freshly ground black pepper
2 tablespoons double cream	

Bring port to the boil in a small saucepan. Turn the heat down as low as it will go and stir in the Stilton and cream. Stir until the cheese melts and the sauce is thick. If the mixture curdles, add a little hot water and whisk thoroughly.

Season with the lemon rind and pepper. Serve immediately.

Buttered Semolina and Nut Pudding

serves 4 £

Anatolian villagers assure me that this rich, earthy pudding, which they call *irmik helvası*, is the best thing to happen to most of them all winter.

I picked the recipe up from the grandmother of a Turkish friend, Murat Kemaloğlu, and assumed a feeling of proprietorship over it, particularly since it was one of the very first recipes I had published. I see now, however, that it bears an uncanny resemblance to the *basbousa bil loz* in Claudia Roden's *Book of Middle Eastern Food*.

3 oz granulated white sugar	1½ oz butter
5 fl oz water	1 oz blanched almonds
5 fl oz milk	3½ oz semolina
1 oz pine kernels	

In a saucepan over a low heat, dissolve sugar in the water and milk. Bring to the boil and cook gently for 10 minutes to make a light syrup. Set aside.

Cut the blanched almonds into slivers the size of the pine kernels. Melt butter in another, heavy pan. Throw in pine kernels and almonds and stir over medium heat for 3-4 minutes until they begin to colour. Add semolina and stir until it darkens a few shades and the whole contents of the pan look golden (10-20 minutes).

Lower heat and stir in half of the syrup. When it has been absorbed, continue stirring while you gradually add the rest of the syrup. When it is all added, the mixture should be quite sloppy.

Take off the heat, cover the pan and leave to stand for 20-30 minutes to settle. A moist, spoonable paste, it can be eaten warm (not hot) or at room temperature, preferably with great globs of clotted cream. You should feel your heart slowing down after the first couple of mouthfuls.

Caramel Orange Tart

serves 4 £

A plain, rimless disc of thick almondy biscuit, so short as to be almost non-existent, covered with chunks of fresh orange and a brittle caramel lattice. As with most puddings, cream – crème fraîche for preference – can be taken or left. In this case, it does provide good lubrication.

Make the base no more than 4 hours in advance as it goes soft fairly quickly. Final assembly of the tart should be immediately before serving since it begins to self-destruct after about 15 minutes.

Alternative approaches are to make the base by blind-baking either the classic French sweetened pastry, pâte sucré, or, even tougher, a British shortbread. Also, try other sweet citrus fruits for the filling and brush the base with melted and sieved jam instead of egg white against juices soaking through.

pastry:
4 oz plain flour
pinch salt
3 oz butter – chilled or softened (see method)
1 oz caster sugar
1 teaspoon grated orange peel
1 large egg – separated
1 oz ground almonds

filling:
3 large sweet oranges
1 tablespoon spirit (brandy, fruit liqueur or eau de vie)
caramel:
4 oz caster sugar
1 teaspoon melted butter
2 tablespoons orange juice

If you have a food-processor the pastry is easy. Sift the flour and salt into the bowl fitted with the metal blade. Add chilled butter (cut into small pieces). Process for a few seconds until mixture resembles fine breadcrumbs. Add sugar, peel, yolk and almonds. Whizz again until it all comes together into a coherent ball.

To make the pastry by hand, sift flour and salt into a bowl. Sprinkle over the almonds. Make a well in the centre for the sugar, beaten yolk and peel, which should then be mixed together with the tips of your fingers until creamy. Add butter, softened, and continue mixing, gradually drawing in the flour and almonds. Knead gently until it forms a paste. Press lightly into a ball.

Which ever way you have made the dough, wrap it in clingfilm and chill in the fridge for half an hour.

Heat oven to Gas 6/200°C/400°F. Using a greaseproof paper template, roll and trim dough on a baking sheet into a 6in diameter circle. Bake for about 15 minutes, until it looks like a very large pale biscuit. Whip a long knife underneath the disc, to loosen it from the sheet, and, when it has cooled enough to have set, slide it on to a wire rack, brush top with a film of beaten egg white and leave to cool fully.

Peel oranges with a sharp knife, cutting straight through skin, pith and outer membrane to the flesh. Cut the peeled fruit into rough 1in cubes, gathering enough juice from this operation for the caramel. Put fruit to chill.

Start the final assembly by arranging fruit in an even, closely packed layer over the whole pastry base. Sprinkle with the spirit.

For the caramel, pour juice and butter into a heavy saucepan with the sugar and stir gently over a medium-low flame. The syrup will start to bubble and foam. Continue cooking, occasionally drawing a spoon through the mixture, until the syrup begins to colour. Remove from the heat when the cloudy caramel is a good mid-brown. Pour immediately in cross-hatched trails all over the oranges.

Transfer to a serving plate as soon as the caramel is hard and brittle. Serve in wide wedges.

FEBRUARY

Funny month, February – sometimes unmemorably bland and grey, throwing in odd bright patches to illuminate banks of snow-drops that will already have faded by mid-month; sometimes an Arctic colony, with the first really cold snaps of the winter. When that happens, supply lines are thrown into chaos, unpicked vege-tables and stored fruit and vegetables go to ruin; the supermarkets reduced-price shelves are full of rotting, frost-bitten greens and black mushy bananas.

VEGETABLES

A good frost is considered beneficial for some crops – tightening up and concentrating the sweetness of sprouts and mellowing kale and parsnips. But a degree or three more of frost, and leeks can be writ-ten off and even Jersey cauliflowers suffer.

Watercress is always one of the first vegetables to become scarce in bad weather as the beds ice over, but re-establishes itself quickly in milder conditions. It makes the season's simplest salad partnered with slices of fresh orange. No dressing is necessary – just salt and freshly ground black pepper. An arrangement of Belgian chicory leaves with toasted and roughly pounded pine kernels or hazelnuts and a dressing of olive oil and dark, rich balsamic vinegar, perhaps sweetened with a few drops of port, makes a more sophisticated salad.

Or, to return to delicious basics, try very finely shredded red cabbage with a basic oil and lemon juice dressing, as the Turks do with their kebabs all winter.

Shopping list
Avocados, **beetroot**, **Belgian chicory**, Broccoli (calabrese), **Brussels sprouts**, **Brussels tops**, cabbages (red, **Savoy**, **white** and **winter green** varieties), **carrots**, cauliflowers, **celeriac**, celery, chilli peppers, Chinese leaves, courgettes, cucumbers, **curly kale**, **fennel**, **garlic**, green beans (French), **greens**, **Jerusalem artichokes**, herbs (parsley), **kohlrabi**, **leeks**, lettuce and some salad leaves, mooli, mushrooms (cultivated), **okra**, **onions**, **parsnips**, **potatoes**, pumpkins (imported), **salsify**, **scorzonera**, **shallots**, **swedes**, **sweet potatoes**, **turnips**, watercress

New imports in good condition should include flat green beans from Africa and the Canaries, new-season carrots from Spain and Israel, Israeli cherry tomatoes, Moroccan mange-touts, Spanish celery hearts and new potatoes from Cyprus. If our weather affects staple crops, Spain and Italy can usually come to the rescue with leeks, cauliflowers and Brussels sprouts. **Butternut squash** is still coming in from America and dudis from Kenya. Seasonal rarities from closer to home are cardoon, **chard**, Chinese artichokes and **seakale** – snap them up if you find them. This is the last full month for prime fresh black truffles from France or Spain. Also look for arrowhead and **bamboo shoots**.

FRUIT

Satsumas are the first of the soft citrus fruits to disappear after Christmas; clementines will tail off towards the end of the month. Ardent marmaladiers will know that the Seville orange season generally ends about the middle of the month. Some of the finest eating oranges around should be Italian Ruby Red bloods.

Crumbles made with the pink forced rhubarb, now at its best, should be very fine – or make a fool, experimenting with added flavourings like ginger, orange, cinnamon, lemon – even Pernod, as suggested by Margaret Costa.

Conjure up the sun, even if only in pale reflection, by buying well-matched tropical and exotic fruits for a fruit salad. Various contributions might be Peruvian mangoes, Antiguan Gallia melon, American Red Emperor grapes and **physalis**, or Chinese gooseberry. Taste anything you are not familiar with as you go along. It is almost impossible to end up with a truly disgusting combination. The best of the fresh lychees will soon be over: a gigantic bowl of these still in their shells and, if possible, on the branch too, if you can find them in a Chinese greengrocer, makes a dramatic and luxurious finish to a social dinner.

Shopping list
Apples (UK – Cox and Bramley; import – North American reds), Asian pears (nashi), bananas, **clementines**, **coconuts**, grapefruit, **kumquats**, lemons, limes, **lychees**, **mineolas**, oranges (Shamouti and Navel), **ortaniques**, pears (UK and import – Comice and Conference), **pineapples**, **pomelo**, **rhubarb** (forced), **Seville oranges**, **sharon fruit**, **ugli fruit**

The better grades of last season's **dried apricots**, **prunes**, **figs** and **dates** remain good until the end of the month; the best are often sold loose.

FISH

Most flat fish – and especially lemon sole – are in fine nick until they start to put their energies into spawning at the end of the month. Haddock is tailing off. Plaice are pretty poor already or roey, the term used by Chris Ramus, a Yorkshire fishmonger with two first-class shops in Harrogate.

Cod is excellent just now. Plainly cooked thick steaks, cut across the whole fish, can take very strong flavours; try a chilli-hot sweet and sour sauce, or a curry spiked with fennel on a cold evening. Farmed salmon is also particularly good, although, in my book, it always has a tendency to woolly blandness. February also marks the beginning of the rod season for wild salmon; there used to be as much palaver about the first landings as about the first grouse of 'the glorious twelfth'. This should be excellent, firm and lean with a more complex flavour than farmed, but also extraordinarily expensive.

Most of the live mussels presently in the shops are good enough to eat raw as long as you can be sure they are from immaculate sources. Opening them, cutting the flesh out of the shells and pulling off the little black beard can be a frustrating business. They don't even need lemon – just a twist of black pepper.

Shopping list
Brill, clams, cockles, **cod**, **conger eel**, **coley**, dab, **Dover sole**, eel, **flounder**, **grey mullet**, **gurnard**, **haddock**, **hake**, **halibut**, **herring**, **huss**, **John Dory**, langoustines (Dublin Bay prawns or scampi), **lemon sole**, **ling**, **mackerel**, monkfish, **mussels**, **oysters** (**native** and Pacific), salmon (wild and farmed), **scallops**, sea bass, **skate**, **smelt**, **sprats** (**fresh and smoked**), tuna, **turbot**, **whitebait**, **whiting**, winkles, **witch**

The winter dip in supplies of prawns from around the British coast has encouraged fresh imports from further and further afield. Some operators are now flying in large cold-water prawns, cooked but not frozen, from the coast of Maine.

MEAT

Feathered game has virtually come to an end. The condition of the remaining pigeons will depend on how bad a time the weather has given them; the same applies to rabbit and hare. Mr Feller, who runs the best butcher's in Oxford, recommends hogget as some of the month's best meat. This is lamb coming up to its first birthday, firm, juicy and red, so perfect for curries and strongly flavoured Middle Eastern dishes.

Chicken tends to be good value at this time of year. Try frying seasoned breasts, dipped in flour, in butter until well coloured. Add strips of fresh sage (imports from Israel are widely available throughout the winter) and a big splash of dry white vermouth. Boil and stir until the sauce is syrupy.

Shopping list

Beef, **chicken**, duck (farmed), guinea-fowl, hare, **lamb** (**mature**), mallard, **pigeon**, **pork**, **rabbit**, turkey, veal, venison

In the long run-up to British lambing, many chains are air-freighting chilled (not frozen) new-season lamb from New Zealand.

CHEESE

This is the low point of the year for English cheeses, with a few noble exceptions. Blue Cheshire is good and some of the farm-house Cheddars that were made around last April should now be fine eating – often tasting more mature than examples from the months just before, when the weather was colder and the grass poor or non-existent. Some Cotherstone, a cheese from the York-shire Dales, may now have ripened into unusual succulence (it can be rather bland and soapy).

Parisian cheese authorities say that the situation is similar in France. The French idea of a poor season, however, is somewhat grander than ours. Look in specialist shops for Beaufort, Bleu des Causses, Brie de Meaux, Brie de Melun, Laguiole, Langres, Maroilles, Mimolette, Neufchâtel, Pont-l'Evêque, Roquefort, Saint-Marcellin and Tomme Arlésienne. Goat's milk cheeses are not good in the winter months, apart from ones that have been kept macerating in oil, herbs and aromatics since the end of their last season. Vâcherin Mont d'Or disappears around the end of the month.

Look out for good, mature specimens of Gorgonzola and its milder, creamier relation, Dolcelatte, from Italy. These also come in *torta* versions, layered with marscarpone cream cheese, a fabulously rich winter indulgence when supplies of other good cheeses are short.

Mussel and Potato Stew

serves 4 £

In Belgium, the modest mussel is a national obsession, served with splendour in even the meanest cafés. Belgians think nothing of day-trips to places with particularly elevated reputations for moules 'en casserole'. The neat little town of Sluis, just across the border in the Netherlands, has established a whole economy on mussel restaurants aimed at Belgians who pop over to buy pornography and butter, respectively harder and cheaper than at home.

Another place of pilgrimage is the down-to-earth Chez Léon – a few hundred yards from the Grande Place in Brussels. The 'moules spéciale frites' – a vast pile of mussels steamed open for perhaps 5 minutes in a covered cast-iron casserole with masses of chopped celery tops and parsley, sautéed and seasoned with nothing more than the juice that came out of the mussels and served with a separate pile of chips, another high-point of Belgian cuisine – is a feast that takes some beating.

This tangy stew does not approach such heights. But with a salad of winter vegetables, crusty white bread and some fruit to follow, it makes a robust supper. Vary by adding diced fennel bulb to the potato and apple. Try a sprig of fresh tarragon in the stock if you can get hold of it, or substitute dry cider or apple juice for the wine.

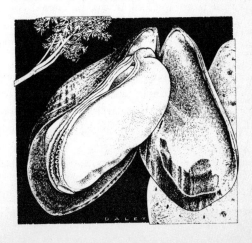

A little fresh nutmeg grated over each bowl before serving adds an off-beat note.

1 medium onion – peeled but left whole and stuck with 3 cloves

2 carrots – peeled and roughly chopped

1 medium leek – trimmed and roughly chopped

1 stick celery – roughly chopped

few parsley stalks

1 bay leaf

1 teaspoon mixed peppercorns (black, white, green, red and allspice)

2 slices lemon

sprig thyme or pinch dried leaves

1 pint water

½ bottle dry white wine

2 pints live mussels (about 60) – cleaned (see page 303)

1½ oz butter

2 cloves garlic – peeled and minced

3 medium-sized waxy potatoes – peeled and cut into fairly neat ¼ in dice (about 1 lb prepared weight)

1 dessert apple – peeled and diced

salt

5 tablespoons chopped parsley

3 egg yolks

5 fl oz double cream

freshly ground black pepper

To make the stock, put onion, carrot, leek, celery, parsley stalks, bay leaf, peppercorns, lemon slices and thyme in a saucepan with the water and wine. Bring to a vigorous boil, maintain for a couple of minutes, then turn down the heat, cover loosely and let the pan bubble gently for an hour. When ready, strain off and discard the vegetable matter.

Put the mussels in a large dry saucepan over a hot flame. Cook, with the lid on, for about three minutes, shaking the contents briskly from time to time. Cook in two batches if you only have a small pan. When all the shells are well open, tip the mussels in batches into a colander over a jug and remove the meat. Discard the shells. Set the mussel juice and meat aside.

Melt butter in a clean saucepan and throw in the garlic to sizzle for a minute or two. Add the potatoes, apple and a little salt. Stir to coat the ingredients evenly, then carefully pour in the mussel juice (leaving all the grit behind on the bottom of the jug) and a measured 1½ pints of the stock. Bring to the boil, cover, and let cook for about 30 minutes until the potato is tender but still holding together.

Scatter in the mussels just to heat through. Stir in the parsley. Turn the heat down to low. Beat the yolks with the cream in a small bowl, then add a ladle of juice from the saucepan and beat thoroughly. Pour back into the pan and stir until the stew thickens. It must not boil or the sauce will curdle. Adjust seasoning.

Ladle into bowls to serve.

Fresh Pasta

serves 2-3 £

Most retail fresh pasta is a granular, compacted, wet-cardboard travesty (I know of only one truly excellent outlet in London: Lina's in Soho). So real pastaphiles have no option but DIY.

In any case, making pasta is easy, satisfying and, contrary to what fancy kitchen shops would have you believe, needs no special equipment – just a little time and space. The results have a fine, slippery texture, a firm bite and incomparable flavour.

Most of the best Italian recipes agree on about 3½ oz flour to each egg (size 3). Some add a pinch of salt, although arch-purist Marcella Hazan can't see the point. She also rages against the addition of olive oil and every flavouring, colouring or other additive except chard leaf or spinach purée for *pasta verde*. Her irreplaceable books give all the arguments.

Some recipes advise strong (that is, higher gluten) flour for a firmer, smoother pasta. This makes the dough very difficult to knead properly. I prefer the texture of pasta made with softer flour, described as 'downy' by Marcella Hazan, who acknowledges both flours as making what she calls 'valid' pasta. A compromise would be to mix flours – 80% ordinary plain to 20% strong, unbleached bread-making flour works pretty well.

7 oz plain flour (not strong)   2 eggs (size 3)

Pile flour on work surface. Make well in top and break in eggs. Beat these lightly with a fork or mix with your hands, gradually drawing in flour until a dough is formed. The consistency should be such that you can stick your finger in fairly easily and it comes out clean, with no stickiness; the exact amount of flour you need will vary according to the flour itself, the humidity of the room, the freshness of the eggs and so on.

Form dough into a ball.

With clean, dry hands, knead dough on a lightly floured surface; holding edge of ball nearest you with fingers of one hand, push rest of ball away with heel of other hand, then roll extended edge back toward you with palm of that hand. Turn the dough through 90 degrees and repeat. At first it will stick and tear. Persevere, lightly flouring hands and surface as necessary, until the dough is quite elastic and you can stretch it a long way across the work surface. This may seem hopeless for the first 5 minutes, but it shouldn't take longer than 10 minutes.

Just to make sure, knead it some more, until, when rolled into a ball, its surface has a silky texture like a baby's cheek. Cover ball in clingfilm and leave to rest at room temperature for at least 1 hour (3 hours at most).

Unwrap, knead again for a minute or two, cut in half and place one piece on a large, immaculately clean, scantily floured, dry surface. Very lightly push a rolling pin, floured in the same way, across surface away from you. Turn dough through 90 degrees and repeat. Continue working, exerting almost no pressure at all downwards, and only rolling away from you, until you can see the work surface through sheet. Repeat with other sheet. (A length of clean, untreated broom handle is easier to control and allows you to roll out bigger sheets.)

Brush sheets very lightly with flour and hang on rails or over chair backs for half an hour to dry a little. Then roll each one up loosely like a Swiss roll and cut across into narrow strips. Unravel the noodles and sprinkle loosely on a clean cloth to dry for another 10 minutes.

Cook by plunging into plenty of boiling salted water. Stir so noodles don't stick together. Start timing from when they rise to the surface and the water boils again. Push them around so that they cook evenly. Depending on your taste, they will be cooked in 1-5 minutes. Drain (do not over-drain – a little extraneous cooking water lubricates many pasta dishes beautifully) and toss immediately in olive oil or butter with plenty of black pepper.

The noodles are now ready for eating, perhaps just with more butter or oil and freshly grated Parmesan, or with a sauce such as the one below.

Blue Cheese Pasta Sauce

serves 2-3 £

Easy, creamy sauce which adds just enough interest to show off fresh pasta at its best. I prefer the subtler dolcelatte *torta* version. This is one of the pasta dishes that does not benefit from the addition of Parmesan at the table.

4 oz button mushrooms – finely sliced
1 oz butter
4 fl oz dry white wine (the fuller bodied the better)
4 oz Gorgonzola or Dolcelatte *torta* – cut into small cubes
2 oz cooked peas – bottled French petits pois are best, or resort to briefly blanched frozen

one quantity fresh pasta, cut into medium-thin noodles (see recipe page 57)
freshly ground black pepper
optional coarsely pounded walnuts

Fry mushrooms in butter until they have given off all their liquid and this has reduced away to nothing again. Splash in the wine and reduce again, leaving just a syrupy film.

Take off the heat and stir in the cheese and peas so that the cheese melts but doesn't cook and the peas just heat through. Slip in your freshly cooked, drained noodles with lots of black pepper. Toss thoroughly.

Sprinkle with walnuts if you like.

Scallops with Rhubarb Sauce

serves 4 £££££

A couple of years ago, innovative restaurant chefs started using rhubarb in a similar way to sorrel, to sharpen buttery sauces for fish and meat dishes. The simplest version, first published in *The Good Food Guide 1985*, is from Franco Taruschio of the Walnut Tree Inn near Abergavenny (long cited by fans as the only source of good restaurant-food in Wales), who spooned it over quickly pan-fried salmon.

In Ian McAndrew's fine book, *A Feast of Fish*, he gives one of his former Canterbury restaurant's most popular dishes: sautéed scallops with rhubarb butter sauce. The sauce is quite complicated – involving sugar syrups, puréeing and passing through muslin, then beating in small pieces of butter to emulsify and thicken – but the combination with scallops is magical. So here is an adaptation of Franco's sauce with Ian's scallops.

12 fresh raw scallops (frozen will not do)

salt and freshly ground black pepper

1 oz butter

3 oz newest pink forced rhubarb – cut into 1in long and ¼in thick batons

3 tablespoons water

3 fl oz double cream

optional fresh chervil leaves to garnish

Having shelled, trimmed, washed and dried the scallops well (see page 304), cut the white meat across into halves, leaving the roe attached to one half. Season with salt and pepper. Heat butter in a frying pan and sauté scallops for about 1½ minutes on each side. Do not overcook, or they will shrink and toughen. Remove from pan with a slotted spoon, allowing fat to drain back into pan, then keep warm while you prepare the sauce.

Put rhubarb batons into same pan with the remaining fat, water and a pinch of salt. Bring to the boil, then turn down heat and simmer for 2-5 minutes until cooked through but not mushy. Remove rhubarb with slotted spoon and put to keep warm.

Add cream to the juices in the pan and cook until slightly thickened. Check seasoning.

Arrange scallops on warm plates. Spoon sauce over, then decorate with rhubarb and chervil, if you can find it.

Middle Eastern Flat Bread
makes 2 large pieces serving 4-6 £

Every village in every Middle Eastern country has its own versions
of flat bread. Some are smaller, puffed up tear-shaped pieces, such
as we call pitta, some larger and thicker, like every Indian
restaurant's nan; some versions add oil to soften the dough, some
glaze with egg, some sprinkle with sesame seeds or make distinct
finger-tip patterns in the top. In most places they are baked in clay
ovens – sometimes built above ground, sometimes a charcoal-
heated pit in the earth. In Gaziantep (south central Turkey) in the
spring, they add a generous measure of fresh tarragon leaves
kneaded into the dough to give a special fragrance.

Here is a simple version, very basic but still the best accompaniment to a spread of Eastern Mediterranean or Middle Eastern *meze*
such as taramasalata, houmus and the like. This bread does not
keep, so make it no more than an hour before you need it and keep
it warm by wrapping in foil or a clean cloth. It is most important to
pre-heat the oven and baking trays.

¼ oz dried yeast
½ pint warm water
1 teaspoon sugar
1 lb plain white or chapatti flour
 (not ordinary wholemeal)

1 teaspoon salt
nigella (kalonji or black onion
 seed)

Dissolve yeast in less than half of the warm water. Stir in the sugar
and allow the mixture to stand for 10 minutes until it froths.

Sift flour and salt into a bowl. Make a well in the centre and pour
in the yeast mixture. Mix with as much of the remaining warm
water as forms a good softish, almost fluffy dough. Knead on a
floured work surface for about 10 minutes until smooth and elastic
(see Fresh Pasta recipe on page 57 for kneading technique). Roll
into a ball, place back in the bowl, cover and leave to stand in a
warm place for about an hour or until almost doubled in bulk.

Set oven to maximum temperature – probably Gas
9/240°C/475°F – in good time. Also put in two large baking sheets
to heat through at the same time.

Punch the dough down. Knead again briefly. Pull into two

pieces, then roll flat on a generously floured surface or cloth. Pull each into an oval, which should be about a foot long, 8in wide and ¼in-½in thick.

Quickly take baking sheets out of oven and flick them with water. Then, immediately, slap a bread on to each, wet one hand in cold water and make jabbing motions all over the surface, leaving only a ½in rim smooth. This jabbing serves the functions of flattening the bread a bit more, pushing it into a good final shape, patterning the surface and brushing it with water to prevent too abrupt browning. It should be over in the wink of an eye. Without pausing, sprinkle the surface conservatively with nigella seeds and bang the sheets back into the oven.

Do not open the oven door for 8 minutes. The breads will be ready in 8-12 minutes. They will be quite hard on the outside and just beginning to brown.

Chicken and Salsify Phyllo Pie

serves 6-8 £

A party or informal supper dish, this is good served hot or warm with a green salad. The filling is a loose adaptation of a French one quoted in Jane Grigson's *Vegetable Book*, but the basic construction of the pie will work with any well-flavoured, moist but un-runny filling that doesn't need much cooking. The classic Greek *spanakopitta* uses chopped raw spinach, beaten eggs and crumbled feta cheese. A simple Turkish *börek* might use just crumbled white cheese, a beaten egg and lots of chopped flat-leaf parsley.

The packs of phyllo pastry most commonly available in supermarkets and delis, which weigh 400g, contain about 15 leaves. To follow this recipe using such a pack, thaw it for 3 hours. You need about 10 of the leaves – immediately fold the rest back into the pack to refreeze. You cannot repeat this operation, as the leaves dry out and become brittle. Use de-frosted phyllo as soon as possible after opening.

The alternative is to make your own. The method is very similar to making fresh pasta (see page 57), although you will need a length of untreated broom handle to roll out the dough properly. Then, having rolled it as thinly as you can, you should pick the sheet up on the backs of your hands and, moving your hands gently apart from the centre of the sheet, stretch it gently until it is gossamer fine. A Turkish recipe for such a dough, which they call *yufka*, is 1 egg (size 3), 14 oz flour, 4-5 fl oz water and 1 teaspoon salt, plus perhaps a little oil to make the dough less fragile. Mix, knead for 10 minutes until really elastic, then, for another 10 minutes, repeatedly hold the dough like a hammer and slap it down at an angle across the work surface until it stretches a good 2-3 feet without breaking (very therapeutic). Rest dough for an hour, closely covered, knead again briefly, then roll, (as described on page 228.) Use immediately. Also suitable for any kind of strudel.

Spare ends of phyllo are good brushed with oil, wrapped into cigar shapes around a tablespoon of *börek* filling and then shallow-fried in oil until golden all over. These are the Turkish *sigara böreği*.

1 lb salsify
splash lemon juice or wine vinegar
salt
splash bland salad oil
10 sheets phyllo pastry – an inch or so bigger all round than your roasting tin, half cut to the size of the tin
1 large onion – peeled and finely chopped
2 oz butter plus 3 oz melted butter
1 lb skinned and boned chicken breasts – thinly sliced across the grain

1 teaspoon cornflour
½ lb mushrooms – sliced
freshly ground black or white pepper
pinch ground nutmeg
smaller pinch ground cloves
12 black olives – stoned and roughly chopped
handful roughly chopped parsley
optional few leaves fresh tarragon

Scrub salsify under cold running water, cut off tops and tails, scrape off the skin and cut the vegetable into 3in lengths. Keep prepared pieces in cold water, acidulated with a little lemon juice or wine vinegar to prevent discoloration. Steam or boil in salted, acidulated water, with a film of oil on the surface (again to keep the salsify white) for 20 minutes. Drain.

Fry chopped onions in 2 oz butter over a medium flame until soft. Throw in chicken breast and cook through. Sprinkle in the flour and add sliced mushrooms. Cook and stir for a few minutes.

Add salt, pepper, nutmeg and cloves. As the mushrooms loose their juice, it amalgamates with the flour to make enough thick sauce to coat all the ingredients. Stir in the olives, parsley and tarragon, if you can get it. Adjust seasoning to taste.

Cover the phyllo leaves with a sheet of greaseproof paper wrung out under the tap. Keep the pile covered as you work with each sheet. Brush the bottom of a standard 10in x 12in x 1½in roasting tin with melted butter. Lay in a sheet of phyllo, which should overhang the tin at both ends and come up almost to the top of the tin at the sides. Brush liberally with melted butter. Lay another sheet over, brush with butter. Continue until you have 5 layers.

Spread with the chicken mixture and salsify. Lay one of the smaller sheets over the filling. Brush with butter. Continue with the other 4 sheets. When complete, fold the overhanging edges from the bottom sheets over the top. Brush with butter again.

Bake at pre-heated Gas 4/180°C/350°F for 40-45 minutes until the pie is golden. Cut in generous squares to serve or turn upside down onto a big platter to present whole.

Sausage with Lentils

serves 4 *££-£££*

A hearty starter, lunch or supper dish co-written with one of my favourite London chefs, Simon Hopkinson, whose restaurant, Bibendum, is in the stylishy reappointed old Michelin building on Fulham Road. Another version of this was first published in *Elle*.

Use green or brown lentils not the little orange ones. The best lentils, but difficult to find, are the tiny *lentilles du Puy*.

Instead of the *zampone* (boned and stuffed pig's trotter, available from Italian delicatessens), you could use other French or Italian semi-cured sausages such as *cotechino*, or excellent, coarse-textured, cereal-free fresh pork sausages, or a mixture. The vinaigrette enhances and lifts the flavours.

big knob goose fat or dripping
1 onion – peeled, quartered and
  stuck with 2 cloves

1 carrot – peeled and quartered
  lengthways

1 stick celery – trimmed and broken to fit in the pan
2 cloves garlic – peeled and minced
1 bay leaf
pinch ground allspice
12 oz lentils – picked over and rinsed
1½ pints boiling water
salt and freshly ground black pepper
about 1 lb *zampone*
3 tbsp good vinaigrette containing 1 raw shallot, peeled and very finely chopped
chopped parsley

Melt fat in a large heavy pan. Throw in the onion, carrot and celery. Sauté for 10-15 minutes until well caramelised. Add garlic and let sizzle for a minute or two. Add bay leaf, allspice and lentils; stir to coat, then pour in boiling water.

Turn flame to low, cover pan and cook for about an hour or until the lentils are tender but still whole, and almost all the liquid has been absorbed. Season to taste.

If using *zampone* or other semi-cured sausage, poach separately, following manufacturer's or retailer's instructions. If using fresh sausage, add raw to the lentil mixture about half an hour before the end of cooking time.

Serve a pile of lentils on each plate, topped with thick slices of sausage and a little of the shallot vinaigrette dribbled over the whole thing. Sprinkle with chopped parsley.

Lamb and Cracked Wheat Pilau

serves 4 ££

Taking the theme of hogget, mature lamb, as an excellent meat for curries and Middle Eastern dishes, here is a very simple cracked wheat pilau.

1 lb lean lamb – cut into ½in cubes
3 oz butter
8 oz onion – finely diced
2 cloves garlic – crushed
4 oz green sweet pepper – diced
2 fresh hot green chilli peppers or 2 dried hot red ones
2 tablespoons tomato paste
salt and freshly ground black pepper
4 fl oz plus 1 pint water
12 oz cracked wheat (bulgur, bulgar and many other spellings)

In a heavy, well seasoned casserole, over a medium-high flame, brown meat thoroughly without the addition of any fat.

Remove meat, set aside, turn the flame down a little and put in 1 oz of the butter. In this, fry the onion until soft and beginning to brown. Add the garlic and let it sizzle for a minute or two, then the green pepper, chilli and tomato paste. Cook for about 5 minutes, stirring from time to time, then put the meat back, season the mixture well and pour in the 4 fl oz water.

Stir thoroughly, scraping the bottom of the pan with the spatula to dissolve any caked-on burnt bits. Turn heat down to a friendly simmer, cover the pan and leave to cook for about an hour until the meat is tender. You may need to splash in a little more water from time to time if the mixture starts sticking to the bottom again.

When the meat is cooked, take the lid off and boil any remaining liquid to reduce it down to almost nothing. Now add the rest of the butter, pour in the cracked wheat and stir over medium heat for about 5 minutes, stirring constantly, until the bulgur is well coated.

Add the pint of water, stir, bring to a decent boil, cover and leave to cook for 5 minutes. Turn heat down to low, stir again, cover and cook for about 15 minutes until most of the liquid is absorbed. Jam the lid on tightly, with foil or a cloth, take the pan off the heat and leave in a warm place for another 20-30 minutes for the grains to settle.

Serve very warm rather than hot.

Grilled Köfte

serves 2-4 ££

Grilled meatballs are another good use for the flavoursome mature lamb around in February.

1 lb leanish lamb – finely minced
1 small onion – peeled and grated
1 tablespoon finely chopped
   parsley (preferably flat-leaf)
½ teaspoon cumin seeds – roasted
   in a dry saucepan then ground
½ teaspoon ground allspice

¼ teaspoon cayenne pepper
½ teaspoon salt
½ teaspoon freshly ground black
   pepper
optional finely sliced mild onion
   and sumac powder for garnish

Knead all ingredients together thoroughly with your hands. Shape into walnut-sized balls, roll them a bit so that they are more egg-shaped, then flatten them between your palms.

Grill over charcoal, on a pre-heated griddle, or under a grill pre-heated to its maximum setting. Turn once. At the end of cooking, the *köfte* should be well-browned on both sides.

Eat with pitta or home-made flat bread (see page 61), the Kars salad of carrot and mooli (see page 44) and, if you like, a garnish of the sliced onion mixed with a large pinch of sour sumac powder and left to marinate for half an hour.

Lemon Meringue Pie

serves 6 £

Nestlé has been manufacturing cans of sweetened condensed milk for more than a century. This lemon meringue pie, along with a gooey fudge, was one of the recipe suggestions to be printed first on the side of the tin and later in the brand's cookery pamphlets. The original name, as tested and approved by a Mrs D. Cottington-Taylor, then director of the Good Housekeeping Institute, for a thirties publication called *MAGIC...In The Kitchen*, was – you guessed it – 'Magic ... Lemon Meringue Pie'. Of course it went on to become a staple of popular family dining after the war and lives on in the memories of a certain stratum of post-war babies as one of childhood's Sunday lunch highlights.

I am grateful to fellow fan, Christine O'Neill, for bringing it all back more recently. Away with all those wobbly yellow cornflour versions – this is the lemon meringue pie to grow up on.

The recipe is also excellent made with lime juice and rind, when it comes close to American Key-lime pie, although this is only authentically sharp when made with the correct variety of Florida lime.

either about 12 gingernut or plain digestive (wheatmeal) biscuits and a big knob butter

or 4 oz shortcrust pastry – see page 212

2 eggs (size 3)

a little less than a 14 oz (400 g)
   tin sweetened condensed milk
   (Nestlé's is thickest)

5 fl oz lemon juice (juice of about
   3 lemons)
grated rind of 1 lemon
2 oz caster sugar

If using biscuits for the crust, break them up roughly then whizz in
a food processor, or pulverise in a solid bowl with the end of a
wooden rolling pin, or put in a heavy-duty plastic bag and smash
into fine crumbs with something weighty. Melt the butter, mix
well with the biscuit crumbs then press firmly across the bottom of
a shallow, lightly greased flan tin.

If using pastry, roll it out and line the tin with it, prick all over
with a fork and bake blind for about 20 minutes at Gas
5/190°C/375°F until it has no more translucent patches.

Separate the eggs. Beat yolks then mix thoroughly with condensed milk, lemon juice and lemon rind. Pour mixture on to prepared base.

Whisk egg whites until stiff, fold in caster sugar, then pile onto
lemon mixture and fork up into dramatic peaks.

Bake slowly at a pre-heated Gas 3-4/160-180°C/325-350°F until
lemon mixture has set and the meringue started to colour. Test
after about 30-40 minutes.

An alternative school of thought bakes at Gas 5/190°C/375°F for
20-25 minutes. By this method, the surface of the meringue may
turn a more attractive golden colour, but it does not stay firm for as
long if there is any left over for another day.

Good warm or cold.

Butternut Squash Pie

serves 4-6 £

A late winter version of pumpkin pie made more luxurious by using the close-textured, delicious butternut squash.

1¼ lb butternut squash flesh –
  cubed, steamed until tender and
  mashed
4 oz sugar
¾ teaspoon ground nutmeg
¾ teaspoon ground ginger
½ teaspoon salt

3 eggs
5 fl oz double cream
dash milk
1×9in pie or flan tin lined with
  shortcrust pastry (see page 212)
  – unbaked

Mix squash, sugar, spices and salt together thoroughly. Beat eggs together with cream and add to the mixture with a little milk, if necessary, to form a good soft paste. Pour into the shell.

Bake at Gas 7/220°C/425°F for 15 minutes, then reduce temperature to Gas 4/180°C/350°F and bake for about another 35-40 minutes or until a knife stuck into the middle comes out clean.

Serve with whipped cream.

Extra Creamy Yoghurt

This is a relatively thick, mild high-fat luxury version, good chilled for breakfast with a swirl of acacia honey and some toasted almonds.

1¼ pints Channel Island milk
  (gold top)
1 tablespoon dried milk powder or
  granules

1 tablespoon yoghurt

Boil the milk in a pan large enough to keep it from boiling over, until it has reduced to a pint. Stir in the dried milk powder. Let it cool until you can hold your finger in for a couple of seconds before the heat hurts (the official temperature is 42°C/113°F). Whisk a little of this milk with the yoghurt in a cup, then pour into the rest of the milk and mix thoroughly.

Pour into a vacuum flask, seal and leave for 4-8 hours or overnight. Tip into a bowl and chill in the fridge. It will thicken further over the next couple of days. Pour off any liquid on the top, or stir back in for a thinner yoghurt.

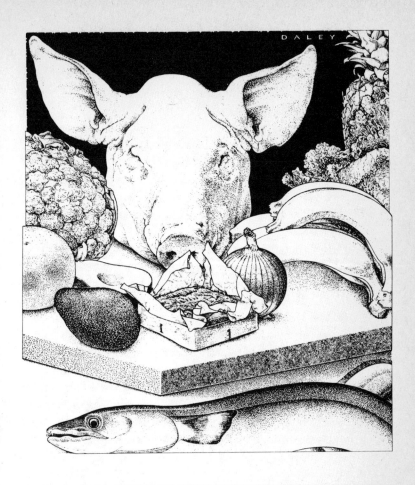

MARCH

March is the bleakest month for fresh foods; winter staples are tailing off and most spring supplies have not quite started. Fine fish from the chilly late-spring waters is still easy to find if you have access to a half-way decent fishmonger. Some imported fruit is at its very best. For vegetables, muddle through on the last of the season's greens and roots, remembering how delicious the prospect of a good parsnip will seem at the beginning of next September.

VEGETABLES

The Brussels sprout season is ending; some are still in good condition, but look carefully for loosely hearted, yellowing, tough old monsters. There are few things in cookery less appealing than a sub-standard sprout.

Even if recent weather has been severe, there should be fit spring greens from Kent and Cornwall. Watercress may be at its scarcest and ropiest. But fat, ageing, late-season leeks – fine for stews, bakes or thinly sliced in a stir-fry – generally manage to rally successfully in the worst conditions. If English cauliflower has suffered, look to French and Italian imports until fine Jersey specimens appear at the end of the month.

The end of March sometimes sees the first of the new-season English carrots, vigorous young spring onions and good, over-wintered crops of spinach. These may all be late in cold years. English hot-house cucumbers and tomatoes have already started to appear, but will not have much flavour until they've had more sun.

Use the last of the winter's good roots in baked purées. Parsnip is particularly good by itself mashed with lashings of butter and sprinkled with toasted sesame seeds. Or experiment with mixtures of different proportions of several cooked and mashed vegetables spiked up with cooked onions or leeks, spices such as cardamom, generous seasoning and butter. Top with slivered almonds, then brown and heat through in a medium oven. Parsnip also fries into good soggy chips.

Shopping list

Asparagus, aubergines, **avocado**, **beetroot**, **Belgian chicory**, broccoli (calabrese **purple sprouting**), **Brussels sprouts**, cabbages (including red, **white**, and **winter green** varieties), **Cape broccoli**, **carrots**, cauliflowers, **celeriac**, celery, chilli peppers, Chinese leaves, courgettes, cucumbers, **curly kale**, fennel, garlic, green beans (French), **greens**, herbs (mint, parsley, tarragon), lettuce and some salad leaves, **Jerusalem artichokes**, **leeks**, mange-touts, mooli, mushrooms (cultivated), **okra**, **onions**, **parsnips**, **potatoes**, pumpkins (imported), red cabbage, **salsify**, **spinach**, **spring onions**, **swedes**, **sweet potatoes**, **turnips**, watercress

Good speciality imports should include green beans from the

Canaries, Dutch pak choi and American **butternut squash** plus **bamboo shoots**, chard and black truffles. Some of the month's best new potatoes are from Egypt. If only they were more readily available, **seakale** and rocket would be two of our native seasonal treats.

FRUIT

Ivory Coast pineapples should now be excellent value. It is a shame to do more than remove the skins and eat the flesh in great unadulterated chunks so that the sweet juice runs down your chin. Or try freshly cut chunks or slices spiked with golden rum. The best bananas this month are from the Windward Isles.

As Coxes near the end of their storage season, Jonagold – a cross between Golden Delicious and Jonathan which keeps particularly well – will take over the market for home-produced apples.

The short season for blood oranges is about over, although there should be plenty of other citrus around. Lemons are simple to preserve. Cram them into a sterilised jar and cover with white wine vinegar or good olive oil (improve the shelf-life of this preparation by sticking each lemon with half a dozen cloves first). Or cut ripe lemons or limes in half, roll in handfuls of dry salt and pack tightly into a jar, with more lemon juice to cover, for a few weeks. For best results, buy organically grown fruit (the Israeli Biotop label, for example), which have skins untreated with wax and ammonia.

Eat kumquats whole, peel and all, for a sour/sweet smack of citrus, or leave them for at least a month in sterilised preserving jars in a liquor of half sugar syrup, half gin.

Shopping list
Apples (UK – Cox, Jonagold and Bramley; import – French Granny Smith), Asian pears (nashi), bananas, coconuts, grapefruit, **kumquats**, lemons, limes, mangoes, mineolas, oranges (Shamouti and Navels), **ortaniques**, pears, **pineapples**, **rhubarb** (forced and outdoor), ugli fruit

Apart from Israeli easy-peel tangerine crosses, look for Mandora from Cyprus, and Kara and Wilkings – both from Spain. **Physalis** (Chinese gooseberry) continues to be one of the most exciting finds in specialist shops.

FISH AND SEAFOOD

Mussels and scallops should both get cheaper as quality falls towards the end of their season. Mackerel is often very good by the end of the month. Many flat fish are now spawning and consequently not good to eat, although brill, dab, flounder and lemon sole defy the general pattern. In the south-west of England plaice is not traditionally touched again until May Day.

The vogue for monkfish, which doesn't really have an off-season, continues, although that old chestnut about it being substituted for lobster in restaurants is somewhat out-of-date now, especially with the high prices the fish can command in its own right. A stunning Provençal way of preparing a whole large tail, is to roast it, stuck with garlic and rubbed with olive oil, seasoning and herbs, as if it were a miniature leg of lamb.

Shopping list

Brill, clams, cockles, **conger eel**, dab, eel, **flounder**, **gurnard**, **halibut**, **huss**, **John Dory**, langoustines (Dublin Bay prawns or scampi), **lemon sole**, **mackerel**, monkfish, **mussels**, **oysters** (**native** and Pacific), salmon (wild and farmed), sardines, **scallops**, sea bass, **sea trout** (salmon trout), **shrimps**, **smelt**, **sprats** (**fresh and smoked**), tuna, **whitebait**, winkles, **witch**.

The month's most interesting exotic imports, from the Seychelles, include colourful parrot fish, emperor bream and *rouget barbet*. Look for specimens that have been flown in chilled not frozen.

MEAT, POULTRY AND GAME

Half a century ago, pork was a seasonal meat, killed from September until February or March, and considered unsafe to eat in the summer. The mild flavour and high fat content make it a good medium for assertively mucked-about casseroles and stews. Try garlic, slices of whole fresh or pickled lemon and bruised coriander seed with white wine in a slow braise of cubed pork shoulder.

Economy cuts of beef make ideal comfort food at this bum end of the winter – chuck, blade, shin and skirt for braising and stewing – brisket for slow pot-roasts, salted for boiling. Richest and most satisfying are casseroles of oxtail or heart. Most offal – calves' liver, some sweetbreads and veal kidney are the obvious exceptions – is a bargain most of the time. Explore Britain's culinary base-line with chitterlings, elder (udder), cowheel, tripe with onions, kidneys with onions, or thick slices of liver dredged in seasoned flour then quickly fried with onions.

Shopping list
beef, **chicken**, guinea-fowl, hare, **pork**, rabbit, turkey, veal, venison.

Imports of fresh (not frozen) New Zealand lamb should be plentiful.

CHEESE

British elements in a March cheese board might include the unpasteurised Appleby Cheshire and real Wensleydale, made from half ewe's, half cow's milk and matured since last autumn, as well as Cotherstone from the Yorkshire Dales. Hugh Rance, proprietor of one of our finest cheese emporiums, describes it as, 'soft and flaky, freshly acidic, smelling of clean curd and new hay'.

French names to look for in reputable specialist shops are Beaufort, Pont l'Evêque, Coulommiers, Comte and Banon. March marks the beginning of the French goat cheeses.

Hot Yoghurt Soup

serves 6 £

An everyday Turkish dish, with the authentic taste of small-town and roadside restaurants and kebab-houses all over Anatolia.

As there is little else to this soup, it should be based on a good broth. Ideally, boil a whole chicken for 2 hours in about 4 pints of water with an onion stuck with cloves, a peeled carrot, a stick of celery, a bay leaf, some parsley stalks and black peppercorns. This is not salted so that you can season the dish freely. The chicken is then excellent bland comfort food, surprisingly good eaten plain, or

in pies, bakes, blanquettes, sandwiches and rissoles. Also useful for feeding the cat. This soup is also one of very few dishes I know which is palatable made from a stock of lamb or mutton bones. Brown them off first in the oven to get rid of the worst of the fatty, farmyard smells.

Dried mint is a staple of the Turkish kitchen; for authenticity do not be tempted to use fresh leaves.

3 pints well flavoured chicken,
  lamb, mutton or beef broth
4 oz long-grain rice
3 oz butter
1½-2 tablespoons flour
2 oz cooked chickpeas

2 egg yolks
15 fl oz strained Greek yoghurt
salt and freshly ground black
  pepper
1 tablespoon dried mint
cayenne pepper

Boil stock with rice for 15 minutes. Melt half the butter in a small saucepan, stir in the flour and cook until it turns a pale straw colour. Take off the heat. Ladle in about ½ pint of the boiling stock and whisk until thoroughly incorporated. Pour mixture back into the stock, add the chickpeas and continue boiling for another 15 minutes, stirring often, until the rice is soft. Take off the heat.

Beat egg yolks together with a little of the yoghurt, then mix with the rest of the yoghurt and pour little by little into the hot (not boiling) stock, beating all the time. Season with salt and black pepper, then heat gently until the mixture thickens slightly. Do not let it boil or it will curdle.

Melt the rest of the butter in a small saucepan. When it is bubbling, stir in dried mint and a generous sprinkling of cayenne, then immediately beat this mixture into the soup.

Serve hot with Middle Eastern Flat Bread (see page 61.)

Okra and New Potato Salad

serves 4 £

The okra, left whole, lightly cooked so that it does not become slimey or lose its bite, is the main ingredient in this satisfyingly messy salad with a sharp thick dressing. Serve cold with bread as a starter or light lunch dish, or as a decent hot or warm single accompaniment to plainly grilled fish or meat.

There are numerous variations. Use all onion or leek rather than a mixture, or experiment with spring onions cut into strips and not cooked for as long as the ordinary onions. Coriander seeds and green coriander leaves could not be more different in flavour and are not normally interchangeable, but this dish also works well with the ground spice left out and some of the chopped fresh herb stirred in at the end of cooking. When fresh tomatoes are tastier and cheaper, try leaving out the chilli, orange juice and tomato paste, and add 1 lb of skinned, sliced and seeded tomatoes with the other ingredients after the okra's first fierce heating.

4 large new potatoes (8-10 oz) – scraped
1 lb fresh okra
4-5 tablespoons olive oil
4 oz onion – peeled and finely chopped
3 cloves garlic – peeled and finely chopped
4 oz leek – thinly sliced

optional 1-2 fresh green chillies – thinly sliced
1 teaspoon ground coriander seed
2 tablespoons tomato paste
juice of 1 small orange (4-6 tbsp)
juice of 1 lemon (3-4 tbsp)
salt
freshly ground black pepper

Boil potatoes in salted water until cooked. Drain. Leave to cool, if possible overnight in the fridge. When cold, cut into ½in chunks.

Wash okra pods well. Carefully cut off the hard conical tops and any withered-looking tails without cutting into the interior seed-chambers. Dry thoroughly.

Heat oil in a large heavy frying pan or casserole. Add the onion, garlic and leek; cook until soft and transparent. Add the chillies, if using.

Turn up the heat, throw in the coriander and okra. Stir and cook for about 5 minutes until the onion and leek is beginning to colour and the okra pods are softening. They should still be bright green.

Turn down the heat. Add the potatoes, tomato paste, citrus juices, at least ½ teaspoon of salt and lots of black pepper. Stir thoroughly. The mixture should be just moist, with no surplus liquid. Cover the pan and leave on a very gentle heat for 5 minutes more.

This will keep perfectly warm for about half an hour with the lid on. It can be successfully served at any reasonable temperature. Keeps well in the fridge for up to two days.

Albanian Liver

serves 4-6 £

Otherwise known as *Arnavut ciğeri*. A popular and easy starter to ring the changes on a *meze* table. Serve hot, warm or tepid on a central plate for people to help themselves, or with cocktail sticks for a buffet or snacks with drinks.

1 lb liver (properly lambs', but calves' is even better)	4-5 tablespoons pure olive oil (not virgin or extra-virgin)
1 teaspoon salt	1 cooking onion – peeled and sliced in paper-thin rings
2 tablespoons paprika	
4-5 tablespoons flour seasoned with freshly ground black pepper	2 tablespoons finely chopped parsley

Cut the well trimmed liver into ¾in cubes. Immediately before you are ready to cook, sprinkle all over with the salt and paprika, then toss with the flour in a plastic bag so that each cube of liver is completely coated, dry and separate. If you wait at this stage, the juices seeping out of the offal will leave you with a terrifying raw liver pudding. As you take out each batch of cubes to fry, shake off surplus flour back into the bag.

Heat oil in a large frying pan, throw in as much liver as still has room to be turned happily. Fry over a medium-hot flame until browned on all sides. This should not take more than 3-4 minutes for each batch. The insides of the liver cubes should remain rosy and moist.

Remove with a slotted spoon, drain on kitchen paper, then repeat with the next batch of liver. Pile all the browned cubes onto a serving pate. Toss the slivered onion together with the parsley in a bowl and scatter over the liver.

Conger Eel Bake

serves 4 £

For all the trend toward fish cooked *à point* – just pink along the bone – and *mi-cuit* half-cooked – especially for steaks of best salmon and fillets of fine flat fish such as Dover sole, brill and turbot – nothing can beat a long slow braise for rich flavour and plush texture. This is admirably suited to the much neglected conger eel.

Mr Crispin, who runs a fish and greengrocery shop in Kingsbridge, Devon, recommends the regional, south-western way of cutting it up, boiling it and serving it with butter. This hearty, family-supper alternative is hardly more complicated.

1½-2 lb conger eel pieces –
  skinned and boned
butter
salt and pepper

8 oz onion – peeled and sliced
1 lb potatoes – peeled and sliced
milk

Pack the prepared conger tightly into a buttered oven dish. Season well. Cover with the sliced onion and potatoes, making sure that the top is mostly potato. Season the top, dot with little pieces of butter, then pour in enough boiling milk to drown the fish and come right up to the level of the top potato layer.

Bake, uncovered, at Gas 4/180°C/350°F for about an hour until the potatoes are tender.

Pot-Roast Caribbean Pork

serves 4 ££

A shameless bastardisation of an already dubious Puerto Rican recipe – the original uses 1½ lb sugar and three bottles of the non-alcoholic and highly nutritious drink, *malta*, this joint comes out of the pot looking like a lurid plum bread and tastes as strange as it sounds. Best served hot with its thin black gravy, plus boiled or steamed carrots and potatoes – or red beans and sweet potatoes. It isn't too bad served cold either – it certainly slices better – with a garlicky spinach salad squeezed over with lots of lemon juice.

For the pork, use a boned, prepared joint suitable for roasting, such as prime hand or quarter leg. This recipe does not require the leanest, slightly more expensive cuts.

While some dried herbs are useless, others – including thyme and sage – perform well in stews or braises. Dried oregano is a Puerto Rican staple.

3 lb joint of pork
12 green cocktail olives stuffed
   with pimento
6 large pitted prunes
20 whole black peppercorns
2 teaspoons salt

1-2 teaspoons dried oregano
4 cloves garlic – peeled
1 tablespoon olive oil
1 tablespoon wine or cider vinegar
¼ pint stout
2 teaspoons demerara sugar

Cut the string off the prepared joint, open it out and remove the rind and as much exterior fat as you can. Cut 24 deep, narrow slits all over the meat and insert an olive or half a pitted prune into each. Roll up the joint neatly and tie with string.

Crush the peppercorns with a pestle and mortar. Add the salt, oregano and garlic. Mash to a paste. Stir in the olive oil and vinegar. Rub this mixture over all the surfaces of the meat.

In a heavy casserole, on a medium flame, brown the meat all over. Turn down the heat and pour in the stout and sugar. When the liquid is bubbling gently, cover the casserole and cook for 2 hours, turning the joint over half-way through the cooking time.

To serve, take off the string and cut across the joint in thick slices. Adjust the seasoning of the gravy and pour it over the slices on the plate (there should only be a couple of spoonfuls each).

Hot and Sour Venison

serves 6 ££

The immediate thought when cooking venison cuts of less than roasting or griddling quality is to stew or casserole them with olde Englishe disguising agents such as juniper, red wine, orange peel and redcurrant jelly. Cream sometimes then appears in an attempt to lubricate what can be a rather dense, dry meat and the whole thing becomes indigestibly rich and heavy.

This is an attempt to go in the opposite direction by cutting through venison's fragrant hint of decomposition with brutal elements stolen from Goanese vindaloo techniques.

2 teaspoons cumin seed – roasted in a dry saucepan until brown and aromatic, then ground
1 teaspoon ground cinnamon
½ teaspoon ground cloves
½ teaspoon cardamom seeds (the small black grains cut out of the pale pods)
½ teaspoon freshly ground black pepper
6 tablespoons wine vinegar
10 tablespoons vegetable oil

3 lb lean stewing venison – trimmed and cut into 1in cubes
2 teaspoons whole black mustard seeds (*sarson*)
1 tablespoon cayenne pepper
1 teaspoon turmeric
2 teaspoons ground coriander
3 teaspoons paprika
12 oz onions – peeled and finely chopped
10 cloves garlic – peeled and finely chopped

1 tablespoon peeled and finely grated fresh root ginger	6 softish pitted dried apricots – chopped
2 teaspoons salt	3 tablespoons lemon juice
	1 pint water

In a glass, pottery or stainless steel bowl, mix the cumin, cinnamon, cloves, cardamom, black pepper, wine vinegar and 4 tablespoons of the oil. Toss the venison in this marinade and leave for at least 8 hours or for up to a day in the fridge, turning from time to time.

Heat the other 6 tablespoons of oil in a large, heavy saucepan. Remove the meat from the marinade with a slotted spoon, shake any liquid back into the bowl and keep for later. Fry the meat in batches until well browned on all sides (about 10 minutes for each batch), then remove from the pan with a slotted spoon, draining extraneous oil back into the saucepan.

With the oil still hot and the saucepan over a medium flame, tip in the mustard seeds. Stir them around for a few seconds, then tip in the cayenne pepper, turmeric, coriander and paprika all together. Stir for another few seconds, then tip in the onions, garlic and ginger. Cook, stirring continuously until these have softened and are well flecked with brown.

Add the browned meat, any remaining marinade, salt, apricots, lemon juice and water. Stir thoroughly, scraping the bottom of the pan with your spatula or spoon to dissolve any burnt bits. Bring to the boil. Boil hard for 10 minutes, then turn down to a lively simmer, partially cover the pan and cook for 1½-2 hours, stirring from time to time, until the meat is tender.

If necessary, boil hard again at the end of cooking time to reduce the liquid to a thick gravy. Serve with plain steamed or boiled rice.

Curried Parsnip and Leek Cakes

serves 4 £

A request from readers for a good dish to mark the last of the winter vegetables produced a dozen versions of fried parsnip and leek cakes. Here is one that blends – and possibly compromises – ideas from several of them.

Good eaten with fried bacon or plainly grilled, meat, poultry or fish. Also fine, accompanied perhaps with a watercress salad or hot spinach and mushrooms, for a vegetarian lunch or supper dish.

½ lb leeks – trimmed and very finely sliced
1 oz butter
1 teaspoon curry powder – any strength
salt and freshly ground black pepper

1 lb parsnips – trimmed and peeled
2 pieces wholemeal bread – toasted and finely crumbed
1 egg – beaten
groundnut oil

Sauté the leeks in the butter until softened and beginning to colour. Add the curry powder and continue cooking for a minute or two, stirring all the time. Season.

Steam the parsnips until tender, then drain well until completely dry. Mash or purée in a food processor. Season.

Mix leeks thoroughly with parsnip purée, then beat in enough of the breadcrumbs and enough of the beaten egg to form a stiff, glossy paste. Form into cakes and shallow fry in medium-hot oil for 5 or more minutes on each side until golden.

You can also bake these on oiled baking sheets; with the addition of another egg they will rise slightly.

Flavouring Carrots

The sweet clean taste of carrots shows off even minute quantities of other flavourings to great effect. Use larger, older carrots for these simple preparations.

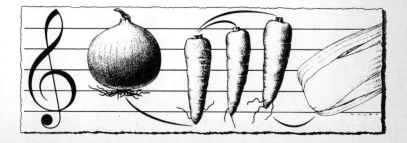

Carrots with Roasted Cumin

serves 2-4 £

1 lb carrots – peeled
½ tablespoon groundnut oil
4-5 spring onions – trimmed and
  thinly sliced (both white and
  green parts)

¼-½ teaspoon cumin seeds –
  roasted in a dry pan until brown
  and aromatic, then ground
pinch salt
pinch cayenne pepper
squeeze lemon juice

Cut carrots into 2in lengths, then into thin lengthways slices, then again lengthways to form matchsticks. Heat the oil in a heavy pan over a medium flame, toss in the carrots and spring onions and stir-fry for 3-5 minutes until the carrot is wilting but still retains some bite. Stir in the ground, roasted cumin, salt, pepper and lemon juice. Serve hot. Good with grilled fish.

Honeyed Carrots with Mint

serves 2-4 £

1 lb carrots – peeled
small knob butter
½ teaspoon light honey (such as
  acacia or orange flower)
2 tablespoons freshly squeezed
  orange juice

1 tablespoon finely chopped fresh
  mint leaves
pinch salt
freshly ground black pepper

Cut the carrots into matchsticks. In a dry, well tempered wok or non-stick frying pan over high heat, stir-fry the carrot sticks until wilting and colouring at the edges. Take off the heat and add the butter, honey, juice, mint, salt and pepper all at once. Keep stirring, as the ingredients sizzle, until the carrots are glazed with them. Serve immediately. Good with ham.

Pineapple Pudding

serves 6 £

The roasted hazelnuts, brandy, fresh rather than tinned fruit, and absence of glacé cherries take this dinner-party version of that old family favourite, pineapple upside-down cake, up a notch or two without quite laying the friendly ghost of Saturday high-tea with great aunt Dottie. Very easy to make.

topping:
half a large ripe pineapple
3 oz slightly salted butter
3 oz caster sugar
1 tablespoon brandy
½ tablespoon lemon juice
cake:
4 oz butter

4 oz caster sugar
3½ oz self-raising flour
1 level teaspoon baking powder
1 oz hazelnuts – roasted, papery
   skins rubbed off, then ground in
   a liquidiser or food-processor
2 eggs (size 3)
1 tablespoon brandy

With a large, sharp, stainless steel knife, cut the top, stem, skin, core and eyes from the pineapple. Slice the fruit crossways to make thin half-rings.

For the topping, melt the butter in a one-piece, straight-sided, 9in diameter and 1¾in deep cake or pie tin – preferably non-stick – over a low flame. Swish the butter around to coat the sides if the tin is not non-stick. Add the sugar, brandy and lemon juice. Stir gently as the mixture boils and foams. After a few minutes it will start to colour. Continue stirring until it is an even, pale toffee-brown.

Take off the heat. Arrange the pineapple slices in the sauce, over-lapping, to cover the whole bottom of the tin.

Whizz all the cake ingredients in the food processor until smooth and creamy, or beat them energetically by hand. Pour the mixture over the pineapple and smooth over the surface with a spatula. Bake at Gas 5/190°C/375°F for 45 minutes, lowering the heat to Gas 4/180°C/350°F after half an hour if the mixture is already well risen and deep brown. When it is cooked, the cake will have contracted slightly from the sides of the tin, and a skewer pushed in at an angle across the cake will come out clean.

Take out of the oven and let sit for a few minutes. Pass a knife round the sides to make sure nothing has stuck. Place an inverted serving plate over the tin then turn the whole thing upside down in one swift movement.

Serve hot, warm or cold with whipped double cream, thick strained yoghurt or crème fraîche.

Linda Sue's Chocolate Cheesecake

serves 6-8 ££

Linda Sue Park, the first winner of *The Independent* cookery competition, sponsored by Taittinger champagne, later sent this gorgeous, rich, highly compact, marbled chocolate cheesecake to the paper in response to a request for favourite recipes. It is her adaptation of a recipe from the extraordinarily successful American book *The Joy of Cooking* by Irma S. Rombauer and Marion Rombauer Becker. Every home should have one.

crust:
12 oz plain digestive (wheatmeal)
    biscuits
6 oz butter
2 tablespoons ground almonds
8 oz vanilla caster sugar (or 8 oz
    sugar and ½ teaspoon vanilla
    essence)
3 eggs
5 fl oz double cream

2 oz caster sugar
filling:
1 lb soft Philadelphia cheese (two
    7 oz/200 g tubs)

1-2 packets Meunier chocolate –
    ordinary size
topping:
11 fl oz soured cream (two tubs)
2 tablespoons sugar

For the crust, crush the biscuits, melt the butter, then mix together with the almonds and sugar. Pack firmly with a fork on to the bottom and a little way up the sides of a large tin (a 13in x 9in roasting pan is ideal). Chill.

For the filling, cream the cheese and sugar together. Gradually mix in the well beaten eggs, blending thoroughly. Stir in the cream. Pour half of this mixture into the chilled crust. Melt the chocolate and stir into the remaining filling. Drop by dollops into the crust, marbling the chocolate and vanilla mixtures together with a knife. Bake at Gas 4/180°C/350°F for 30 minutes until filling is set. Let cake cool to room temperature.

For the topping, mix the soured cream and sugar, then spread evenly over the cake. Bake for 5-8 minutes at Gas 7/220°C/425°F to form a glaze. Chill the whole thing for several hours. Remove from the fridge an hour or two before serving.

Russian Jelly

serves 6 £

On an unsophisticated note similar to last month's lemon meringue pie, this sharp tasting pudding, which I have always known as Russian jelly although I have no idea of the source, is basically lemon flavoured curds and whey with the addition of egg and gelatine to sort out the texture. As the curds and whey separate out in the setting, the bottom layer becomes a clear jelly and the top a coarse mousse.

3 lemons   ½ lb sugar
1 pint milk   3 eggs – separated
½ oz gelatine

With a sharp knife, carefully peel just the yellow zest from the
lemons.

Put a little of the milk into a cup and sprinkle on the gelatine.
Leave until it has absorbed the liquid and become spongy.

Put milk, sugar, egg yolks, strips of lemon zest and proved gelatine into a saucepan. Slowly bring to the boil. It will curdle. Strain
off the lemon zest and let the liquid cool.

Whip egg whites until stiff then fold into mixture. Stir in the
juice of all the lemons.

Leave to set, which takes at least 2 hours in the fridge.

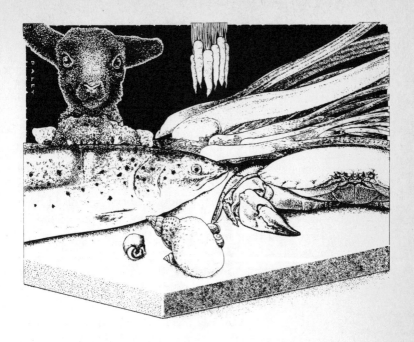

APRIL

The sap is rising. Crisp young carrots will soon be buzzing with it, new spinach leaves lazily unfurling with it and glorious English asparagus quite explicitly erecting itself with it. By May, winter should be left quite behind. In the meantime, some of the best April news is sea trout and new-season lamb.

On the negative side, the month sometimes keeps a last serious cold patch and occasionally a severe few inches of snow up its sleeve. Fruit is mostly imported at this opposite end of the year from harvest festivals.

VEGETABLES

Even if conditions have been bad and British-grown produce runs a couple of weeks late, milder weather and a bit of sun in the second half of the month will quickly bridge the gap. If all goes well, there should be English asparagus by the last week of April, even though the official open season for the crop does not start until 1 May. At worst, Spanish and American imports provide a reasonable second best.

Purple sprouting broccoli should be at its prime this month. These are most often off-puttingly sold, as Jane Grigson says, 'hugger-mugger in boxes', although unprepossessing appearances may belie excellent quality. Some supermarkets are now making some concession with see-through plastic cartons. Cape broccoli is a British-grown variety, not, as it sounds, calabrese imported from South Africa, which looks like a cauliflower with purple florets. Spring cabbages and their unhearted brothers, spring greens, are taking over from winter varieties (although, confusingly, most greens are now sold as 'spring-greens' throughout the rest of the year). Good home-produced spinach should be abundant by the end of the month.

Roots are very much on their last legs, although if the weather is kind, tiny new-season English carrots, sold in bunches with their feathery tops still on, might be around. The first, expensive Jersey Royals – most delicious of new potatoes – should be coming in by the end of April.

As temperatures rise, the growth rate of cultivated mushrooms gets harder to control and the price goes down. Hot-house English salad crops – cucumbers, tomatoes and lettuce – are more generally available, as well as Dutch imports, although these are often pretty tasteless and pappy. For the revelatory real taste of sweet juicy cucumbers, search out the small new-season imports from Cyprus and the Mediterranean.

Shopping list
Asparagus, aubergines, **avocados,** beetroot, Belgian chicory, broad beans, broccoli (calabrese, **purple sprouting**), cabbages (including red, **white** and **spring green** varieties), **Cape broccoli, carrots, cauliflowers,** celeriac, celery, chilli peppers, Chinese leaves, **courgettes, cucumbers,** curly kale, fennel, garlic, globe artichokes, green beans (French and flat), herbs (basil, chervil, dill, mint, parsley, rosemary, sage, tarragon) **leeks, lettuce,** mange-touts, mushrooms (cultivated), okra, onions, **parsnips,** potatoes, **rad-**

ishes, **salsify, spinach, spring greens, spring onions, swedes,** sweet
potatoes, tomatoes, turnips, **watercress**

During the build up to Jersey Royals, Morocco sends us about
the best of the month's new potatoes. This is the last full month for
American **butternut squash** and for Israeli avocados, so this is the
month to make use of particularly cheap, very ripe or slightly
imperfect specimens.

A real treat for mycophiles with access to a good specialist
retailer is the start of the short season for **morels,** those fleshy wild
mushrooms with deeply indented caps and a wonderfully fine flavour. Also look for **bamboo shoots,** chard, rocket and samphire.

FRUIT

Iberia steals the thunder of our own spring and summer crops by
being able to export all our favourites a few weeks in advance of the
British season. The flavour tends not to be as good, although not
always as hopeless as sometimes made out: Spanish strawberries
can be particularly good. The price should fall dramatically in
April.

The Caribbean banana season is now at its peak. Prime quality
imports seem to have extra sweetness and tang. Otherwise, with
the season's best apples and pears coming from the southern hemisphere, this is not a stimulating month for fruit.

Shopping list
Asian pears (nashi), **bananas,** coconuts, grapefruit, kumquats,
lemons, limes, lognab mangoes, mineolas, oranges, **ortaniques,**
pears, physalis, **pineapples, rhubarb** (outdoor), strawberries
(import), topaz, ugli fruit

FISH AND SEAFOOD

The first good month for crustacea for a while. Crab, especially, is
getting back on form after its winter break. Sea trout sometimes-
called salmon trout, which some people think a cheat, although it
seems a perfectly fair anglicisation of its Latin name – *Salmo trutta*
– is a fine beast for showy meals. Of the meaty, firm-fleshed white
fish, conger eel remains excellent value.

Shopping list

Brill, clams, cockles, **conger eel, crab, crawfish** (spiny lobster), dab, eel, **gurnard,** hake, **halibut,** huss, langoustines (Dublin Bay prawns or scampi), **lemon sole,** ling, **lobster, mackerel,** monkfish, **oysters (native** and Pacific), **prawns, salmon (wild and farmed),** sardines, **sea trout** (salmon trout), **shrimps,** tuna, **whelks, whitebait,** winkles, **witch**

St Peter's fish, or tilepia (as caught in the Sea of Galilee), is widely farmed in Israel, and now also in Belgium, from where it sometimes comes to British wet-fish counters at this time of year.

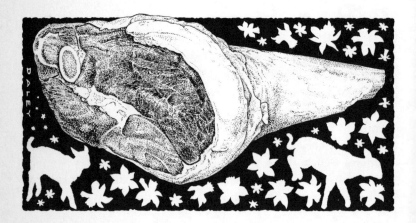

MEAT

Some of the world's best new-season lamb is raised in the mountains of Powys in central Wales. The sheep of the area are fine-boned, with sweet meat, feeding on open pastures and long established, traditional herbage rather than the new grasses introduced elsewhere. Some are pure bred Welsh Mountain, others have been crossed with Down rams, to give a more developed musculature and leaner meat. The main flush of lambs is now being reared for dressing in three to four months' time: at the height of the season in June and July, an abbatoir might kill 4,000 animals a week.

Some lambs are purpose-bred indoors for the Easter market and these should now be coming into the shops. Local producer Edward Hamer, who has a beautiful Victorian butchery at Llanidloes, recommends shoulders on the bone, roasted a little on the pink side and accompanied by leeks casseroled in the oven with bacon.

Shopping list
beef, chicken, guinea-fowl, **new-season lamb,** pork, quail (farmed), rabbit, turkey, veal

CHEESE

Some of the best French varieties to look for in specialist shops during April are Beaufort, Bleu des Causses, Boules des Moines, Camembert and the fresh new goat's milk cheeses, such as Charolais, Montrachet and the various Chevrotins. From Britain, try the Single Gloucester and Double Berkley made by Charles Martell, who also has a cheese stall in Cirencester market on Mondays and Fridays. The curds for the Double Berkley are divided, then half are dyed orange before being cut back into the untreated portion, so giving the cheese a marbled effect.

Mashing Avocados

Avocado dips were the *sine qua non* of the mid-seventies suburban party, as fuelled by recipes in glossy cookery books on entertaining and free hand-outs from greengrocers. The movement peaked with the invention of avotara – a grey paste of avocado and fluffy, pink supermarket taramasalata blended together with extra lemon juice and pepper. Soon enough, complete-snack-and-savoury hostesses realised the avocado was no longer chic and, of course, that taramasalata was no longer taramasalata, my dear, unless you made it yourself.

The end result of all this is that the avocado has been unjustly maligned. It is time for a revival. There is no need to think of it as watery and flavourless. One taste of a small, rough, dark-skinned, yieldingly ripe Hass – the best of the four main varieties – should convert the most cynical.

Arguments about what constitutes 'proper' guacamole tend to be bloody and long drawn out. One camp accepts nothing but oil, lemon or lime juice, salt, black and cayenne peppers and occasionally fresh green coriander in a smooth purée, even resorting to the food processor for an extra velvety texture. The other comes up with chunky mixtures, which purists call just *salsa cruda*.

Both are good as a side relish with tacos, tamales and other Mexican or Tex-Mex food. Or with plainly grilled fish and poultry. Or even as a suburban party dip.

Guacamole/Salsa Cruda

serves 2 as a dip £

1 Hass avocado, ripe and soft but not mushy

1 large tomato (beef or marmande) or 4 ordinary salad tomatoes

1 tablespoon finely chopped fresh green coriander

1 clove garlic – peeled and minced

1-2 fresh hot green chilli peppers – seeds removed, flesh finely minced

1 tablespoon freshly squeezed lemon juice

1-2 tablespoons best olive oil

salt and freshly ground black pepper

cayenne pepper

Cut the avocado in half lengthways around the stone. Twist to separate the two halves. Lever out the stone with the point of a knife. Spoon out the flesh on to a board, scraping the inside of the skin clean. Chop up the flesh quite finely and scrape into a bowl.

Skin the tomatoes. This is made easier by loosening the skin first, either by scalding them briefly in boiling water or by skewering them on a carving fork and holding them over a naked gas flame until the skin chars and splits.

Cut out the hard stem-join bit of the tomatoes. Cut the fruit in half crossways. Scrape out all the pockets of seeds with your fingers and discard. Finely dice the remaining flesh and add to the bowl with the coriander, garlic, chillies, lemon juice, olive oil and seasonings.

Mix thoroughly. Chill for up to 30 minutes, then serve before the dip begins to discolour.

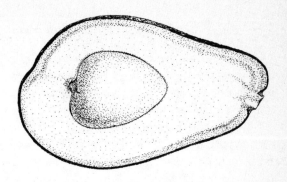

Guaca-Texacana

serves 2 as a dip £

1 Hass avocado – as soft and ripe as you like

1 tablespoon fresh green coriander – finely chopped

1-2 pickled jalapeño or tinned serrano peppers – finely diced

1 tablespoon freshly squeezed lime juice

1 tablespoon olive oil

3 spring onions – trimmed and finely sliced (both white and green parts)

salt

For this slight variation, mash the avocado flesh smoothly. Stir in the lime juice and oil, then all the other ingredients.

Marinating Raw Fish

Small quantities of thinly sliced raw fish, partly 'cooked' by the action of some applied agent – acid, salt, alcohol, herbs – then artfully arranged on the plate, can make an upbeat first course. British food champion, Henrietta Green, cuts fine, real, undyed, cold-smoked haddock at a slant into tissue-paper-thin slices which she layers with finely chopped spring onion and black pepper before dribbling olive oil over, to serve half an hour later with wodges of brown bread. Others seem to have forged their entire early careers on style-conscious dinner parties with exquisite positionings of raw scallop, salmon and monkfish marinated in vodka and fresh lime.

Ian McAndrew – a tall, good-humoured Geordie, who used to run the best restaurant in Kent, before setting up in London – bases his menus on imaginative, modern ideas executed with great care and panache. One of his early spring dishes is a starter assortment of marinated raw fish – scallops in lime juice, gravadlax, turbot in a tomato-based marinade, sea bass in olive oil, and a salmon tartare – arranged on a large plate around a pile of small, raw vegetable batons tossed in garlicky mayonnaise. Here are three of the components, each suitable for serving alone as well as in combination.

It is *essential* that all the fish used be absolutely fresh, and that you work with a flexible, sharp knife. Neither sea bass nor turbot are amongst the fish on this month's shopping list, not being officially at their best, but you should be able to find good examples at reputable fishmongers. If not, substitute halibut, brill or one of the exotic species, such as jobs jaune, vara vara or red grouper, which are flown in from the Seychelles.

Work on a total of 3 oz salmon and 4 oz of other fish per person. If you are loath to attempt it, get your fishmonger to take on the skinning and filleting.

Sea Bass with Herbs

serves 4 ££-£££

quantities for 1 lb of sliced fish
1 teaspoon sea salt plus another 1
   teaspoon for serving
freshly ground black pepper

fresh herbs such as tarragon,
   chervil, dill, chives and flat-leaf
   parsley – stalks removed but
   leaves left whole
4 fl oz olive oil

Skin and fillet the sea bass, then cut very thinly at a slant to form large, translucent slices. The knife must be razor sharp.

Season each slice and scatter fairly generously with mixed fresh herb leaves. Layer slices in a dish, sprinkling each herbed layer with olive oil. Make sure there is enough oil to cover the top slice, then leave for 12-36 hours in the fridge.

Bring up to room temperature before serving. Lift slices out of the dish with the herb leaves still in place. Drape across individual plates. Sprinkle with the extra salt and spoon over a little of the olive oil marinade.

Turbot with Tomato

serves 4 £££

quantities for 1 lb of sliced fish
6 tomatoes – roughly chopped,
    plus extra peeled tomato for
    garnish
salt and freshly ground white
    pepper

3 tablespoons walnut oil
1 tablespoon sherry vinegar
tarragon leaves for garnish

Skin and fillet the turbot. Slice the fillets straight across the grain into thin slivers. Liquidise the tomatoes with lavish seasoning, plus the walnut oil and vinegar. Pass the purée through a sieve, to get rid of the skin and pip debris.

Marinate fish pieces in the tomato mixture for 6-12 hours. Lift fish out of bowl, shaking off excess marinade.

Arrange on serving plates with a teaspoon of the marinade splodged on top in a decorative manner (you may need to beat this first if it has separated), plus a sprinkling of tarragon leaves and a neat strip of peeled tomato flesh or two to garnish.

Salmon with Cucumber and Dill

serves 4 £££-££££

quantities for 12 oz skinned and
  filleted fish
freshly squeezed juice of 2 limes
salt and freshly ground white
    pepper
grated lime zest
4 oz cucumber – peeled and
  seeded

2 tablespoons plain yoghurt –
    beaten to make it creamy
½ tablespoon finely chopped fresh
    dill plus extra sprigs for garnish

Finely dice the salmon. Season with some of the lime juice, salt and pepper and a tiny scraping of finely grated lime zest. This mixture does not need to be left marinating for more than a minute or two. The ingredients take their effect almost immediately.

Finely dice the cucumber and stir in just enough yoghurt to give it a pearly sheen. Season very lightly and add a slug of lime juice and the chopped dill.

To serve, spoon a small pile of the cucumber mixture on to each plate. Make little fishburgers with the salmon, and arrange half-on, half-off the cucumber mounds. Garnish with dill.

Eggs au Miroir

serves 6 £

William Verrall was master of the White Hart Inn, Lewes, from 1737 until about 1760. He had been apprentice to the French chef St Clouet and picked up and developed many ways with food that make him stand apart from contemporaries such as Hannah Glasse. Some of the ideas published in his *Complete System of Cookery* (1759) are strikingly modern and would grace any restaurant menu today – turkey braised with chestnuts, teal with olives, rabbit collops with champagne, peach fritters with hock.

This recipe, adapted by Michelle Berriedale-Johnson for *The British Museum Cookbook*, shows Verrall's passion for cream. But combined here with the green of the onion and parsley and citrus tang of the juices, it makes a surprisingly fresh-tasting first course or lunch dish.

1 oz butter	10 fl oz double cream
10-12 finely chopped trimmed	juice of 3 small oranges
spring onions	juice of 2 small lemons
3 handfuls finely chopped parsley	salt and freshly ground white
6 large eggs	pepper

Butter the bottom of a flan dish large enough to hold the eggs. Sprinkle over the onions and parsley. Carefully break in the eggs, side by side.

Mix cream and citrus juices, season generously and pour over the eggs. Bake at Gas 3/160°C/325°F for 15 minutes or until the whites of the eggs are just set.

Serve warm or cold with brown bread or toast.

Michelle Berriedale-Johnson advises that if you want to double the number of eggs, you should only increase quantities of the other ingredients by a third.

Garlic Custard

serves 4 £

Steam king, Jacques Manière, who has taught his techniques to many of the top-name chefs in France, came to London in 1988 to act as consultant to David Chambers, executive head chef of Le Meridien hotel in Piccadilly. His ideas are often healthy – for example, using oil as a last-minute seasoning rather than the cooking medium for sometimes heavy dishes such as ratatouille. But Manière is no ascetic crank, as illustrated by this gutsy savoury custard, an excellent accompaniment for roast lamb.

I haven't tried any variations, but don't see why the idea shouldn't work with other flavoursome main ingredients such as morels or other fresh wild mushrooms (or reconstituted dried ones), dried tomatoes, black olives, or strips of bulb fennel (although it would be essential that all extraneous liquid was drained and pressed out before these were puréed).

2 whole heads garlic – separated
 into bulbs, then peeled and
 trimmed
1 whole egg
1 egg white

1 teaspoon potato flour
salt and freshly ground pepper
4 tablespoons crème fraîche or
 fromage blanc
about ¼ oz butter

Cut each clove of garlic in half and discard any green centres. Steam for 15 minutes over rapidly boiling water. Mash with a fork, or purée in a food mill. Put in a bowl with the egg and egg white. Whisk lightly.

Add the potato flour and whisk lightly again. Season. Add the crème fraîche or fromage blanc and whisk again.

Use the butter to grease 4 ramekins. Divide the mixture between the ramekins. Cover with foil. Steam for 15 minutes – 10 with the steamer lid tightly on, 5 with it half-open.

Turn custards out to serve. Eat hot.

Steaming Dough

The idea of steamed breads has held a weird fascination for me ever since my introduction to dim-sum – the Chinese midday and after-noon snacks that are eaten with tea – during snatched Soho lunch-breaks. Drew Smith, my first real employer and editor of *The Good Food Guide*, would enthusiastically act as courier, taking me off to vast eating palaces, like the Chuen Cheng Ku in Wardour Street and New World in Gerrard Place, and guiding me through the contents of the rattan steamer baskets piled on chrome trolleys and pushed up and down by bored-looking waitresses.

Apart from the whelks in black bean sauce, shark's fin dumplings and lotus leaves stuffed with sticky savoury rice, it was always the little pure white buns of steamed dough stuffed with aromatic roast pork in a fragrant, sweetish red sauce which made the imminent return to paper-shuffling seem an especially dismal prospect.

Chinese Split Buns

serves 4 £

As yet, I haven't mastered the technique of making these buns with their stuffing already inside, but the following recipes provide a fair compromise. The diners stuff them themselves at the table.

This can be a messy first course to a fancy Chineseish meal or an elaborate and time-consuming snack. The buns would also be good as an accompaniment to sloppy, rich, highly flavoured stews, or make up your own filling. I've always fancied one with oysters and spring onions in chilli-hot, thick, dark sauce but haven't experimented yet.

1 teaspoon dried yeast	1 teaspoon baking powder
1 teaspoon caster sugar	¼ oz lard
¼ pint warm water	sesame oil
8 oz plain flour	

Mix yeast, sugar and water and leave for about 10 minutes to foam. Sift flour and baking powder together and rub in the fat. Mix in the frothy yeast liquid and knead well. Cover loosely with clingfilm and leave until doubled in volume (about 1 hour).

Knock back dough and form into 12 equal balls. Flatten slightly. Put each on to a little square of lightly oiled greaseproof paper. Brush with sesame oil and fold in half to make a sort of sideways bun shape. Cover loosely with clingfilm and leave to rise again for 30 minutes.

Steam, with the steamer partially covered, over fiercely boiling water for 20 minutes. Serve hot from the steamer. These buns are tough and indigestible when cold.

Prawn Filling

serves 4 ££

8 oz Chinese leaves – finely shredded	1 tablespoon rice wine or dry sherry
1 teaspoon salt	1 tablespoon dark soy sauce
1 tablespoon vegetable oil	2 tablespoon hoisin or barbecue sauce
1 teaspoon fresh root ginger – peeled and finely grated	1 tablespoon sesame oil
2 cloves garlic – peeled and minced	8 oz prawns – cooked and shelled
3 oz spring onions – trimmed and finely chopped	

Sprinkle the shredded Chinese leaves with the salt and leave to degorge for 20 minutes. Rinse well under cold running water, then squeeze out dry in your fist.

Heat vegetable oil in a small frying pan. In it, fry the ginger, garlic and onion for a minute or two, stirring all the time. Add rice wine or sherry, soy, hoisin and sesame oil, then reduce until the sauce is very thick and syrupy. Stir in the squeezed out leaves and prawns.

Serve sauce hot with the buns straight from the steamer. The guests grab a bun, split them and spoon in some of the filling. These should be eaten with the fingers.

Syrian Orthodox Easter Bread

serves 4-6 £

The Paschal lamb served with roast potatoes and two veg has always struck me as rather shocking in its insensitivity to symbolism. Eastern sects take a more sophisticated approach to the emblematic.

Overlooking the northernmost plains of Mesopotamia, the Syrian Orthodox monasteries and churches around Mardin and Midyat start their Easter liturgy either an hour before midnight on Saturday or at dawn on Sunday, depending on the curfew. After the service, the community, which still speaks Aramaic – the language of Christ – plays a game similar to conkers with eggs painted red. Their Lenten fast has eschewed all animal products. (On my brief visit, it seemed to consist of nothing but plain lentils boiled in salty water.)

Breakfast on Easter Sunday is of white foods – yoghurt, cheese, eggs and milk puddings – and round, oval or plaited flat loaves of this mildly spiced bread. Similar recipes can be found in all Orthodox cuisines and are, I suppose, not a million miles distant from hot-cross buns.

1½ teaspoons dry yeast (about half the normal packet)
2 tablespoons sugar
5 tablespoons warm water plus another 5 fl oz
1 lb plain white flour
1 teaspoon ground spices (most importantly cinnamon, perhaps cloves and allspice too)

4 oz salted butter
big pinch bicarbonate of soda
1 beaten egg to glaze
optional blanched almonds to decorate

Beat yeast and half a teaspoon of the sugar with the 5 tablespoons of warm water. Leave in a warm place for 10 minutes or so to froth.

If you have access to a food processor, whizz the flour and spices with the butter (cut into small cubes) for a few seconds until the mixture resembles fine breadcrumbs. Mix in the bicarb and rest of the sugar, then the yeast mixture. Now, with the machine running, gradually add warm water until you have a medium-soft dough.

This takes anything from a couple of tablespoons under the quarter pint, to 5 or 6 tablespoons over. When the texture is right, exchange the metal blade for the plastic one and process until smooth and well 'kneaded' (1-2 minutes).

If you're not using a processor, rub the butter into the flour and spice mixture. Stir in the bicarb, sugar, foamy yeast and water. Then knead for about 10 minutes.

Put dough in a loosely covered bowl in a warm place until it has doubled in size and the surface has begun to crack. Then knock it down, knead briefly again and cut into three pieces. Form each of these into a ball. Roll the balls out into flat circles about ½ in thick and put on oiled baking sheets. Cover with a cloth and leave to rise again for 20 minutes or so. Just before baking, press almonds into the surface in hearts, crosses, stars and flowers, or indent similar shapes with your fingertips, keeping the patterns appropriately crude, primal and ageless – however hi-tech your kitchen may be. Brush all over with beaten egg.

Bake in a hot oven (Gas 7-8/220-230°C/425-450°F) for 15-20 minutes.

Sweetening Rice

For every person put off the food of their childhood for life, there is another left with a deep need for regular fixes. Rice pudding seems a common bête noire, although the luckiest of us remember only succulent beds of creamy rice with a golden skin, flecked black and tasting richly of caramel.

From Greece to India, cold rice pudding is a popular and refreshing treat, made either in a saucepan and poured into individual serving bowls before chilling, or baked separately in the oven so that each helping has its own crust. The texture is much looser than the moulded French rice rings – sometimes just a sweet sauce with a few grains of rice lurking at the bottom.

The quality of the milk used is one of the most important factors in the regional variety (try using gold-top from the Channel Islands in the following recipes) and each cuisine adds its own flavouring. Greece and Turkey settle for fragrant mastic resin and sometimes cinnamon, an Arab version dribbles honey syrup over the top, and in India raisins are cooked with the rice and the finished dish is decorated with vark (silver or gold leaf beaten so thin as to be edible).

The best rice pudding I've ever eaten was high up in the lushest green meadows of the Pontic Alps behind Trabzon, Ancient Trebizond, in Eastern Turkey. The little village of Hamsiköy, which stands on the main road over the pass onto the Anatolian plateau and the desolate city of Erzurum, is famous throughout the country for its dairy produce. Every passing bus, lorry and car in the know stops at the biggest café in the centre for its passengers to remind themselves to what gastronomic heights a modest rice pudding can ascend.

The first, runny version below is one of the best recipes from Helen Saberi's *Noshe Djan: Afghan Food and Cookery*. The second is a baked Turkish version; the mastic resin you need for it can be bought in Greek Cypriot and Turkish shops.

Afghan Rice Pudding

serves 6 £

4 oz short-grain pudding rice
1 pint water
18 fl oz milk
4 oz sugar
2 teaspoons rose-water
¼ teaspoon ground cardamom
   seeds (just the black grains
   inside the pods)

1 oz unsalted shelled pistachio
   nuts or almonds – finely
   chopped

Wash rice and bring to the boil in the water in a heavy pan. Turn down heat and boil gently, stirring from time to time to prevent sticking, until rice is soft and all the water has evaporated.

Add the milk and bring back to the boil. Cook gently until the mixture thickens slightly, then add the sugar. Continue cooking and stirring until the sugar has dissolved and the texture is a little thicker still. Add cardamom and rose-water; heat for another couple of minutes until the flavours are well incorporated. Take off the heat and when cool leave to chill in the fridge.

Afghans serve this on a flat plate decorated with the ground nuts.

Turkish Rice Pudding

serves 6 £

1½ pints milk
8 oz sugar
5 oz cooked short-grain pudding
   rice

½ teaspoon crystals of mastic resin
   – pulverised
1½ rounded tablespoons cornflour
2 small egg yolks – beaten

Bring the milk to the boil in a large saucepan. Stir in the sugar and rice. Take the pan off the heat, then, stirring all the time, sprinkle in the mastic powder. The pan should still be steaming hot, but should not come back to the boil after this has been added, or the mastic gets hard and stringy.

Mix the cornflour with a little water to form a thin paste. Whisk this with the egg yolks into the hot milk, then stir – over a low flame if necessary – until the mixture thickens.

Pour into individual oven-proof bowls and let the mixture cool to blood temperature. Arrange the bowls in a deep oven tray, pour a little cold water into the tray, then pack ice-cubes around the bowls. This is to prevent the mixture boiling while the crust browns.

Place the tray towards the top of a pre-heated oven – about Gas 6/200°C/400°F – for half an hour or so until the top is dark golden brown. Chill the puddings before serving.

MAY

A perfect May banquet would start with English asparagus, at room temperature and only just cooked through, so that the delicate heads offer more resistance to the teeth than the silky stems. Next would come simply prepared wild river trout, sea trout or salmon with a small pile of sorrel leaves briefly wilted in butter.

The main course is new-season lamb – a mountain breed with sweet flesh, either pink and juicy or well roasted so that the crust is charred and the meat tender enough to be cut with a fork – served with Jersey Royal new potatoes, young broad beans and, perhaps, tiny new-season carrots and turnips. Pudding need not be anything more complicated than a bowl of that most elusive of fruits, the loquat.

Back in the real world, the asparagus and potatoes alone are feast enough. They are the epitome of excellent seasonal food: incomparable and available for no more than six weeks in a bad year, so you are pushed to make the most of them while they are around.

VEGETABLES

May often seems to be the best month of the year. Long, bright days and rising temperatures quickly make up for previous bad weather. The markets should be bursting with produce.

Good cauliflowers and greens should be in glut. The winter and early spring varieties of cabbage are now looking a little ropy, but are soon replaced by the big-hearted, green, round Primo. British grown peas should appear toward the end of the month; the first and sweetest broad beans a little earlier.

The English asparagus 'open' season starts on 1 May and, if we are lucky, will last through until the end of June. The special finesse of flavour compared with that of imports is apparently due to the slower growth rate in our climate. Now is the peak season for English cucumbers and spring onions. The first lot of outdoor-grown Jersey Royal new potatoes is usually brought over at the very beginning of May, with the official launch of the season a week or two later, and the first outdoor Jersey tomatoes are due, with about twice the flavour of the English hot-house varieties.

This is the last month for the small dark Hass avocado, which to my mind has the best and nuttiest flavour of the four varieties commonly available here. Purple sprouting and Cape broccolis are flourishing. If British crops of new-season carrots and turnips are a little slow, they should be preceded by French and Dutch imports.

Shopping list
Asparagus, aubergines, **avocados**, beetroot, Belgian chicory, **broad beans**, broccoli (calabrese, **purple sprouting) cabbages (spring/summer varieties,** white) **Cape broccoli, carrots** (new-season), **cauliflowers**, celery, chilli peppers, **Chinese leaves, courgettes, cucumbers**, curly kale, fennel, garlic, green beans (French, flat), herbs (basil, **chervil, dill**, fennel, marjoram, **mint, parsley**, rosemary, sage, tarragon, thyme), leeks, **lettuce**, mange-touts, marrows and squashes, mushrooms (cultivated), **okra**, onions, peas, peppers (capsicums), **potatoes** (new), **radishes**, salsify, **spinach, spring greens, spring onions**, swedes, sweetcorn, tomatoes, **turnips** (new season), **watercress**

Majorcan new potatoes remain cheap and plentiful at the beginning of the month while Jersey Royals are still scarce and expensive, although the flavour cannot compete. May sees the end of the brief **morel** season, with no more wild mushrooms in view until the end of the summer. Spanish peas herald our own season. Although not yet at their height, globe artichokes – including the tiny bite-sized variety – are imported in good condition for much of the year. The flavour goes particularly well with new-season lamb. Also look for rocket, **samphire** and sorrel.

FRUIT

Another thin month for fruit. Gooseberries may come through by the very end of May, but should not be depended upon until June. Elderflowers should be out all over the country by the end of the month. Free-food addicts can start preparing deep pans of fat for summery fritters made with the whole heads dipped in batter, fried until golden, then served with a sprinkling of lemon juice and sugar. Loquats are a brief early summer treat in the Mediterranean – the more bruised and battered looking, the better the flavour – with sporadic imports available here. Pineapples are still good and cheap. Bananas from Jamaica and the Windward Isles should be excellent. There may be good Spanish, plus a few English hot-house, strawberries around.

Shopping list
Apricots, **bananas**, grapefruit, lemons, limes, **loquats, pineapples, rhubarb**, strawberries
    Apricots from the States and Tunisia arrive toward the end of the month, but do not buy any until you find ones that are a rich deep yellow tinged with red. This is the lowest time of the year for apples but, if you must have them, decent new season imports from the southern hemisphere include Cox and Gala from New Zealand, Brazilian Gala, and Chilean Red Delicious and Granny Smiths. Look for labels or ask to be sure of places of origin. In exceptionally early years for soft fruits, Spanish nectarines and peaches, American cherries plus half a dozen varieties of melon should creep into some stores over the month. Good exotica might include mangoes from Venezuela, Mexico and Puerto Rico, and physalis.

FISH AND SEAFOOD

Salmon, sea trout and river trout are at their best. Dover sole and lobster come back after their low season. Crabs and other crustacea are in excellent nick. Imports of good red mullet and squid are stepping up, although most of what is sold here is still frozen. This is also traditionally the high season for whitebait (the very small fry of herrings and sprats, not a separate species), although most of it now goes to freezing plants. Another shame is the export of most of our waters' crawfish (spiny lobster) to the appreciative Spaniards and Italians.

May and June mackerel, with its roe, is an acquired taste but a definite preference with some people.

Shopping list

Clams, cockles, conger eel, **crab, crawfish** (spiny lobster), dab, Dover sole, **haddock**, huss, langoustines (Dublin Bay prawns or scampi), **lobster, mackerel**, mock halibut (Greenland halibut), monkfish, oysters (Pacific), plaice, **prawns**, red mullet, river trout, **salmon (wild and farmed)** sardines, **sea trout** (salmon trout), **shrimps**, squid, tuna, turbot, **whelks, whitebait**

MEAT AND GAME

New-season lamb gets steadily more plentiful. The most controversial young meat, veal, for many years tarred with the brush of cruel rearing, is starting to be more humanely produced on a larger scale.

Shopping list

beef, chicken, duck (farmed), **lamb (new-season)**, pork, quail (farmed), rabbit, turkey, **veal**

Many of the big retailers are beginning to feature meats suitable for simple grilling or barbecues – steaks, chops, chicken drumsticks and the like.

CHEESE

Cheese-master Michael Day suggests, as some of the month's best Gallic imports, Reblochon, Bleu d'Auvergne, Cantal and Tomme de Savoie. Hugh Rance, for Britain, recommends Welsh Caerphilly – the one made at Fferm Glyneithinog is particularly good – and new-season English soft cheeses such as Sharpham, Bonchester and Wheatland.

Cucumber and Prawn Soup

serves 4 (depending on the prawns) *££-££££*

Cucumber soup sounds such a good idea – refreshing, delicate, ideal for elegant lunches on the lawn – but the reality generally turns out to be at best faintly metallic, at worst one of the culinary blights of the British summer. Otherwise perfectly rational cooks, who would not expect to get carrot soup by grating carrots into yoghurt, or chicken soup by chopping cold chicken into cream mixed with a chicken stock-cube, nevertheless plough on with recipes that promise magical transformations of raw cucumber by such means. In the recipe below the cooked vegetable provides the soup's texture and a mellow support for the predominant taste of prawns. In sad acceptance of the fact that cooked prawns are all that most of us have easy access to, this recipe is written to use them. Why on earth good, raw, unfrozen prawns are so hard to come by remains a mystery, although I have a conspiracy theory which connects shellfish suppliers, the catering industry and giant drums of Marie Rose sauce.

Any size of prawn works, from ordinary small to finger-length

Mediterranean, but it is essential that the prawns used be bought complete with heads and shells. Colin Spencer, *The Guardian* food columnist, wrote to me after this recipe was published to point out that since raw prawns have to be headless – immediately a prawn is dead, apparently, its head becomes susceptible to contamination – they would be no good for this recipe anyway.

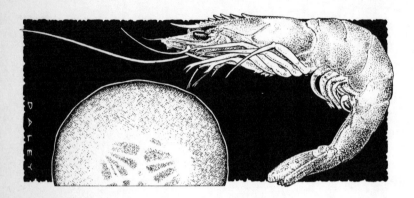

2 large cucumbers
small knob butter (to serve hot)
   or dribble of bland oil (to serve
   cold)
2 cloves garlic – minced
8 oz prawns (in shell, plus heads)
8 fl oz dry white wine
12 fl oz water
2 tablespoons lemon juice
parsley stalks – bruised

1 small onion – peeled and
   quartered
tiny pinch freshly grated nutmeg
few whole black peppercorns
1 teaspoon cumin seeds – roasted
   in a dry pan until dark and
   aromatic, then ground
2 tablespoons double cream or
   crème fraîche
salt

Top, tail and peel the cucumbers. Cut them in half lengthways. Scrape out all the seeds with a teaspoon. Finely dice the flesh. Heat the butter (if the soup is to be served hot) or oil (if cold) in a heavy saucepan. Add the garlic. Stir the pieces about until they are just turning pale gold, then tip in the cucumber. Turn the flame down to very low. Cover the pan tightly and let the vegetable sweat for about 30 minutes, until it is soft and translucent.

Shell the prawns, removing any dark thread of gut. If using very large prawns, cut them in half lengthways. Set aside.

Bring the prawn shells and heads to the boil in a pan with the wine, water, lemon juice, parsley stalks, onion, nutmeg and peppercorns. Cover and leave to bubble away for 20 minutes.

Strain the stock from the prawn shells onto the cooked cucumber. Boil together for a minute or two, then pass the mixture through a sieve or whizz up in a food processor. The texture should still be grainy.

To serve cold: chill the soup. Just before serving, stir in the cream and prawns. Season. Garnish with a few pinches of ground roast cumin seed.

To serve hot: return the soup to the flame from the seive or food processor. Add the cream. Stir in the prawns and give them time to heat through properly. Season. Garnish with cumin.

Stewing Broad Beans

The broad bean season is keenly anticipated each spring all over the Middle East. The most popular Turkish way of preparing the first young specimens, 'no thicker than a lady's finger', according to cooks' lore, is this *zeytinyağlı*, or 'olive-oily' method.

A favourite way of massacring everything from leeks or fresh green beans to stuffed green peppers or cabbage leaves, it involves stewing the vegetables for an hour or two with olive oil and water and then serving them cold, either as part of a meze (hors d'oeuvres) table or as a separate course after the main meat dish. After living in Turkey for a while, you begin to get used to, and soon positively yearn for, such long-over-cooked vegetables.

Zeytinyağlı dishes never contain meat or dairy produce and so are always suitable for vegans. These broad beans, however, differ from the usual run by being more watery, containing a distinctive herb and, more often than not, being eaten with dollops of yoghurt stirred through with crushed garlic. Bad luck, vegans.

Cold Olive-Oily Broad Beans in their Pods

serves 6-8 £

2 lb young fresh broad beans in
  pods – strings and stems cut off
2 onions – peeled and chopped
5 fl oz pure olive oil (not virgin or
  extra-virgin)
2 tablespoons lemon juice
big pinch sugar

salt
8 fl oz boiling water
2 tablespoons chopped fresh dill
  weed
10 fl oz strained Greek-style
  yoghurt
2 cloves garlic – peeled and
  minced

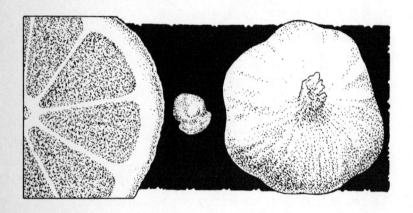

Wash whole beans thoroughly. Drain. Sauté the chopped onion for
a few minutes in the oil in a large, heavy, lidded saucepan over a
medium flame, to soften but not colour. Turn heat down to low,
add the beans in their pods, the lemon juice, sugar and a pinch of
salt. Stir, cover pan and leave to stew for 15 minutes, stirring from
time to time.

    Add water and 1 tablespoon of the dill, adjust heat so that liquid
simmers gently, cover pan again and leave to cook for another 1-1½
hours until the pods are very tender. Take off the heat. Leave to
cool.

When fully cold, stir in the other tablespoon of dill and turn beans out, with all their liquid, on to a dish.

Stir yoghurt and garlic together with a little salt.

As is the form with *meze*, diners help themselves from the central dish, slopping on their own helping of yoghurt. Added pleasure is in dipping pieces of bread in the central dish juices. Keeps well for a couple of days in the fridge.

Broad Bean and Artichoke Salad

serves 4-6 £

If the previous recipe sounds too barbarous, here is a yuppy compression of the *zeytinyağı* method, bringing in the magical marriage of broad beans with globe artichokes familiar from Jane Grigson's *Vegetable Book*. The tiny artichokes are sometimes available in flagship branches of major supermarket chains. Serve as a starter with warm French bread. This recipe is okay for vegans.

1 lb tiny fresh globe artichokes
4 tablespoons best olive oil
3 cloves garlic – peeled and cut in thin slivers
1 lb shelled broad beans – washed
1 tablespoon finely chopped fresh dill or marjoram

2 tablespoons lemon juice
2 tablespoons water
salt and freshly ground black pepper

Wash artichokes and trim down to the tenderer parts of the leaves (up to an inch sliced off the top of the globe, then judicious snipping with kitchen scissors all round). Quarter each trimmed artichoke.

Heat oil over medium flame in a large, heavy, lidded saucepan. Add the garlic slivers, then, after a few seconds, the artichokes. Sauté for 10 minutes or so until beginning to soften and colour. Add the beans, herb, lemon juice, water and generous seasoning. Stir.

Jam lid on tightly and leave for 20 minutes without peeking. Stir, test vegetables for doneness (cook a little longer with a splash more water if necessary). Let cool in the pan. Serve at room temperature.

Spinach with Eggs

serves 2 as a main dish, 4 as a starter £

A crude Anatolian incarnation of Oeufs Florentine. Wayside caffs on the steppes have dozens of versions, many including minced meat, sweet peppers, tomatoes, spices and, invariably, eggs rock-hard from having stood around for hours. Few dabble with cheese, but this is one I like. The Turkish equivalent of Greek feta is *beyaz peynir*, literally 'white cheese'; Caerphilly or Wensleydale are good substitutes.

1 lb fresh leaf spinach – picked
  over, trimmed
1 oz butter
1 clove garlic – peeled and minced
salt and freshly ground black
  pepper

4 eggs
4 oz feta cheese – crumbled
5-6 spring onions – finely sliced
  (both green and white parts)

Wash spinach well. Do not shake dry. Place wet leaves in large lidded saucepan over moderate heat. Cover tightly and leave to cook down. Check after 5 minutes, stir. When all the leaves are wilted and the volume of spinach has reduced considerably, take off the heat.

In a large, heavy, lidded frying pan, over a medium-low flame, melt the butter and sizzle the garlic for a few seconds. Remove spinach from its pan to the frying pan with a slotted spoon, squeezing out as much liquid as possible as you go. Season well. Stir so leaves are cooking evenly in the butter, then make four depressions in the spinach with the back of a spoon. Break an egg into each and sprinkle with more black pepper.

Scatter crumbled cheese all over the surface. When the pan is steaming happily, jam on the lid. Leave for about 5 minutes for soft yolks, up to 10 minutes for hard.

Sprinkle whole dish with spring onions. To serve, hot or warm, scrape up each egg with its spinach base to plonk on the plates in a single wodge.

Cooking Asparagus

Reckon on 6-10 spears per person for a first course, depending on thickness; 12-20 if you're serving sprue. Nothing beats the tried and trusted ways of serving this most regal vegetable:

hot or warm: with melted butter seasoned with rock salt and freshly ground black pepper, then spiked while still foaming with a squeeze of lemon juice before being poured into a bowl for dipping or gravy boat for pouring; or with hollandaise sauce or its close relation maltaise sauce (with orange juice and zest – especially good if you can get blood oranges).

tepid or cold: with olive oil and lemon juice, either handed separately or mixed together in a light vinaigrette, perhaps with the addition of a little grated orange rind and a squeeze of orange juice (especially if you can get blood oranges); or with a blandish mayonnaise

Preparing the spears for cooking is simple but exacting. The following method is not necessary for the slender sprue varieties, which just need plunging into boiling salted water in a roasting pan on top of the stove and boiling for 3-5 minutes until relatively flexible, before draining.

For fatter spears, first snip them out of their bunches. Wash thoroughly to remove sand and dirt from the shafts and hold the tips carefully under quite strongly running cold water to dislodge grit from the closely packed buds.

Cut off the very bottom of the spears and equalise the lengths. Perfectionists should now gauge from how far down the outer skin of the spears will be inedibly tough when cooked and shave it off with a potato peeler. Sluggards will leave their guests to suck the tender interior from these hard bits whilst eating.

Now tie the spears into bundles of ten or so (depending on thickness), with one piece of string an inch or so down from the tip and another about a third of the way up from the bottom of the spear. Do not tie too tightly.

If you have an asparagus kettle, you shouldn't need to be reading this. If you haven't, choose a relatively high-sided saucepan large enough to take all the bundles standing up. Stand the bundles in it and pour in water up to about 3in from the top. Form a double thickness of kitchen foil into a dome, which will sit with its edges crumpled around the rim of the saucepan, to seal in the steam and cover the tips completely.

Have the dome ready. Take the asparagus out of the still cold water and have it ready.

Salt the water and bring it to the boil. Stand the bundles in it, bring quickly back to bubbling, then regulate the heat to remain at a merry boil. Quickly fit the dome. Cook for 10 minutes before testing.

A sharp knife point should pass easily though the thickest part of the bottom of the spear, while the tips should be just wilted but still retain some snap. Depending on the thickness of your spears, the cooking time might be from 10-30 minutes, although I have never been lucky enough to find any so massive that they require more than 12 minutes.

When they are done, remove from the water. Drain well and snip out of the bunches again. It is most important now to lay the spears flat, with their bottom two-thirds between several thicknesses of kitchen paper or a spotlessly clean folded tea-towel or napkin. This is to absorb the excess water which lurk in the spears and can considerably dilute the pleasure of eating them.

Serve soon, if you're having the spears hot. Or leave between the paper or cloth until cooler.

Save the water in which you've cooked asparagus for boiling new potatoes. It adds a terrific, subtle flavour.

Asparagus is traditionally eaten with your fingers. Attack it with a knife and fork and, oh dear, the imperceptible sound of lowering estimations round some dinner tables – especially if you are American.

Lamb's Kidney and Sprue Stir-Fry

serves 2 £££

Free the wok! Use it for more than just that token twice-yearly ethnic dinner party: its vast expanse of easily heated steel makes it the best utensil for both the quick cooking of any suitably cut vegetable, meat or fish, and the fast reduction of liquids to make well flavoured sauces.

This is a non-oriental stir-fry of pencil-thin, relatively cheap sprue asparagus, red pepper (capsicum) and lamb's kidney, lightly glazed with red wine sauce.

4 lambs' kidneys
2 teaspoons onion juice –
    extracted by squeezing chopped
    peeled onion in a garlic press
5 tablespoons red wine
1 teaspoon lemon juice
1 clove garlic – peeled and minced
1 tablespoon best olive oil
freshly ground black pepper

bunch sprue asparagus
1 red sweet pepper – cut into
    long, thin strips, discarding
    stalk, seeds and pith
1 teaspoon groundnut or other
    bland oil
salt

By pushing a sharp knife or kitchen scissors into the concave side of the kidneys, snip out as much of the tough white tubing as you can without cutting the whole organs in half. Wash. Pat dry. Put in a mug to marinate for at least an hour with the onion juice, wine, lemon juice, garlic, olive oil and some black pepper.

Wash the sprue well – the heads are often very sandy. Dry thoroughly. Cut off the top 2 in of the stalks for use in this recipe. (The rest of the stalks are good for soup, or steamed and puréed for light sauces, or sliced finely, fried briefly in butter, then made into an omelette.)

Heat bland oil in wok over fairly fierce flame until it begins to smoke. Tip in the sprue tops. Push them around so that they cook evenly. Scoop out as soon as they begin to relax but are still bright green.

Repeat process with the pepper strips, this time letting them get quite soft. Remove.

Take kidneys from marinade, shaking to remove excess liquid. Pat dry. Quickly sear whole kidneys on all sides in the wok. Remove. Slice thinly cross-ways. The insides should still be raw.

Turn heat under wok down a bit. Tip marinade in and let it boil and reduce down almost to nothing. Return sprue, pepper and kidney slices to wok with a pinch of salt. Toss until evenly glossed. Thirty seconds will be enough to finish the kidneys. Serve immediately.

Baked Sea Trout

serves 6-8   £££

One early summer, I got by on a single dinner party menu again and again: pistachios, olives, radishes and slices of smoked Spanish sausage with drinks; cold asparagus with olive oil and lemon juice; warm sea trout with cucumber sauce – the recipe is given below – and Jersey Royal new potatoes; lightly dressed salad leaves with toasted pine kernels as a separate course; an enormous cheese board; a vast dish piled high with one or two kinds of fine rare fruit (sometimes loquats and physalis, sometimes proper English strawberries and sweet tropical granadillas); finally, home-made Turkish delight and coffee. This took two hours preparation on each evening I served it and seemed to work pretty well. The scheme depended on this way with salmon trout which does not rely on a fish kettle.

1 sea trout weighing 3½-4 lb –
   gutted and scaled
olive oil
	optional herbs, slices of lime etc
	rock salt and freshly ground black
	   pepper

Rub the whole fish with olive oil and season well, remembering to oil and season the belly cavity too. If you like, put a sprig or two of fresh herbs and slices of lime or lemon in the belly as well. Wrap loosely in foil and bake in the oven at Gas 7/220°C/425°F for 12-18 minutes. Take out of the oven, but don't open the foil for an hour, by which time the fish should be cooked *à point* (just enough to lift off the bone, but very succulent) and still be tepid. Serve it at this temperature or let the fish stand until cold.

You can serve the fish hot, although the flesh will not have the same delicacy: bake in foil at a lower temperature for longer, say Gas 5/190°C/375°F for 30-45 minutes.

Before serving, pull off the skin, leaving head and tail in place, if you like, as a decorative feature. Or skin and fillet the whole fish, then reassemble back into something like its original shape on a serving platter. Be careful to remove the nasty little line of blubber that runs down the backbone.

Serve tepid or hot with a fresh, lukewarm sauce, such as this cucumber and dill one, or with a stiff hollandaise. When cold, it is better served with mayonnaise.

Cucumber and Dill Sauce

makes about ½ pint £

A fresh alternative to hollandaise or mayonnaise for serving with sea trout or salmon.

1 large cucumber – peeled, de-seeded and very finely diced
small knob butter or splash bland oil
4 fl oz dry white wine
3 tablespoons finely chopped fresh chervil or dill weed

salt and freshly ground black pepper
4 tablespoons fromage frais (with chervil) or soured cream (with dill)

Sweat the cucumber in the butter or oil for a minute or two, until translucent but not soft. Add the wine, bring to the boil and reduce until the cucumber is quite dry. Stir in the chervil and fromage frais, or dill and soured cream, and seasoning. Serve immediately.

Calves' Tongue

serves 4 as a main course £££

Tongue is the richest and most luxurious of meats. The only tricky bit of the preparation is peeling it after poaching: too soon and you burn your fingers, but leave it too long and the skin seems to knit back on to the muscle.

The main recipe below is adapted from London chef Simon Hopkinson. At Bibendum, he serves it hot, in slices, with a gravy made by reducing half of the strained stock, whisking *beurre manié* (equal quantities of flour and butter kneaded together), into the simmering liquid, little by little, until the desired consistency is reached. The finished gravy is enriched with a little cream and sharpened with the addition of a couple of tablespoons of pickled capers. Simon's favourite accompaniments are boiled new potatoes or peppery mashed potatoes and butter-sautéed spinach.

I prefer to serve the tongue warm, or just at room temperature, with a thick vinaigrette of best olive oil, lemon juice, garlic, mustard, capers and fistfuls of freshly snipped herbs such as flat-leaf parsley, chervil, tarragon and chives.

1 large fresh calves' tongue – about 2 lb in weight	1 bay leaf
	sprig fresh thyme or pinch dried
water	several parsley stalks
1 carrot, peeled	½ teaspoon black peppercorns
1 onion, peeled	½ teaspoon salt
2 sticks celery	2 tablespoons red wine vinegar
3 cloves	

In a large covered stew pan, bring the untrimmed tongue – completely immersed in water – to a lively simmer together with the roughly chopped carrot, onion and celery, plus the cloves, bay leaf, thyme, parsley stalks, pepper, salt and wine vinegar. Skim the surface to remove any dirty scum that rises, then poach for 1¾-2½ hours. When done, a skewer will pass easily through.

Remove tongue from stock, leave to stand for no longer than 10 minutes, then peel immediately and trim off fatty bits and ragged roots. To serve hot, put peeled tongue back into simmering stock until ready to slice. To serve cold, put back in the stock, off the heat, to cool with the liquid.

If you can find small lambs' tongues (sometimes available from Halal butchers), scrub them well and poach in the same way, but without the cloves and vinegar, for 30-35 minutes. Peel, cool in the stock, then serve sliced up with a simple olive oil, lemon juice, garlic and chopped parsley dressing, for a typical addition to a Middle Eastern *meze* table.

Grilled Goat's Cheese

flexible quantities ££

This dish would figure prominently on any checklist of modern restaurant clichés. But carefully dealt with, it still makes an elegant starter, cheese course or light meal by itself. Choose a fresh, soft, mild goat's milk cheese such as Sainte-Maure, which comes in a log; the hard, pungent types are a different sort of thing altogether and not suitable for grilling. Top-quality salad ingredients and a light hand with the dressings are the other keys to success.

This version comes from David Dorricott, top chef at London's Portman Inter-Continental, who runs one of the most underrated hotel kitchens in London. He prepares several other variations on the theme of cheese salads to serve between main and pudding courses of his menus: for example, he has one of raw mild goat's cheese on a salad of batavia leaves and peeled green grapes, simply dressed with lemon juice and best olive oil; another of grilled slices of stronger goat on curly endive and grated celery dressed with 1 part blackcurrant vinegar to 3 parts walnut oil.

bunch watercress	hazelnut oil
flat-leaf parsley sprigs	salt and freshly ground black
fresh tarragon sprigs	pepper
fresh chervil sprigs	½in slice mild goat's milk cheese
champagne vinegar	for each serving

Wash and dry watercress and herbs. Get rid of stalks as far as possible. Toss in dressing made by mixing the vinegar and oil in proportions 1:2 rather than the more usual 1:3-4. This is a very mild vinegar. If you cannot find it, use smaller quantities of white wine vinegar. Season well. Arrange dressed greenery on cold, individual plates.

Pre-heat grill to hot. Cook de-rinded cheese slices on clean, not pre-heated grill pan for a minute or two so that the tops melt and start to colour but the bottoms are just warmed through, keeping their body. Quickly remove cheese from pan with a fish slice and plonk on the piles of salad. Serve immediately.

Elderflower Fritters

serves 2 £

An unusual treatment for elderflowers, originating, it seems, in the seventeenth century, is quoted by Norman Douglas in his extraordinary *jeu d'esprit*, *Venus in the Kitchen*, written under the pen-name Pilaff Bey. This is now unfortunately out of print. My New English Library edition of 1971, retitled *Lovers' Cookbook; the Great*

Classic of Culinary Erotica, has a photograph on the cover of a young woman, naked except for a skimpy pinny, stirring a pudding. Graham Greene's foreword describes it as an 'unserious and shameless . . . collection of aphrodisiac recipes'.

But for all that, the book is more a compilation of gutsy dishes from the lands around Douglas's beloved Mediterranean, ancient Rome and Greece and Renaissance Europe. In an essay on the book in *An Omelette and a Glass of Wine*, Elizabeth David points out that any element of stimulation from these dishes lies in the simple fact that 'this is good cooking; interesting, well-seasoned, appetising, fresh, unmonotonous.' Douglas says this recipe is 'not so bad as it sounds'. I disagree and include an adaptation of his hopelessly unspecific instructions, more as a curiosity than a recommendation.

Having tasted it, you may be more inclined to leave the creamy florets on the bush for free-winesters to turn into a hedgerow stand-in for Alsatian gewurtztraminer. Their faces may be contorted in an agony of indecision: if they leave the flowers until the autumn, the berries are transformable into indigo nectar, a rustic equivalent of cabernet sauvignon.

4-6 elderflower heads (8
  tablespoons separated blooms) –
  washed well
3 tablespoons cream cheese
3 tablespoons curd cheese
2 tablespoons freshly-grated
  Parmesan

1 egg – beaten
pinch ground cinnamon
2-3 drops rose-water
butter for frying
sugar for sprinkling

Pound flowers to a beige mush in a mortar. Mix in the cheeses, beaten egg, cinnamon and rose-water.

Drop tablespoons of the batter into a hot frying pan containing a little foaming butter. Turn once, carefully. Both sides should be a light, golden colour. Sprinkle with sugar and serve hot.

JUNE

Hey ho! Another month of asparagus, salmon and strawberries. The brilliance of trees' new green is wearing off; the ubiquitous fields of day-glo rape have faded; it doesn't get truly dark in the gardens of country pubs until nearly closing time.

More prosaically, retail chains launch the summer sales push on the idea of outdoor eating: jazzy little stickers, claiming 'Suitable for BBQs', appear on the meanest shrink-wrapped pork chop and packet of sausages while meat-counters scale wild heights of imagination on the wooden skewer and kebab front. Men who wouldn't dream of letting *delice de volaille grillé aux crudités de saison* anywhere near their lips nevertheless don hilarious pinnies to toss salads and watch over blackened drumsticks that sullenly spit with each application of their own special barbecue sauce, which always has a 'secret ingredient', which always turns out to be Tabasco.

VEGETABLES

Make the best of the unbeatable English asparagus; it's sometimes over by the third week of the month. New potatoes are best bought only in quantities to be cooked as soon as possible: in just a couple of days they lose half their flavour and begin to go soft. Stick with the Jersey Royals as long as they hold out, although some of the British-grown varieties that follow are also impressive.

English courgettes, mange-touts and broad beans should be plentiful by the end of the month. Pick-your-own farmers generally throw open their pea fields in the middle of June.

Hispi and Primo are the season's best cabbages. Good home-produced salad stuff includes celery, cucumbers, fresh herbs, radishes and watercress. There will also be decent English lettuces (Cos, Webb's, iceberg and the brilliant Little Gem), tomatoes and cherry tomatoes about. When buying the latter, check the label to make sure that these are the genuine article, not just tiny ordinary tomatoes which do not have anything like the full flavour. The last week of June sometimes sees a gap in the supply of spring onions.

Shopping list

Asparagus, aubergines, avocados, beetroot, Belgian chicory, **broad beans, broccoli** (calabrese), **cabbages (green spring** and **early summer** varieties, white), **carrots** (new-season), **cauliflower**, celery, chilli peppers, **Chinese leaves, courgettes, cucumbers**, fennel, garlic, **globe artichokes, green beans**, (French and flat), herbs (**basil,** chervil, **dill**, fennel, marjoram, **parsley, rosemary**, sage, **tarragon, mint, thyme**), **lettuce and other salad leaves, mange-touts**, marrows and squashes, mushrooms (cultivated), **okra**, onions, **peas**, peppers (capsicums), **potatoes** (new), **radishes, spinach**, spring greens, **spring onions**, sweetcorn, **tomatoes** (including cherry), **turnips** (new-season), **watercress**

If British-grown broad beans and courgettes are late, French and Spanish imports will hold the supply. Sorrel is not commonly available although you might try very specialist greengrocers. It is, however, one of the easiest things to grow yourself, even in a window-box. Remove just the most mature leaves for cooking from time to time and the plant keeps going. Also look for rocket and samphire.

FRUIT

Apricots are improving and British cherries are on the horizon, but June really belongs to the strawberry. The earliest English varieties from Hampshire and the Cheddar Gorge are available through a few specialist retailers in the first week or so of June; supplies from Kent following on by mid-month. The main flush of outdoor crops and the pick-your-own farms will be open by the second or third weeks of the month. Gooseberries should be in full flood by then too. There may be a few raspberries by the very end of the month.

Of imported fruits, the quality of bananas coming in from the Caribbean and Central America should be high, while the summer flood of melons starts with cantaloup, Gallia and yellow honeydew, mostly from Spain. The best of the season's grapes are seedless varieties from Israel and Cyprus.

Shopping list
Apricots, Asian pears (nashi), **bananas, cherries**, coconut, **gooseberries**, grapefruit, **grapes**, lemons, limes, **melons**, rhubarb, **strawberries**

Prices of soft fruit now on sale in the larger chain-stores can be very volatile; this is especially true for peaches and nectarines from Spain and Italy, cherries from the United States, Greece and Turkey, and English strawberries. Enemies of seasonality will be promoting pears and Braeburn apples from New Zealand, which also sends nashi (crisp Asian pears) at this time of year. If you're set on international fruit, look for the excellent greeny red mangoes air-freighted from Guatemala.

FISH AND SEAFOOD

The pick of the season this month, as last, is salmon, sea trout and shellfish – either cheap crab and shrimps, or expensive lobster and langoustines. Sardine is Miss Barbecue Fish of the Month, although mackerel gets the runner-up's cheque and the chance to sit on tart little puddles of gooseberry sauce all summer long.

Shopping list
Clams, cockles, **crab, crawfish** (spiny lobster), dab, Dover sole, **grilse, haddock, hake**, langoustines (Dublin Bay prawns or scampi), **lobster, mackerel**, mock halibut (Greenland halibut), monkfish, oysters (Pacific), plaice, **prawns**, red mullet, river trout, **salmon** (wild and farmed), **sardines, sea bream, sea trout** (salmon trout), **shrimps, squid**, tuna, turbot, **whelks, whitebait**

MEAT AND GAME

All cynicism about barbecues melts away at the first sniff of well marinated meat, fish or vegetables cooking over charcoal in the open air. Any good cut of meat is suitable: thick slices from across a boned leg of lamb, pig's kidneys cut almost in half and held in a butterfly shape with a couple of skewers, whole quail split along the backbone and squashed flat. Even cubes of the most appallingly flavourless modern chicken come back to life if they are soaked in good olive oil, lemon juice, garlic and seasoning for a couple of hours, pushed on to skewers with the odd bayleaf, then lightly charred.

Shopping list
Beef, chicken, duck (farmed), **lamb**, pork, quail (farmed), rabbit, veal

CHEESE

If you are lucky enough to have access to one of the rare retailers who knows and cares about cheese, ask for June's most glorious French imports: Gratte Paille, a luscious, mild brick with a soft white rind, Saint-Marcellin rouge, creamy and fresh tasting, and

Pont l'Evêque, best bought by the piece from a large, bulging 'cutting' cheese because it tends to ripen better than the small versions in little wooden boxes. The blue ewe's milk cheese, Roquefort, is coming deliciously to the end of its season. One bite of a well kept specimen and real cheese fanatics won't want to eat anything else all June. Gabriel Coulet is the only hand-made *marque*, but, Papillon is also good.

Almost any time is a good time for English farmhouse Cheddar. One of the best is Denhay Cheddar, a veteran of the trophy for excellence in cheesemaking awarded at the Royal Bath and West Agricultural Show, the foremost showcase of good Cheddar.

Ox-Heart Sticks

serves 4 as a starter or 8 as a snack

Chunks of charcoal-grilled ox-heart, a pretty macho sounding kind of a cocktail nibble, are popular street-food from outside the bull-ring in Lima, Peru, according to Elisabeth Lambert Ortiz's *Book of Latin American Cooking*. The recipe below is a very loose adaptation. The flavour is actually quite refined and fools even dedicated offal-loathers.

1 lb slices ox heart – trimmed well and cut into 1in cubes (about 48 cubes)
5 cloves garlic – peeled and crushed
3 fresh, hot red or green chilli peppers – seeded and very finely chopped
1½ teaspoons cayenne

½ teaspoon paprika
½ teaspoon ground cumin
½ teaspoon dried oregano
2 teaspoons groundnut oil
3 tablespoons red wine vinegar
big pinch salt
generous milling black pepper

Marinate heart cubes in mixture of all the other ingredients, covered in the fridge, for 24 hours. Thread 3 pieces on to each of about 16 small wooden skewers and barbecue or cook under grill, heated to its fiercest, for 4-5 minutes until well coloured, splashing on any remaining marinade as you turn the skewers. Eat hot.

Asparagus Cigars

serves 2 as a starter, 6 to nibble

Boulestin restaurant in London's Covent Garden, set up originally in 1926 by Marcel Boulestin – the most famous chef of his day and the first TV cook – has experienced quite a renaissance under its present chef, Kevin Kennedy, who started here in 1978. He was one of the first British harbingers of the eighties' return to old-fashioned restaurant values, with, for example, his tornedos Rossini: fillet steak topped with a thick slice of foie gras in a truffled Madeira Sauce – no packets, no pâté, no stinting. With its generous cooking, elegantly sober surroundings and unintrusive but attentive service, Boulestin, along with the Connaught and Bibendum, is still one of the capital's very few restaurants for grown-ups – it neither patronises nor panders.

This is my version of one of Kevin Kennedy's ideas.

12 spears asparagus

2 sheets phyllo pastry, roughly 12inx18in from 400 g pack frozen phyllo pastry – see page 62 for details

olive oil for brushing on pastry

2 heaped teaspoons freshly grated Parmesan

freshly ground black pepper

Cut about 4in from the tip of each asparagus spear. Keep the rest of the stalks for another use. Wash the tips well, then rinse in boiling water to blanch. Drain very well and pat dry with cloth or kitchen paper.

Lay out the sheets of phyllo pastry on a board. Brush generously with olive oil. Cut each in half lengthways, then across three times so you are left with 12 leaves about 6in × 6in. Sprinkle evenly with the Parmesan.

Lay an asparagus tip along one side of each square, about 1in in from the edge. Sprinkle spear with black pepper. Fold the 1in of phyllo over the spear, then fold in the two adjacent edges at a slight angle along their whole lengths, so that the far edge is now shorter than the asparagus spear. Roll up spear like a neat cigar. Brush with more olive oil.

Bake in an oven, pre-heated to Gas 6/200°C/400°F for 10-15 minutes, turning once so that the pastry browns evenly. Eat hot or warm in your fingers.

Crab and Aubergine Noodles

serves 2 ££

This speedy, faintly oriental assemblage gives upward mobility to the one-course supper. The noodles are the thin, easy-cook Chinese sort, made with egg, sometimes called thread egg noodles, that can be bought dried from specialist stores or, increasingly, from half-way adventurous supermarkets.

Frozen or pre-packed chilled crabmeat will do for this preparation. Of course, nothing comes close to the flavour of really fresh crab, bought live, cooked yourself and eaten the same day, but if you have one, don't waste it on this recipe.

6 oz thin egg noodles
1 aubergine (about 8 oz)
3 tablespoons groundnut or other bland oil
2 cloves garlic – peeled and minced
¼in thick slice fresh root ginger – peeled and finely chopped
½-1 small fresh green chilli – finely chopped

6 spring onions – trimmed, roughly sliced
8 oz brown and white crab meat (from a medium-sized crab, about 1¼ lb)
1 tablespoon light soy sauce
1 teaspoon lemon juice
1 tablespoon chopped fresh coriander leaves
few drops sesame oil

Cook noodles according to instructions on packet. They are generally put in boiling water, off the heat, for 4-6 minutes. Drain.

Cut aubergine into stubby sticks with the dimensions of a plump cigarette (do not take off skin). Heat 2 tablespoons oil in a wok until just smoking. Toss in the aubergine and stir-fry until soft and well coloured all over – about 5 minutes. Remove.

Heat the other tablespoon of oil until beginning to smoke. Add garlic and stir, the ginger and stir, the chilli and stir, the spring onion and stir, then the drained noodles. Toss around together for a minute, then stir in the well mashed brown and roughly chopped white crab meat and the cooked aubergine.

Sprinkle on the soy sauce, lemon juice, chopped coriander leaves and sesame oil to taste. Stir again briefly to mix the flavours. Serve immediately.

Making Sandwiches

Britons tend to come over all superior about sandwiches just because some eponymous English blue-blood is supposed to have invented them. In my experience, there are few other countries that would willingly accept the horrifying specimens sold from kiosks, buffets and caffs all over Britain. The fact that Marks and Spencer should have been so quickly able to establish its pre-packed versions as the standard by which all other bought sand-wiches are now judged should tell us something.

The roots of the problem are twofold. First, there is the lingering post-war British obsession with butter, once a rationed luxury now spread on every slice we can lay our hands on. Second, there is the awe-inspiring British capacity to compromise on food quality for the thrill of saving a penny or two. This meanness is especially pre-valent with foods that we don't take seriously because they are not eaten around a table. If we can buy economy loaves of pre-sliced pap, margarine at a third the price of butter, pink slices of water-injected, mechanically recovered, re-formed pork shoulder more cheaply than ham, we will do so. Thus the British Rail 'ham sand-wich' was born.

Hardly surprising, then, that Americans, Belgians, Italians, Danes, even Turks for goodness sake, weep when they are pre-sented with a British sandwich. Often, they sensibly throw the whole thing in a bin after the first bite. They cannot believe that both slices of the blotting-paper bread are always buttered, or mar-garined, even though the flavour of the fat just does not suit many fillings – cheese, for example, or mixtures with mayonnaise such as egg salad.

Their disbelief deepens as they realise that the fillings ring the same joyless rounds: plastic cheese, spongy ham, fibrous beef, fart-smelling egg, pulpy tomato, jammy pickle, abrasive salad cream, soggy fish paste, watery tinned prawns, vinegary sardines, ageing lettuce, gritty mustard and cress. This is a shame as fine examples of all these ingredients become more and more widely available.

Possible saviours of our sandwich self-respect are properly made examples of the following classics: smoked salmon – generous slices seasoned with cayenne, black pepper and lemon juice, between good brown bread smeared lightly with cream cheese, chicken – juicy slices of cold roast breast between thickly cut, home-made white bread spread with mayonnaise and chopped tarragon; cucumber – wafer-thin slices degorged with salt and dressed with lemon juice, olive oil and white pepper, between very thin slices of buttered white bread. Personal favourites include raw mushrooms and anchovy fillets with lemon juice and chopped dill on granary bread spread thickly with soured cream, or yesterday's left-over cold new potatoes and tinned smoked mussels on warm toast scraped with raw garlic and thinly spread with mayonnaise.

Victor Gordon goes several stages better in his *English Cookbook* with the following assemblage for eating with 'heroic quantities of very pink gin'. Thickly cover one piece of hot, lightly buttered toast with smoked salmon. Spread thinly with mango chutney (I prefer lime pickle). Lay several rashers of hot, crisply grilled streaky bacon on top and sprinkle with cayenne pepper. Cover with another slice of hot, lightly buttered toast. Worth a knighthood, I'd say, especially if Charles Forte deserved ennoblement for peddling the other sort of sandwich.

The much loved plain bacon sandwich is, of course, a subject which arouses strong opinion: does it taste better made from smoked or unsmoked bacon, floppy fried back or crisply grilled streaky, with or without rind, on toasted or untoasted bread, with or without tomato ketchup? And so on. The search for the authentic chip butty arouses just as much debate.

It is the Americans, however, who, as with most other forms of convenience food, have taken the sandwich to sublime heights. Here are two personal adaptations – the first from a family-diner bastardisation of a Louisiana way with fish, the second a Kentucky grandmother's version of a down-home modern staple.

Blackened Chicken Sandwich

fills 4 soft sesame baps £

2 chicken breasts (ie all the breast meat from one bird)

1½ level teaspoons salt

1 teaspoon freshly ground black pepper

1 teaspoon cayenne pepper

2 teaspoons paprika

1 teaspoon ground cumin

½ teaspoon dried basil (this dish is the only excuse that I know for dried basil)

½ teaspoon dried thyme

½ teaspoon dried oregano

1 teaspoon sugar

1 tablespoon lemon juice

1 tablespoon Worcestershire sauce

1 teaspoon Tabasco sauce

pure olive oil (not virgin or extra-virgin)

shredded iceberg lettuce

Hellman's mayonnaise

I would not attempt this dish on electricity because it is far too hot to control. Cut each breast in half lengthways and flatten between sheets of greaseproof paper, with a blunt instrument, to form thin 'schnitzels'. Mix all the other ingredients together, except the oil, lettuce and mayo. Stir in enough olive oil to make a basting liquid.

Pre-heat a heavy, dry, clean, cast-iron frying pan or griddle over a high flame until it is as hot as it will go. This will take at least 5 minutes. Do not chicken out. It should be hot enough to scare the life out of you. Make sure the windows are open and the extractor fan on, or the whole place will be smoked out.

Dip the flattened chicken breast pieces in the spice and oil mixture to coat completely, then slap them down immediately on to the white-hot surface, holding each for a few seconds with a spatula. Give them 2-3 minutes on each side until thoroughly black. Then turn the heat right down and leave to cook for another 5 minutes or so, until cooked through.

Split the baps. Toast lightly on the opened side, spread with Hellman's, pile on the shredded lettuce and bung a chicken piece in each. Eat hot.

Tuna Salad Sandwich

fills 2 rounds (ie 4 slices of white or wholemeal sandwich loaf) £

7 oz tin good quality tuna in oil

1 apple – peeled and cut into medium dice

1 stick celery – stringed and finely chopped

½ teaspoon curry powder

salt and freshly ground black pepper

2 tablespoons Hellman's mayonnaise

Mash all ingredients together and sandwich between unbuttered slices of bread. The filling should be very deep. To be eaten with egg salad sandwiches and potato crisps washed down by cans of coke.

Courgette and Mushroom Salade Tiède

serves 2 £

The principle of a *salade tiède* is to put something hot and flavoursome on cold dressed salad leaves – the combination amuses the palate and enhances the flavours. Commonly seen examples of this Great Modern Restaurant Cliché include chicken liver with little strips of bacon on a salad dressed with hazelnut oil, poached or boiled quail's eggs with bacon on raw baby spinach leaves, slices of rare pigeon breast with toasted pine nuts on fancy chicories or goat's cheese on just about anything – as described on page 122.

The best and most sophisticated *salade tiède* I've ever tasted, prepared by David Doricott of London's Portman Inter-Continental Hotel was of asparagus spears, wafered radish, carrot and mushroom dressed with champagne vinaigrette, served with a neat slab of hot pan-fried skate, served alongside another salad of dandelion, red radicchio, claytonia, garlic flowers, blanched lime and orange zests, little pieces of duck confit and slivers of raw, marinated duck fillet dressed with blackcurrant vinaigrette.

The diverse elements married together perfectly. I also like the most basic stews – from chilli con carne to carbonnade de boeuf – slopped on to robustly dressed salad leaves. This homely dish falls somewhere between the two extremes. The leaves don't need dressing because you are effectively making a hot vinaigrette in the pan.

mixed salad leaves
4 tablespoons olive oil
4 rashers smoked streaky bacon – de-rinded and cut into short, thin strips
2 cloves garlic – peeled and minced

8 oz courgettes – topped, tailed and cut into thick slices
8 oz button mushrooms – cut in half
salt and freshly ground black pepper

4 fl oz red wine

2 slices crustless white bread –
fried until crisp in olive oil,
then cut into small croûtons

Pile the salad leaves on two large plates. Heat the olive oil in a frying pan and in it fry the bacon until crisp. Throw in the garlic, courgettes, mushrooms and season well. Fry until everything is well coloured but the courgettes still retain some bite.

Slosh in the wine and let it bubble down until syrupy, then tip the entire contents of the pan over the plates of salad. Chuck on the croûtons.

Salmon and Sorrel Soufflé

serves 4 £££

A hot soufflé is just a white sauce, enriched with egg yolks, flavoured with something, folded into beaten egg whites and baked. The knack is easy to acquire. You need a certain amount of care, but the process requires sure, firm handling rather than mincing about.

2 oz butter plus extra for greasing
½ tablespoon finely grated
　　Parmesan
½ pint milk
1 bay leaf
1 slice peeled onion
1 clove
small pinch grated nutmeg
6 peppercorns

2 oz plain flour
salt
4 eggs (size 3) – separated
5 oz cold cooked salmon – flaked
4 oz sorrel leaves – wilted in
　　butter, drained thoroughly then
　　puréed
pinch cayenne pepper
1½ oz grated Gruyère

Butter a 2½ pint soufflé dish (about 6in in diameter) and toss a little grated Parmesan cheese in it to lightly coat the whole interior.

Heat the milk very gently in a pan with the bay leaf, onion slice, clove, nutmeg and peppercorns for about 20 minutes for the flavours to infuse. Only bring it to the boil when you are about to use it.

Melt the butter in a saucepan. Add the flour and cook for a minute or two without letting it colour. Take off the heat, strain in the boiling milk all at once and whisk energetically. Add salt, return to the heat and boil gently for a few minutes, stirring all the time, to cook out the taste of the flour.

Take off the heat and beat in the egg yolks, then stir in the salmon, sorrel purée, cayenne and grated Gruyère. Leave to cool until lukewarm.

Whisk the egg whites with a pinch of salt until they stand in soft peaks but are still nice and glossy. Add a couple of tablespoons of the whisked whites to the salmon and sorrel mixture, stirring in thoroughly to lighten the texture. Then fold the mixture lightly into the whites with a large metal spoon, using regular, downward, figure-of-eight movements through the mixture, to incorporate it fully while losing as little air as possible.

Pour the mixture into the prepared mould. Smooth the surface. Sprinkle with a little more Parmesan and cayenne pepper. Put into the middle of an oven pre-heated to Gas 6/200°C/400°F. Immediately, turn the heat down to Gas 5/190°C/375°F and leave for 30 minutes without opening the oven door. It should then be well risen, brown on top and just firm to the touch. The inside should still be oozing and creamy.

Home-Smoked Monkfish with Mustard Sauce

serves 6 ££

A proper smoke-box is not necessary for small quantities of relatively delicate home-smoked food. The Chinese smoke duck like this, on a steamer-rack in a lidded wok over dry tea. The method is also good with large prawns.

This really is quite an exacting dish, but worth it.

fish:
2-3 small monkfish tails (about 1½ lb total weight)
2 tablespoons fresh grapefruit juice
salt and freshly ground white pepper

3 tablespoons dry tea (Oolong or a black variety such as Keemun)
3 tablespoons white rice (any kind will do)
2 tablespoons sugar

sauce:
6 fl oz full-bodied dry white wine
4 tablespoons water
1 slice peeled onion
sprig fresh summer savory or
   thyme
1 bay leaf
3 eggs (size 2)
3 tablespoons fresh grapefruit
   juice
1½ level teaspoons dry English
   mustard
1 teaspoon Dijon mustard

salt and freshly ground white
   pepper
garnish:
handful broad beans – podded,
   then the individual beans
   poached, peeled of their grey
   jackets and kept warm
12 pieces potato – turned (cut
   into little barrel shapes),
   steamed and kept warm
needles of grapefruit zest –
   slivered off peel and blanched
6 tiny sprigs fresh summer savory
   or thyme

Skin fish, removing all the gossamer membrane or this will contract in the smoking and distort the fish. Cut the fillets from each side of the central bones (keep these). Put the fish fillets on a plate, sprinkle with the grapefruit juice and lightly with salt and pepper. Leave to marinate for 30 minutes.

Line the bottom of a lidded wok with a double-thickness of foil. Put in the tea leaves, rice and sugar, mixed together. Put fish on metal steamer-rack above the tea mixture. Seal wok fully with lid and more foil.

Put wok on a very high flame. After 4 minutes, turn heat down to medium. After another 3 minutes, turn off the flame and leave the wok undisturbed and covered for 10 minutes.

Chop up each fish backbone into 2 or 3 pieces. Put in a saucepan with the wine, water, onion and herbs. Bring to the boil, jam on the lid and boil fiercely for 3 minutes. Turn the heat down, fish out all the bones, then continue boiling until there are only about 5 tablespoons of liquid left. Strain to remove onion, herbs and any stray flakes of fish.

In a bowl over a pan of hot, but not boiling, water, whisk the eggs until thick. Whisking all the time (a hand-held electric beater is the best tool for this job), add the reduced wine liquor, the grapefruit juice, mustards and seasoning. Beat until thick enough to coat the back of a spoon.

Serve arranged on heated plates, one per person. Cut fish into angled ¼in slices and lay in rows down the centre of each plate. Put a dollop of sauce to one side, just covering that edge of the fish.

Arrange two pieces of turned potato and a little pile of the broad beans to the other side. Garnish fish with grapefruit zest and herb sprig.

Stuffed Mackerel

serves 2-4 ££

The official show-off version of this Turkish dish involves removing the entire contents of the mackerel's skin-sack through the gills or a tiny hole in the fish's chin. But even the brusque method outlined below turns the mackerel, plentiful and cheap now, into a real star turn.

2-2½ lb mackerel (2-4 whole fish) – scaled but not headed or gutted

4 tablespoons good olive oil, plus more for frying

1 large onion (about 6 oz) – peeled and finely chopped

4 heaped tablespoons pine kernels

2 heaped tablespoons seedless raisins

big pinch ground allspice

big pinch ground cloves

big pinch ground cinnamon

salt and freshly ground black pepper

2 tablespoons finely chopped parsley

beaten egg

flour seasoned with salt and pepper

Wash the fish. Do not slice along the underbelly, but cut off the head and scoop out all the guts with your fingers. Wash the cavity well. Break the backbone, without tearing the skin, a little way up from the tail. Now loosen the flesh inside the skin by repeatedly pushing all over the outside surface of the fish with your thumbs until you feel it give, being careful not to split the delicate underbelly.

By pushing and squeezing up from the tail – as if the mackerel were a tube of toothpaste – force all the contents of the skin-sack out at the head end. You should be able to get the backbone out in one piece.

Carefully pick over the flesh to get rid of any bones. Roughly chop flesh. Tidy up the empty skin-sacks by pulling or snipping off the fins and tearing out any bony bits left inside. The odd tiny tear is not too much of a problem. Discard bones, heads and guts.

Heat olive oil in a heavy pan. Fry onions and nuts gently together until onion is soft and transparent and nuts have taken on some colour. Add chopped fish, raisins, spices and parsley, mix and fry together for a few minutes until fish is cooked. Season this stuffing then pack quite loosely back into the mackerel skins. There is no need to sew up the opening, but you can thread a thin skewer through twice for appearances' sake.

The tastiest way of serving the fish is fried – or rather, dipped in beaten egg, then seasoned flour, then fried gently in olive oil until golden all over. If cooked at too high a heat, the fish split like sausages. You also can bake the fish in a medium oven or grill them, if you like.

Serve hot, warm or cold with lemon wedges. Good accompaniments are new potatoes, and a tomato and cucumber salad dressed simply with lemon juice and olive oil.

Double-Steamed Couscous

serves 4 ££

A light, fragrant version of this North African dish. Instead of making a stew over which to steam the couscous, the meat and vegetables are steamed too. The recipe specifies pre-cooked couscous, but don't worry if the packets you find don't mention this. They are almost certain to be so since it is very difficult to buy any other kind outside North Africa or France. Harissa paste is available in tubes from delicatessens and specialist stores. You also need a spacious two-tiered steamer.

1½ lb lamb neck fillet – trimmed and cut into 1in cubes
1 medium onion – peeled
juice of 1 lemon
1 teaspoon salt plus extra pinch
½ teaspoon ground cinnamon

1in cube fresh root ginger – peeled and grated
8 small new-season turnips – trimmed
8 small new-season carrots – scraped and trimmed

1 medium aubergine – half peeled in alternate strips lengthways, then cut into 1in cubes

4 small courgettes – trimmed and cut in half lengthways

4 fresh dates – skinned, pitted and cut into quarters

4 heaped tablespoons cooked chickpeas (these may be tinned)

1 lb pre-cooked couscous

3 tablespoons melted butter

1-2 tablespoons harissa paste

Marinate lamb for 30 minutes in a sloppy paste made either by puréeing the onion with the lemon juice, salt, cinnamon and ginger in a food processor, or by grating the onion finely and mixing with the other four ingredients.

Pour 3in-4in water in a saucepan over which you can fit a closely fitting two-tier steamer with lid. Bring water to the boil.

Pick out pieces of meat from the marinade without scraping off any of the paste that sticks to them. Arrange in the bottom tier of the steamer. Set this, with its lid on, over the boiling water and let steam for 30 minutes. Check from time to time that the water has not boiled dangerously low.

Add the turnips, carrots, aubergine, courgettes, dates and chickpeas to the meat. Cover and steam for 20 minutes more.

Meanwhile, put couscous in a large bowl. Pour on a mean ¾ pint lukewarm water and leave grains to swell for 10 minutes, stirring occasionally to stop lumps forming.

Ten minutes before the meat and vegetables are to be ready, put the couscous in the upper tier of the steamer to heat through uncovered. It is done when the steam begins to penetrate the surface. If this has not happened by the time the meat and vegetables cooking time is up, take out the bottom tier and put the couscous straight on to the saucepan.

Toss hot couscous in the melted butter and extra pinch of salt.

Pile couscous on to serving platter. Arrange the meat and vegetables on top. Dilute 1-2 tablespoons harissa (depending on heat required) with ½ pint of the hot steaming water and hand separately for guests to spoon over their portions as required. Taste the rest of the steaming liquid – depending on how concentrated the dripped flavours are from the meat and vegetables, you may like to hand round a bowl of this, as well as a thin gravy.

Sweet Olive Mousse

serves 6 £

This is a domestic adaptation of Roger Vergé's extraordinary dessert mousse made from green olives, as prepared by young chef John Murray after his scholarship year training in Provence. Ordinary green olives in brine – such as can be bought already pitted in ring-pull tins from supermarkets – are perfectly suitable. This recipe includes the tricky procedure of making Italian meringue.

olives:
7 oz pitted green olives
½ pint water
4 oz sugar
mousse:
5 level teaspoons gelatine
2 tablespoons water

whites of 2 eggs (size 3)
4 oz sugar
½ pint double cream
sauce:
¼ pint single cream
1 teaspoon icing sugar
1 teaspoon Pernod

Drain olives, rinse under cold running water. Cover with fresh water in a saucepan. Bring to the boil, drain, rinse. Repeat this process three more times.

Return olives to pan with the measured half-pint of cold fresh water and 4 oz sugar. Bring to the boil. Cook gently for 5 minutes. Pour contents of pan into a bowl and leave olives soaking in the sugar syrup for a day.

Sprinkle gelatine granules into bottom of small pan. Add 2 tablespoons water and leave to soak until it has become spongy.

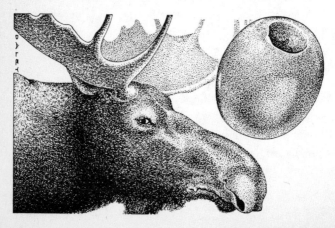

Beat egg whites until they stand in soft peaks. Melt the second 4 oz sugar in a heavy saucepan and boil until a few drops of the syrup dripped into cold water form a soft ball (121°C on a sugar thermometer). Continue whipping egg whites as you pour in the boiling sugar in a steady stream.

Whip the cream up into soft peaks. Melt the soaked gelatine over a gentle heat until runny, then fold into the meringue. Fold cream into this mixture. Drain olives of their syrup, reserving 6 whole. Chop the rest finely and fold into the cream mixture. Pour to a depth of about an inch into moulds – one or two per person – made by nesting 3 paper fairy-cake cases together.

If serving within a few hours, put the mousses into the freezer until an hour before you want them, then into the fridge to thaw out. If serving the next day, they can be put straight into the fridge to set.

Unmould on to individual plates. Spoon slightly sweetened cream scented with Pernod around them. Serve topped with whole crystallised olives and accompanied by delicate plain biscuits such as langue de chat.

Baked Gooseberry Flan

serves 8 £

Adapted from a recipe from the southern states of America in Bill Neal's book *Southern Cooking*.

pastry:
6 oz flour
½ teaspoon salt
1 teaspoon sugar
1½ oz butter
1½ oz lard
4 tablespoons cold water (possibly
  a little more)

filling:
12 oz sugar
2 tablespoons flour
2 eggs – well beaten
1 lb sharp gooseberries – topped
  and tailed

Mix flour, salt and sugar. Rub in the fat. Add water to form a dough that will just hold together. Wrap in clingfilm and refrigerate for 30 minutes.

Roll thinly on floured board and line an 11in flan tin. Prick all over with a fork and bake blind for 10-15 minutes at the bottom of an oven set to Gas 5/190°C/375°F until there are no translucent patches.

Thoroughly mix the sugar and flour for the filling. Stir in the eggs, then the gooseberries. Pour mixture into pie crust and bake at Gas 5/190°C/375°F, in the middle of the oven, for 30 minutes or until the eggs have set.

Serve warm with whipped cream.

JULY

Many years, it seems, after a fine May and dull June, just as the idea of picnics seems a wash-out, the sun appears and people start moaning about the heat.

I am not a fan of eating outside at the best of times; unless on chairs at a table on the terrace of some restaurant with a view of the Alps and an adjustable sun-shade, it flies in the face of evolution. Certainly, the romanticised English plan – pootling off to a flowery meadow by a clear, lazily flowing stream backed by an inviting wood, with a couple of dressed crabs, a pot of home-made garlic mayonnaise, a mixed salad and a bottle of something fizzy chucked into the insulated cool-box in the boot of the car – is rarely matched by the reality. Nobody washed out the cool-box since that avocado mousse spilt all over the bottom last year, the meadow is full of vast yellow slugs, the stream foams with effluent, the ants and wasps eat more than you do and the wood is surrounded by impassable barbed wire.

The only acceptable British circumstance for a picnic, as far as I'm concerned, is whelks with vinegar and pepper in the car parked on the seafront somewhere, with headscarves on and the windows rolled down.

VEGETABLES

This is the month of almost over-abundant salad stuff. Can it really be only a decade ago that salad inevitably meant wet leaves of flimsy butterhead lettuce? These days supermarkets come on with ever more numerous varieties of interesting and competitively priced leaves – oakleaf, lamb's lettuce and curly endive are becoming more common names at the check-out than their snob-gourmet equivalents, chêne, mâche, and frisée, ever were in Hampstead greengrocers.

Corn on the cob should now be coming in from the Isle of Wight, with supplies from Kent to follow. British grown runner beans should be through by mid-month. Cauliflowers should be looking plumper and healthier than for a while. With courgettes in full spate, their larger cousins, the European marrows and squashes, begin to make their appearance.

Finally, the vegetables which most readily summon up the Mediterranean are now really coming into their own: globe artichokes (including the tiny one-bite varieties), heavy plum tomatoes from Provence and Italy, and fat sweet peppers.

Shopping list
Asparagus, aubergines, avocados, **beetroot** (new-season), **broad beans, broccoli** (calabrese), **cabbages** (**summer varieties**, especially Primo, also white), **carrots, cauliflowers, celery**, chilli peppers, **Chinese leaves, courgettes, cucumbers**, fennel, **green beans** (**French** and **runner**), **garlic, globe artichokes**, greens, herbs (especially **basil**, chervil, chives, dill, **fennel, mint, marjoram, parsley, rosemary, sage, tarragon, thyme**), leeks, **lettuce and many varieties of salad greens, mange-touts**, marrows and squashes, mushrooms (cultivated), **okra**, onions, **peas, peppers** (capsicums), **potatoes** (**new**), **radishes**, spinach, **spring onions, tomatoes** (including beef or marmande, plum and cherry varieties), turnips (new-season), **sweetcorn, watercress**

Many supermarkets now offer passable packs of mixed salad leaves, some with interesting ingredients such as peppery nasturtium flowers or dark green, tangy rocket (arugula). French and Jersey marrows, Italian peas and Spanish runner beans all keep supplies steady while waiting for British crops. Also look for pak choi, and samphire.

FRUIT

Summer pudding is the month's biggest treat. If the weather has held up soft fruits in the latter half of June, they should now catch up and come racing through. The English strawberry season continues in full swing, with the even headier delights of home-produced raspberries following fast behind.

When you get bored with summer pudding made with red and black fruits – raspberries, red currants, blackberries, loganberries, blackcurrants, strawberries, cherries for those who are not purists, and so on – try a stunning variation with pale fruits: white currants, dessert gooseberries and yellow raspberries.

My Lincolnshire grandmother used to marinate raspberries straight from the cane in vinegar and sugar; then strain and boil the lot to make a thick viscous sauce to be bottled and served on Yorkshire pudding throughout the winter, as an invigorating starter before the Sunday roast. The more usual way of capturing July for later consumption is to make red currant and white currant jellies, the colours of garnet and antique topaz, as magical accompaniments to the autumn's game.

Shopping list
Apricots, bananas, **bilberries, blackberries, blackcurrants, blueberries, cherries**, coconuts, **gooseberries**, grapefruit, **grapes**, lemons, limes, **loganberries, melons, nectarines, peaches, raspberries, red currants, strawberries, white currants**

I find most supermarket peaches very disappointing – unsweet and rock hard or juiceless and cottony. Maybe it is the way they are stored. Nectarines don't seem to suffer so badly but, for real pleasure, look for white-fleshed peaches and nectarines from Italy and France. American plums may be making an appearance. Good exotica should include pawpaw (papaya) and the smaller Mexican and large Guatemalan **mangoes**. Passable melons might include

Spanish honeydew and Gallia, French charentais, Spanish early watermelons and Israeli ogen and golden-fleshed watermelons.

FISH AND SEAFOOD

Ken Condon keeps a little fishmonger's shop with a blue and white awning on the Wandsworth Road. In the back yard behind the shop, is a blackened, wooden smoke-house, used by his father and grandfather before him. Here, everyday, he smokes fresh salmon over wood chippings supplied by a local furniture maker. The result is moist, delicate in flavour and gets my vote for the best smoked salmon in the city, particularly good in sandwiches for lazy luxury picnics.

Mr Condon is just as skilled and knowledgeable in his handling of fresh wet fish. For July he recommends grilse, the juvenile salmon, as a good buy – weighing around 6 lb for a whole fish and cheaper per pound than larger adult fish. He says mackerel and the white fish are now thickening up and that plaice is just starting its best period. Squid, some of it from Scotland, is now in prime condition. Crab, lobster, prawns and shrimps continue to surpass themselves in quality.

Shopping list
Brill, clams, cockles, cod, crab, crawfish (spiny lobster), dab, **Dover sole**, flounder, **grey mullet, grilse, gurnard, haddock, hake, halibut, herring**, langoustines (Dublin Bay prawns or scampi), lemon sole, **lobster**, mackerel, monkfish, **plaice, prawns, red mullet, salmon (wild** and **farmed)**, **sardines**, sea bass, **sea bream, sea trout** (salmon trout), **shrimps, squid**, tuna, turbot, **whelks, whitebait**, whiting

MEAT AND POULTRY

Why have meat when the fish is so good? Enjoy it while you can and wait for the game season.

Shopping list
Beef, chicken, duck (farmed), **guinea-fowl, lamb**, pork, quail (farmed), rabbit, veal

CHEESE

The French get fed-up and sleepy as the summer gets hotter. According to Michael Day, of the Huge Cheese Company, the best of the season's Gallic cheeses are light and fragrant in order to buck them up. Fine goat's milk cheeses include Crottin de Chavignol and Valencay, with its subtly mouldy aroma. For a real taste of the mountain grasses, choose Pithiviers au Foin. With picnics in mind, Reblochon – in its malleable rind – stands up well to hot weather; Fourme d'Ambert is a good, light, blue; and Appenzeller is a rich, creamy, hard cheese from Switzerland.

Marinated Kippers

serves 4-6 £

Some dishes are delicious in a big, straightforward, gutsy sort of a way that becomes dangerously addictive. Take the salutary tale of my American friend, Sandra Razelos and these marinated kippers. Sandra, formerly a hosiery heiress, came to London in the mid-sixties via Puerto Rico, Athens and two marriages, with a palate tuned to the better things in life. After falling prey to this edible equivalent of absinthe, at that time the staple of bohemian bistro circles, she lost all her money and ended up working in an East End button-hole factory. Warning signs to look for in friends are protestations that they actually prefer marinated kippers to smoked salmon.

4 whole, small raw kippers –
  skinned and filleted, with all
  stray bones pulled out
1 onion – peeled and thinly sliced
	3 tablespoons white wine vinegar
	  or lemon juice
	9 tablespoons best olive oil
	freshly ground black pepper

Rinse and dry small raw kipper fillets. Layer, alternating with onion slices, in a non-metallic bowl. Pour over a peppery vinaigrette made with the other ingredients. Make sure all the kipper and onion is well coated.

Cover bowl and leave in a cool place for 24 hours, turning the fish from time to time. Eat as a starter with brown bread and butter, perhaps followed by other symptoms of swinging London: coq au vin, green salad, chocolate mousse.

Roasting Peppers

Few transformations effected by the simple action of direct heat are as magical as that in the flavour of fresh sweet peppers (capsicums), when they are charred.

It works with green and any other of the new colours of capsicum that Dutch growers regularly come up with, but the effect is most glorious with the sweetest, ripest, yellow and red peppers.

Crisp, refreshing and more of less bland before, they take on a deep, seductive, woody taste and a silken texture that is usually a revelation to people who could previously take the vegetable or leave it.

It works with hot fresh chilli peppers too, although the heat can obscure the benefits of the process. The Turks grill long, relatively fleshy green chillis until flecked with black, then serve them cold with spoonfuls of chilled garlicky yoghurt, usually to accompany slices of cold fried aubergine, or as a garnish to any kind of grilled kebab. A wonderful recipe for beanless chilli con carne sent in by a reader required the roasting of from 3 to 20 fresh chillis, as well as onions and a whole head of garlic, to peel before adding to the pot.

The basic technique is to char the skin of the pepper all over, without cooking the flesh inside beyond a certain stage of softness (more and it becomes merely scrapeable slime). So the heat has to be close and fierce. I have seen Claudia Roden do it, with onions and aubergines for a fabulous cooked salad, on a baking sheet in a very hot oven, and I have stood – bored out of my mind – for the ages it takes to accomplish by revolving each vegetable in turn on the end of a carving fork over a naked gas flame. But the most efficient way is to grill them under the hottest of pre-heated grills, turning as each side is done.

They are ready when the skin is blistered all over (even right down in the cracks), burnt black in big patches and split in places. The whole pepper should be relaxed and flexible, but not completely floppy. Some cooks advocate sealing the freshly burnt peppers in plastic or brown paper bags, or wrapping them in a cloth, so that they continue steaming, to loosen the skins further. I'm not convinced; the peeling is always a messy and frustrating business.

Cut out the stem and seeds (be careful if you're handling them straight from the grill as the insides will still be red-hot), rub off the charred patches, then pull or scrape away the rest of the skin with a vegetable knife. Rinse off the debris from time to time under running cold water, but don't hold the pepper there for too long or you will wash away a lot of the tasty juices.

Cut into strips, the flesh is good simply dressed with a little salt and best olive oil, left to soak at room temperature for a few hours, garnished with chopped chives or spring onions, then eaten as a starter with perhaps a squeeze of lemon juice and warm white bread for mopping. Beyond that, it is simply a question of personal experiment. Food and wine writer, Aileen Hall, replaces the salt with slivers of anchovy fillet, and adds capers and minced garlic; Italian food expert, Anna del Conte, brings in chopped parsley when she talks of Calabrian and Sicilian *peperoni arrostiti* in her *Gastronomy of Italy;* writer and editor, Vicky Hayward, wraps the whole roasted pepper, sliced down one side, around a filling of griddled spring onions – a substitute for Spanish fresh garlic and fillets of anchovy. One of Marcella Hazan's most delicious pasta sauces, from *Marcella's Italian Kitchen*, is strips of roasted red pepper cooked briefly in olive oil with chopped garlic, then stirred, off the heat, with capers, parsley and shredded tinned tuna.

Here is an undiscriminating mélange as a basis for your own experiments.

Roast Pepper Salad

serves 4 ££

8 spring onions

4 small to medium sweet peppers (the majority red or yellow, with perhaps 1 green for contrast) – roasted, peeled and cut into ½in strips

4 anchovy fillets tinned in oil – cut lengthways into thin slivers

1 tablespoon capers – drained if in brine, rinsed and dried if in dry salt

1 tablespoon finely chopped flat-leaf parsley

8 tablespoons best olive oil

Trim spring onions, cutting off the root fibres without disturbing the bottom of the bulb, which holds the leaves together. Cut each onion in half lengthways. Heat a dry, preferably non-stick frying pan, or wok, until very hot then griddle the spring onions against the surface so that they are flecked with gold and black on the outside. They should wilt slightly but still retain some bite.

Arrange the spring onion with pepper strips and anchovy fillets on a large serving plate. Sprinkle with capers. Beat parsley and olive oil together and dribble over all the ingredients. Cover loosely with clingfilm or an upturned plate and leave to marinate for 12 hours in the fridge. It keeps for another day or two.

Serve with warm, crusty white bread.

The roasted, peeled red pepper purées into an excellent sauce. Liquidise while still hot, then gently reheat with seasoning and a couple of spoons of fromage frais or crème fraîche. This is good with hot fish or chicken quenelles and mousses. Or soften the strips further in reduced stock, then blend and reheat for a dramatic accompaniment to braised fennel or poached fish. Or try this vinaigrette with cold cooked French beans, cold poached white fish, slices of chicken and vegetable terrines or the like.

Roast Pepper Vinaigrette

makes about ½ pint £

2 red sweet peppers – roasted until quite soft, peeled and roughly chopped
1 tablespoon sherry vinegar
4 tablespoons best olive oil

½ clove garlic – peeled and minced
salt and freshly ground black pepper

Whizz up in a blender.

Smoky Aubergine Dip

serves 4-6 £

Subjecting aubergines to a naked flame or a very hot grill has almost as astonishing an effect on them as that on sweet peppers, but in this case the flavour is darker and smokier.

Grilling or turning over a naked flame are equally effective with aubergines; the hot oven method imparts a milder smokiness, which I suppose some people might prefer. Once again, the skin should be blistered all over and charred in large patches. Peeling is as irritating a procedure as for roasted peppers. Do this under cold water, then squeeze out as much potentially bitter juice from the vegetable as you can. Make sure you've removed every little particle of blackened skin. If you work slowly, put each finished peeled aubergine in a basin of cold water acidulated with lemon juice to prevent discoloration. Then squeeze out again before use.

The best use is mashed or puréed in a Middle Eastern dip such as *baba ghanoush*, also known as *moutabal*, (with tahina paste, lemon juice and minced garlic), or in the following Turkish recipe, sometimes rather coyly called 'poor man's caviar'. It is a common part of the *meze* table all over the Eastern Mediterranean and Near East. Some versions include yoghurt, which I think ruins the clean flavour and slippery texture.

2 large aubergines – roasted, peeled and bitter juices squeezed out
juice of l large lemon or more
2 cloves garlic – minced
salt
4 tablespoons olive oil or more
slices of tomato, flat-leaf parsley sprigs and the odd black olive to garnish

Mash with a fork, or whizz in a food processor, the aubergine, lemon juice, garlic and salt. Gradually eat in the olive oil. Taste and adjust lemon juice, salt and oil until you like it.

Spread out in the centre of a flat dish, surrounded by slices of tomato stuck with parsley sprigs and a few black olives. Chill well before serving.

Stuffed Courgettes

serves 4 £

For a simple salad, try griddling halves of baby courgettes and dressing them only with salt and olive oil. This is only slightly more complicated and makes a good starter.

4 medium-large courgettes
olive oil
8 oz feta cheese – crumbled
2 eggs – beaten
2 tablespoons chopped flat-leaf parsley
generous sprig fresh thyme – finely chopped
salt and freshly ground black pepper
cayenne pepper

Scrub courgettes, but do not peel. Cut off stem and little brown dot from the other end. Cut in half lengthways, so that each half will sit flat on its skin side, and scrape out all the seeds with a teaspoon to make boats.

Steam over rapidly boiling water, with the steamer's lid on fully, for about 5 minutes, until the courgettes have relaxed slightly. Arrange as horizontally as possible in a grill pan brushed with olive oil.

Mash all the other ingredients together. Spoon into the boats, sprinkle with a little more cayenne and grill under a medium flame until well browned.

Monkfish and Courgette en Papillotes
serves 4 ££

Another recipe gleaned from Jacques Manière, the steam pioneer, after his visit to work with chef David Chambers at Le Meridien, Piccadilly.

3 courgettes – trimmed and thinly sliced
4 pieces monkfish, each about 5 oz – off the bone and well trimmed of skin and membrane
salt
freshly ground black pepper
paprika
1 teaspoon canned green peppercorns – drained and rinsed then coarsely crushed
1 clove garlic – finely chopped
1 tablespoon finely chopped chives
4 tablespoons crème fraîche
chopped fresh thyme leaves

Steam courgette slices for 5 minutes. Be careful not to overcook. Divide between four 6in squares of foil. Place a piece of fish on each. Sprinkle with salt, pepper, paprika, green peppercorns, garlic and chives. Spread evenly with crème fraîche, then sprinkle with thyme. Draw up the edges of the foil, leaving plenty of room inside, to make packets with air-tight seams.

Steam for 15 minutes – 10 with the steamer lid tightly on and 5 with it half-open. Open the packets only at table for the full aroma to be enjoyed.

Sloppy Joes

serves 4 £

These are basically unformed hamburgers piled between toasted sesame buns and so very messy to eat. Some people might call them tacky. But then tackiness, fortunately, never stopped anything tasting good.

The recipe comes from a young married couple of American born-again Bible-bashers, who lived below us in Oxford. While he took post-graduate classes, she baked cookies – lots of different kinds, from peanut butter to double chocolate. Sometimes there would be brownies, too, or massive hunks of cake smothered in butter frosting. Quite often, Debbie had enough cookies for herself and Rob, so we were the happy recipients of the rest.

Debbie was not quite so interested in savoury dishes. But Sloppy Joes she had mastered. Here is Debbie's 'official' version for guests, quoted verbatim. When she and Rob had Sloppy Joes alone, they left out the Worcestershire and Tabasco sauces and added mushrooms.

1 lb lean minced beef	1 few drops Tabasco sauce
1 medium onion – peeled and chopped	1 teaspoon salt
2 oz trimmed and chopped celery	2-3 tablespoons tomato ketchup
2 oz chopped sweet green pepper	2 fl oz water
1 tablespoon Worcestershire sauce	4 hamburger buns – split and toasted

Brown beef and onion together in a frying pan until well coloured. Drain. Stir in remaining ingredients (except buns). Cover and cook over low heat for 10-15 minutes until vegetables are tender. Fill buns with the mixture.

Peas with Sausages

serves 6 £

As until very recently there were no outstandingly good Spanish or Portuguese restaurants in Britain, DIY was the only answer for anyone wanting to enjoy the true taste of Iberia. For Spanish recipes, I've always liked Penelope Casas's *The Foods and Wines of Spain*, although experts assure me that it is neither comprehensive nor properly authentic. Portugal seems to have had better treatment. Jean Anderson's *The Food of Portugal* includes this traditional recipe, *Ervilhas a Moda de Portimao*, a fine way to treat quantities of the season's fresh peas.

1 medium onion – peeled and coarsely chopped
1 small sweet red pepper – cut into matchstick strips
4 oz garlicky sausage (linguica, chorizo, pepperoni or similar) – very thinly sliced
1 tablespoon olive oil
2 pints shelled fresh peas
2 pints water mixed with 1 tablespoon vinegar
6 eggs (size 3)
salt and freshly ground black pepper
2 tablespoons flat-leaf parsley – minced

Sauté onion, red pepper and sausage in the oil until onion is limp. Turn heat down, cover pan and sweat ingredients for about 20 minutes. Stir in the peas, cover pan and cook until tender – about 8-10 minutes (you may need to add a little water).

In the meantime, bring the acidulated water to a simmer and in it poach the eggs for 3 minutes.

Season peas and sprinkle with parsley. Serve in a mound with the softly poached eggs arranged on top.

Oriental Beef Pot-Roast

serves 4-6 £££

The dry-griddling of small vegetables, as in the garnish to this dish, draws out a delicious earthy aroma. The slow, long cooking of the beef in highly aromatic syrup makes it a rich, tender foil. Eat hot with boiled rice and steamed slices of Chinese leaves tossed in oyster sauce.

2 lb roasting joint of beef – neatly tied
2 tablespoons groundnut or other bland oil
2 tablespoons finely grated fresh root ginger
2 tablespoons peeled and minced garlic

1 tablespoon minced fresh hot green chilli pepper

3 tablespoons rice wine or dry sherry

1 teaspoon brown sugar

3 tablespoons dark soy sauce

big pinch five-spice powder

1 medium sweet red pepper – cut into 12 strips

12 baby corn cobs

12 spring onions – trimmed

Brown the neatly tied joint well on all sides in a very hot, dry wok. It may seem to stick at first, but if you leave the stuck surface for a few more seconds, and the heat is high enough, it will soon loosen. Do not wash the wok, because you need it later.

Heat the oil in a medium-sized, heavy, lidded saucepan or flame-proof casserole, then add the minced ginger, garlic and chilli pepper. Stir until the paste mixture begins to brown, then add the rice wine or sherry and let it boil hard. Lower the heat. Stir in the sugar, soy sauce and five-spice powder, then place the browned joint in the casserole and turn it in the mixture so that all sides are coated. Ensure the heat is at no more than a simmer, cover the pot tightly and cook for 1½ hours, turning the joint from time to time.

About 15 minutes before serving, stir-fry first the red pepper strips, then the baby corn and finally the spring onions in the dry wok over a fierce heat. As you char each batch, remove them to a bowl. All the vegetables should have relaxed slightly and be well flecked with black, but still crisp.

Remove string from meat when ready and slice. Lay slices on serving platter. Toss vegetables in the glossy, dark syrup left at the bottom of the casserole and make sure they are thoroughly heated through, then tip them over the meat and serve immediately.

Soft Fruit Roulade

There are plenty of ways to use up gluts of soft fruit, but those of us without gardens are likely to have only a small quantity of fine berries, either bought or donated, which need stretching out. This recipe for a sweet roulade – essentially a *nouveau riche* Swiss roll with a more delicate, usually flourless sponge and a comparatively perishable filling – uses fresh currants baked into the cake and fresh berries in the filling. It is one good solution to the problem of an unusual midsummer pudding. Loganberries, tayberries and the like are well suited to the filling, as are raspberries and blackberries or a mixture of any of these.

Roulades are best eaten at one sitting. I owe the basic sponge method to Barbara Maher's *Classic Cakes*, although she doesn't include fruit.

melted unsalted butter to brush
  tin
2 oz shelled hazelnuts
3 eggs – separated
2 oz caster sugar
handful red/black/white currants
  or blueberries

½ pint double cream
8 oz fresh berries (as you choose)
optional icing sugar to sweeten
  cream
optional 2 tablespoons sweet
  liqueur for cream

Roast hazelnuts at Gas 6/200°C/400°F for 5-10 minutes until they are golden brown and the papery skins rub off completely. Grind coarsely in a pestle or food processor.

Line a 7 in×12in Swiss roll tin, or shallow baking tin, with foil overhanging at both short ends by a couple of inches. Brush well with melted butter.

Beat the egg yolks and sugar in a bowl set over a pan of simmering water until a ribbon of the mixture, when trailed over the surface, holds its shape for at least 5 seconds. Lift the bowl off the heat and continue beating as it cools. It should almost treble in volume.

Whisk the whites separately until they stand in firm peaks. Fold portions of whisked whites, alternating with spoonfuls of the ground hazelnuts, into the whisked yolks and sugar until all is well combined. Scatter the handful of currants over the mixture and lightly fold them in.

Pour the mixture into the prepared tin and level it out. Bake at Gas 4/180°C/350°F for 15-20 minutes until a good brown colour, but still soft to the touch.

Turn straight out on to silicon-coated baking parchment dredged with caster sugar. Carefully peel off the foil, trim the edges of the sponge, cover with another sheet of parchment and roll the cake up.

Leave on a wire rack to cool, covered with a slightly damp cloth. You need not go on to the next stage for a couple of hours.

Just before serving, whip up the cream and fold in the berries. You may like to sweeten the cream with icing sugar and/or sweet liqueur. Benedictine works well.

Unroll the cake and remove the paper. Spread a layer of the cream and fruit all over, then roll up again. Place seam-side down on serving plate and dredge with more icing sugar. Serve pretty soon.

Blueberry Muffins

makes 12 £

An American breakfast classic, very crumbly and delicate, here adapted from Jane and Michael Stern's *Real American Food*. Blueberries are also good cooked in pancake batter.

10 oz flour	1 level teaspoon grated lemon zest
3 oz sugar	4 tablespoons melted butter –
1 level tablespoon baking powder	cooled but still liquid
½ teaspoon baking soda	4 oz blueberries – dried
½ teaspoon salt	thoroughly and tossed with a
2 eggs – beaten	little flour
8 fl oz buttermilk	

Grease 12 deep mince-pie tin cups.

Mix flour, sugar, baking powder, baking soda and salt. Beat together eggs, buttermilk, lemon zest and melted butter. Stir egg mixture lightly into flour mixture (it will remain lumpy). Fold blueberries into batter. Spoon into cups of the prepared baking trays.

Bake at Gas 6/200°C/400°F for 20-25 minutes until golden. Remove from pan. Serve warm, spread with butter.

Sour Cherry Bread

serves 6 ££

The Turkish equivalent of summer pudding, this only works with sour Morello cherries. They also flavoured one of the Ottoman court's favourite sherbets, or fruit crushes, which has now become a popular soft drink, marketed all over Turkey in little brown bottles labelled *vişne suyu* and relished by snooty tourists as an alternative to coca cola. In contrast, this pudding is rarely found outside the home, except in one or two of Istanbul's grander restaurants. The Divan Hotel near Taksim Gardens does a good version, but my favourite is from Pandeli – a long-established suite of tiled dining-rooms over the entrance to the Spice Bazaar. Here you can also eat proper Iranian black caviar at what must be the cheapest restaurant price in Europe.

6½in thick slices unprocessed white bread	6 tablespoons water
1 lb fresh Morello cherries – stoned	¾ pint double cream
6 oz sugar	5 tablespoons kirsch
	flaked almonds – toasted

With as large a pastry cutter as fits entirely within the crusts, cut a circle from each of the slices of bread. Arrange on a shallow baking tray and toast at Gas 3/160°C/325°F for about an hour, or until completely crisp and a light golden colour.

Heat cherries with sugar and water in a large pan. Bring to the boil, then cook for about 20 minutes until syrupy.

Pour cherries in hot syrup over the hot bread rusks straight from the oven. Put aside to cool.

To serve, arrange one circle of bread, which will have soaked up much of the syrup, on each dessert plate, with some of the cherries on top and a spoonful or so of extra syrup. Whisk the cream with the liqueur until it will hold soft peaks, then dollop a generous pile on top of each cherry bread. Sprinkle with toasted almonds.

AUGUST

August is a relentless month, blowing
Marrows out of proportion, mixing
Old broad beans and new swedes, ending
Spring's reign with dull roots.

High summer sees the end of many of summer's raw materials – the salmon, sea trout, Jersey Royal new potatoes, cherries and first-growth strawberries which all seemed so exciting two months ago. This, rather than September, is cross-over month. The momentum changes and plums, English apples and the first real game birds mark the start of the end of the year.

VEGETABLES

New Covent Garden generally promises Brussels sprouts by the middle of the month (mostly for the catering trade). And so, with parsnips, kohlrabi and the days getting shorter, we might as well get used to the idea of autumn.

But hang on! There are beans first – many English varieties will be in glut this month, home-grown peas should come properly into their own, cauliflowers are also looking healthy enough to eat raw, and a good heavy second crop of 'early' potatoes will keep up the salad supplies. Maris Peer is a particularly good scraper, but the most delectable in flavour – the potato equivalent of the truffle – is the pink fir apple: expensive, grown in relatively small quantities but now widely distributed through the supermarkets.

As for other salad vegetables, supplies of excellent outdoor-grown celery should now continue right through until December. British growers seem to have turned to Chinese leaves in a big way, leading to low prices (although I can take or leave this vapid vegetable). Look for ripe, sweet marmande, or beef, tomatoes.

Shopping list
Aubergines, avocados, **beetroot** (new-season), Belgian chicory, broad beans, **broccoli** (calabrese), **cabbages** (**summer varieties** such as Primo, with Sugarloaf following), **carrots**, **cauliflowers**, **celery**, chilli peppers, **Chinese leaves**, **courgettes**, **cucumbers**, fennel, **garlic**, **globe artichokes**, green beans (**French** and **runner**), greens, herbs (especially **basil**, chives, dill, **fennel**, **marjoram**, **mint**, **parsley**, **rosemary**, **sage**, tarragon, **thyme**), **kohlrabi** (new-season), **leeks** (new-season), **lettuce** and **many varieties of salad leaf**, **mange-touts**, **marrows** and **squashes**, mooli, mushrooms (cultivated), **okra**, **onions** (including **pickling**) **parsnips** (new-season), peas, **peppers** (capsicums), potatoes (second earlies including **pink fir apple**), **radishes**,

spinach, spring onions, swedes (new-season), **sweetcorn**, **tomatoes** (including **large beef** or **marmande**, **plum** and **cherry** varieties), turnips (new season), watercress

Some stores are now making a big thing of baby vegetable varieties – for example leeks, courgettes and kohlrabi. The tiny yellow courgettes are especially pretty. If you like your sweetcorn to live up to its name, look for the Supersweet variety. Also look for pak choi, rocket and **chanterelles.**

FRUIT

A brief respite in the strawberry and raspberry season will be followed by the autumn second-cropping at the end of this month. Look out especially for Scottish raspberries. Connoisseurs are supposed to be able to tell from which side of the country they come by flavour and appearance alone; something to do with the Gulf Stream, I expect.

Peaches, nectarines and melons are at their peak this month. A friend serves them in a salad just sprinkled with Amaretto, the almond flavoured liqueur, or fresh fruit juice with a few drops of ratafia essence, which brings out the sweetness beautifully. Yellow honeydew melons are particularly good at the beginning of August. Watermelons will get larger through the month until they are sold by the slice as well as whole.

The summer abundance is augmented by the appearance of English plums, which I think are jolly good in summer puddings, although most people don't agree with me. Most varieties have a very short season – here one week, gone the next – so it is worth keeping a close eye on the market as the month progresses. Early Laxton, Rivers' Early Prolific, Czar and Opal are among the first, followed by Cambridgeshire Gage, Pershore Yellow Egg and Oullin's Gage toward the end of the month, when the justly famous Victoria also arrives.

Make the best of English cherries and French and Spanish apricots before they tail off mid-month. The kiss of autumn is truly set when the first English apples appear. The earliest commonly available is Discovery – excellent when young and fresh, but not a very good keeper.

Shopping list

Apples (UK – Discovery), **apricots, Asian pears** (nashi), **bananas, bilberries, blackberries, blackcurrants, blueberries, cherries** (including the sour **morello**), **coconuts**, custard apples, **gooseberries, grapes**, lemons, limes, **loganberries, mangoes, melon** (charentais, **Gallia, ogen, cantaloup, honeydew**), **nectarines, peaches, plums, raspberries, red currants, strawberries**, watermelon, **white currants**

FISH AND SEAFOOD

Plaice, sole and haddock join the crustacea as some of the month's best eating. Sea bass is a rare delicacy, steamed whole for a surprisingly short time – about 8 minutes for a 2 lb fish – then sprinkled Chinese-style with needles of fresh root ginger and spring onion and finely dribbled with soy sauce and smoking hot bland oil.

Assuming you are bored with lobster and crab mayonnaise, try a selection of filleted white or flat fish, poached briefly (seconds rather than minutes) in a fragrant stock with wine and herbs, then chilled in the fridge and served with good white bread, cold boiled young carrots and thick home-made mayonnaise beaten with garlic and handfuls of finely chopped fresh herbs such as parsley, chervil, tarragon and dill. Halibut, turbot, plaice and brill are particularly good treated in this way.

Shopping list

Brill, clams, cockles, cod, crab, crawfish (spiny lobster), dab, **Dover sole**, flounder, **grey mullet, gurnard, haddock, hake, halibut, herring**, John Dory, langoustines (Dublin Bay prawns or scampi), lemon sole, **lobster**, mackerel, monkfish, **pilchards, plaice, prawns, red mullet, salmon** (farmed), **sardines, sea bass, sea bream, shrimps, squid**, tuna, **turbot, whelks**, whiting, **witch**

MEAT, POULTRY AND GAME

Just as grouse and snipe were beginning to think we only wanted them for their minds, they learn that it was their bodies we desired all along. The 'glorious twelfth' has, over the last few years, attracted as much rah-rah ballyhoo as the Beaujolais race. Helicopters descend to the lawns of Home County hostelries full of ruddy-cheeked chaps bearing braces still warm from the moors. London restaurants search freezers for last year's cryogenised survivors.

Some commentators protest that game birds are never worth eating until they have been hung for a while (complete with guts, in the case of snipe). Others hold that while this is certainly true for more mature birds, there is a special subtlety in a young bird, roasted rare a few hours after shooting. Whatever your view, nothing can beat the traditional accompaniments of bread sauce and tart currant jelly.

Hare, pigeon and traditionally reared duck will improve from now throughout the autumn. There is also excellent beef and lamb about at the moment.

Shopping list
Beef, **chicken**, duck, **grouse**, **guinea-fowl**, hare, **lamb**, pigeon, pork, **quail** (farmed), **rabbit**, snipe, veal

CHEESE

Undemanding French cheeses for high summer include soft bloomy Chaource, with its faint smell of mushrooms, and fresh, light goat's cheese such as Valencay. In specialist retailers, look out for fine farmhouse Cheddars. Pasteurised will be a consistent product, boring or not depending on the source and particular batch; non-pasteurised can scale great heights but, as it is more of a 'living' product, it can also develop strange taints and off-flavours. A rigorous quality mark is that administered by Mendip Foods for the Milk Marketing Board – the farmhouse logo (three cheeses in a pyramid with the words 'Farmhouse English'). An excellent, non-pasteurised farmhouse Cheddar such as Montgomery, made by old-school craftsman and opera-lover Harold Chase, who plays recordings of Verdi to his cows, is dense, crumbly, nutty, with a long, satisfying after-taste. Chef Peter Kromberg at London's Inter-Continental hotel likes his 'with a tossed salad and a glass of 6-year-old Alsace Riesling'.

Parsley and Gin Soup

serves 2-4 £-££

This soup, a thick greenish mush, is both cooler and inflamer – best eaten in very small portions on hot, humid days by the pool. Behind the cocktail-belt, pan-American touches of canned tomato juice and gin, is a base of onion, celery and green pepper, which Louisiana-born chef Beany Macgregor calls the 'holy trinity' of Creole and Cajun cooking. They give a distinctive, slightly bitter, metallic tone to all the area's most famous dishes, from gumbo to jambalaya. The recipe is an adaptation of a Bloody Mary Soup concocted by Ed Keeling, executive chef of the New Orleans Hyatt Regency.

8 fl oz canned tomato juice
2 oz celery – chopped
3 oz onion – peeled and chopped
2 oz sweet green pepper – de-seeded and chopped

4 heaped tablespoons chopped parsley
2 fl oz gin
salt and freshly ground black pepper

Liquidise. Chill.

Menemen

serves 2 £

Dishes of sautéed peppers and tomatoes scrambled together with eggs are common to many parts of southern Europe and the Mediterranean. The French-Basque version, pipérade, includes onion, but I prefer this Turkish menemen, which doesn't.

A popular quick meal at any time of the day, it is most commonly prepared in a double-handled metal skillet, to order, in small restaurants and pastry shops all over the country. The best peppers to use are long and pale with thin, moderately hot-tasting flesh (they are called *sivri biber* if you should happen to live near a Turkish store). Alternatives in this country are milder green chillies or a mixture of ordinary sweet green pepper and hot green chillies to your own pain threshold. Don't even think of making this if you only have canned tomatoes.

1 oz butter	salt
2 large, heavy, firm, sweet, very red ripe tomatoes – skinned, seeded and cut into strips	4 very fresh, free-range eggs – beaten
4 oz finely sliced sweet green pepper (see above)	

Heat butter in a small frying pan. Add tomatoes and pepper and cook for 5-6 minutes over a medium flame, until the tomato has dried out a bit and the pepper relaxed. Sprinkle generously with salt.

Turn down the heat and stir in the beaten eggs. Keep stirring until they are almost cooked through but still creamy. Serve at once, with warm white bread to mop up the juices.

Emulsified Sauces

Two sauces, warm hollandaise and cold mayonnaise, will serve all of high summer's best seafood – crabs, lobsters, crawfish, langoustines, prawns – and much more besides. Both are luxuriously thick, suave emulsions – suspensions of tiny, closely packed fat droplets in water-based liquids – and have a reputation for being hard to make. Both are also the mother sauces for small families of delicious relatives. The knack of preparing them is worth acquiring.

Use pottery, glass or stainless steel mixing bowls for making all the sauces below, other metals may taint them.

Classic Mayonnaise

makes about ¾ pint to serve 6 generously £

Mayonnaise, Elizabeth David's 'beautiful, shining golden ointment', can be made by hand, with a wooden spoon, wire whisk or hand-held electric beater, or in a liquidiser or food processor. As well as giving the satisfaction of direct involvement with such a magical transformation, the wrist-numbing rigours and saintly patience required to make it with a wooden spoon are rewarded by a matchless, dense, almost jelly-like texture.

However you are preparing it, make sure all the equipment and ingredients are at, or just under, normal room temperature. Take eggs out of fridge in advance. If necessary, warm mixing bowl in hot water and put oil in the airing cupboard for a few minutes to take off any chill.

The most important ingredient is the oil. The finest mayonnaise is made with the sweetest, cleanest tasting olive oils. Many virgin and extra-virgin oils are far too strong, hot and throat-grasping for the purpose. Groundnut oil is the perfectly good, bland alternative. Or blend your own mixture of olive and groundnut.

The recipe that follows is a good start. As you gain experience, you can *either* cut the number of yolks to two, *or* increase the quantity of oil to 15 fl oz. The mustard is to help with the emulsion; leave it out if you like. Some people don't add any acid to the mixture until it has thickened (about half way through adding the oil); they then just add a few drops from time to time to thin and season.

Making mayonnaise by yourself by hand, dripping oil with one hand and beating with the other, leads to difficulties. Having the bowl on a non-slip surface such as damp newspaper helps, or stand it in a heavy casserole or saucepan.

3 egg yolks (size 3)	½ pint oil (as you choose)
about 1 tablespoon wine vinegar or lemon juice, or a mixture of the two	seasoning to taste
	freshly ground black pepper
	prepared Dijon mustard
½ teaspoon salt	extra salt
¼ teaspoon dry English mustard	vinegar or lemon juice

Beat yolks thoroughly until sticky. Add acid, salt and mustard and beat again.

Now, beat constantly but at a moderate pace (too fast leads to as many problems as not beating all the time – Julia Child says about 2 beats of a whisk per second, perhaps a little faster with a wooden spoon). Add oil very slowly at first, literally drop by drop, from a thin-spouted jug or teaspoon. The importance of this cannot be over-emphasised. After a couple of fluid ounces have been added, you can proceed with a minutely thin stream.

At some time between adding a quarter to a half of the oil in this manner, the mixture will suddenly thicken appreciably.

From now on, you don't need to beat so constantly and you can pour the oil in a faster dribble or a couple of tablespoons at a time. Every time the mixture becomes unworkably stiff, add a few drops of vinegar or lemon juice to thin it, then go on with the oil.

When you have added the full half-pint of oil, season with salt, pepper, more mustard and more vinegar or lemon juice until you like the result. This is entirely a question of taste.

Once made, mayonnaise does not take kindly to extremes of heat, cold or agitation.

If you're going to keep it a day or two before using, beat in 2 tablespoons boiling water with the seasoning. Protect against a surface skin forming by covering closely with clingfilm.

If your mayonnaise curdles; warm another mixing bowl. Add *either* another yolk and a pinch of dry mustard *or* 1 teaspoon prepared mustard and 1 tablespoon of the curdled sauce. Beat until they thicken together. Beat in the rest of the curdled mass drop by drop.

For mayonnaise made with a hand-held electric beater, set it to moderate speed and follow the recipe above. Received wisdom about liquidiser mayonnaise is that the extra agitation should be offset with more emulsifying agent, in the form of the albumen proteins in egg white, so you need to add the whole egg (1 to a scant ½ pint oil, other ingredients as recipe) for a sauce that is thinner and less gloriously sticky.

The good news is that food processors are not quite so vicious, so you can follow the recipe for hand-made mayonnaise and end up with something almost as good. Process yolks with salt and mustard for 10 seconds. With the machine running, pour in oil as slow a stream as possible until the mixture thickens. Then add acid. Then continue with the oil, alternating as necessary with more acid to thin. Take off the lid and scrape down the insides of the bowl from time to time to make sure everything is well combined.

variations:

Stir in with the seasoning 3-4 tablespoons of finely chopped fresh herbs, such as chervil, chives, parsley, marjoram, tarragon, basil or watercress, for a fragrant quick green mayonnaise.

Stir in very finely chopped herbs, gherkins, capers and anchovies or anchovy essence for a tangy rémoulade sauce.

For sauce tartare, mash 3 hard-boiled egg yolks with a squeeze of lemon juice to a smooth paste. Stir in a raw yolk, a tablespoon of Dijon mustard and ¼ teaspoon salt. Then proceed as for normal mayonnaise, adding about 8 fl oz oil and more acid to thin as necessary. Stir in chopped gherkins, capers, fresh green herbs and a couple of finely sieved hard-boiled egg whites.

If you stir some minced garlic into your mayonnaise, you will get perfectly nice garlic mayonnaise. This is not the same as aïoli – the Provençal sauce for boiled salt cod, fish soups and the like – which is made by pounding garlic to a very smooth paste (sometimes with soaked and wrung out stale bread), amalgamating this with yolks and salt then beating in the oil. This is a slower and more laborious process than making ordinary mayonnaise, impossible in a processor because the garlic takes on a metallic taste and the mixture becomes too thick. Aïoli is all but solid, thinned slightly at the end with lemon juice. Elizabeth David's quantities for 8 people are 16 large cloves garlic, 3 yolks, a pinch of salt, almost a pint of olive oil and 'a very little' lemon juice.

Classic Béarnaise

makes ½ pint, to serve 4 generously £

While delicate hollandaise is glorious with warm artichoke hearts, plainly-cooked white and flat fish, steamed crab, lobster and other crustacea, chicken, poached eggs and dribbled on to broccoli, its gutsy big brother – sauce béarnaise – is the essential lubrication for grilled or barbecued steaks, poultry and fish. As there is more water base, proper béarnaise is easier to make than hand-made hollandaise.

Perhaps a little neglected during the decade of *nouvelle cuisine*, both sauces are experiencing something of a renaissance with the popularity of Creole and Cajun cooking from the Gulf coast of America. They are the most obvious culinary indicators of the area's Gallic heritage along with mayonnaise, roux (flour and butter thickening) and simple lemon, parsley and butter *meunière* dressings.

Hollandaise, béarnaise and all their relations are meant to be tepid, not hot.

4 tablespoons white wine vinegar and 2 large sprigs fresh tarragon (or 2 tbsps tarragon vinegar)	big pinch salt 3 egg yolks (size 3) 5oz butter at room temperature –
4 tablespoons dry white wine	cut into 24 small cubes
2 shallots (or spring onions) – trimmed and chopped	extra salt and pepper 1-2 tablespoons finely chopped
a few screws of freshly ground black pepper	fresh tarragon

Boil the vinegar, wine, shallots, pepper and salt in a small pan until reduced to about 2 tbsp. Put aside to cool.

In a basin fitted over a saucepan of hot water on a very low flame (the water must never get anywhere near boiling point), beat the yolks with a wire whisk or wooden spoon until sticky. They must heat very gently.

Strain on the cooled vinegar reduction and stir until the mixture is creamy and thickens slightly.

Add one cube of butter and beat for a minute until incorporated smoothly. Continue adding single butter cubes until, when about half are in the pan, the sauce thickens appreciably. Now you can turn up the heat slightly and add the rest of the cubes more quickly. If at any point the sauce looks in danger of overheating, whip out of the water immediately and beat so that the yolks cool.

When all the butter has been added, season to taste and add the chopped tarragon.

Classic béarnaise or hollandaise can go wrong for four reasons.

If the yolks are heated too quickly or to too high a temperature at the beginning of the process, they can go grainy or even scramble. If this happens, start again from the beginning with fresh ingredients.

If the butter is added too quickly in the initial stages, it will simply not be absorbed by the yolks and the sauce will not thicken.

Warm another bowl, put in 1 tsp lemon juice and 1 tbsp of the sauce. Beat until they cream together and thicken. Then beat in the rest of the sauce by half tablespoonfuls, beating until thick between each addition. This works because, as it's being beaten off the heat, the butter cools, creams and thickens. For electric hollandaise, just pour the unthickened mass into a jug, then drip it back slowly into the machine, with the motor running.

If you go on adding butter too quickly, the thickened sauce will curdle. Sometimes beating in 1 tbsp of chilled water will bring it back. If not, put another yolk in a clean bowl, beat with 1 tbsp of the turned sauce until thick, then place the new bowl over the pan of hot water and add the rest of the sauce – drop by drop – beating all the time. For electric hollandaise, empty the jug, whizz up another yolk with a few drops of water, then add the curdled mass drop by drop. If this does not work because the sauce is now too cool, resort to the basin method above.

If you overheat the sauce it may become lumpy. You now have perfectly delicious, very rich scrambled eggs. Cook some more and eat on toast.

variations:
Chervil and parsley are good alternatives to the tarragon in sauce béarnaise, or mint, which makes sauce paloise, excellent with roast lamb.

Beat in about 3 tablespoons tomato paste to finished béarnaise and you have sauce choron – also good with grilled steaks, poultry and fish.

Electric Hollandaise
makes about ¾ pint to serve 6 generously £

Just as good oil is essential to fine flavoured mayonnaise, the delicate quality of hollandaise or béarnaise depends on the butter used. Only best unsalted will do. Use Anchor and you end up with Anchor glop.

Even perfectionist Julia Child admits, in *Mastering the Art of*

French Cooking, that hollandaise made in a liquidiser, 'well within the capabilities of an 8 year old child . . . has much to recommend it'. Absolutely correct hollandaise is just yolks, butter and lemon juice – no vinegar. Here is a slight adaptation of Cumbrian personality, hotelier and restaurateur John Tovey's version.

4 egg yolks (size 3)	8 oz best unsalted butter
big pinch salt	extra salt and freshly ground
3 tablespoons lemon juice	white pepper
1 tablespoon water	

When separating the eggs, leave a little more white than usual adhering to the yolks. Blend yolks and salt for a few seconds in a food processor or liquidiser until sticky. Turn machine off. Bring lemon juice and water to the boil in a small pan, then, with the machine running, trickle the steaming liquid on to the yolks until fully incorporated. Turn machine off.

Heat butter until foaming in small saucepan with a narrow lip. With the machine running, drip hot butter into it, at first literally drop by drop, but soon speeding up to a mean trickle. After you've added about half the butter, the mixture will thicken appreciably, and you can then speed up the addition to a thin stream.

Season. Whizz again for 3 seconds to mix

Use immediately or pour either into a vacuum flask, where it will keep for an hour or so, or into a basin which is standing in a pan of warmish, not hot, water.

variations:

Many flavourings can be stirred into prepared hollandaise: chopped herbs – especially chervil, parsley, chives, tarragon and watercress; finely chopped and sautéed or puréed vegetables or seafood – such as mushrooms, artichoke hearts, asparagus tips, prawns and red peppers.

Equally, it can be enriched or sharpened. Add a couple of tablespoons of whipped double cream just before serving for mousseline sauce – fabulous with asparagus. Replacing some of the initial lemon juice with blood orange juice, then seasoning the finished hollandaise with more orange juice and some grated orange zest, makes sauce maltaise – a terrific complement for asparagus and broccoli.

For a creole sauce Albert – excellent with hot seafood – peel, de-seed and chop a ripe tomato. Sauté with a couple of finely chopped spring onions in a little butter, then stir into the completed hollandaise with some cayenne pepper. Yves Ambroise of London's Cajun and Creole restaurant, Fifty-One Fifty-One, suggests the typical Lousiana use for hollandaise: to mask cooked fish or meat before finally glazing the dish under a very hot grill, as, for example, in a red snapper topped with crab meat and spiced ham before its coating of sauce, and sautéed veal spread with mushrooms duxelles.

Cold Baked Hake

serves 4 ££

Colin au four chambré would be a camper name for this indisputably butch, Greek summer fish dish with its messy sauce. It works with almost any white fish – cod, haddock, halibut and so on – and has a satisfying internal logic to its preparation: each ingredient is chopped up as the last one cooks.

4 tablespoons olive oil
1 medium onion – peeled
1 large carrot (about 5 oz) – peeled
1 medium potato (about 5 oz) – peeled
3 oz bulb fennel
6 cloves garlic – peeled and roughly chopped
2 tablespoons tomato paste
4 fl oz dry white wine
2 tablespoons lemon juice
1 level teaspoon sugar
1 bay leaf
handful fresh basil leaves (at least 4 tablespoons when torn into small pieces)
1½ lb hake fillet
1 teaspoon salt
freshly ground black pepper

Heat oil over medium flame in heavy saucepan. Chop onion finely, then fry until just beginning to colour at edges. Finely dice carrot, then stir into the pot. Finely dice potato, then stir into the onion and carrot. Finely dice fennel, then stir into the other vegetables. Add garlic.

Stir over the flame until the contents of the pan begin to stick and colour. Stir in the tomato purée, wine, lemon juice, sugar and bay leaf. Cover pan and leave to simmer until vegetables are tender (about 15 minutes). Take lid off and boil to reduce liquid until it just coats the vegetables. Discard bay leaf. Stir in the basil off the heat.

Preheat oven to Gas 6/200°C/400°F. Skin hake and make sure there are no bones. Sprinkle with salt and pepper.

Spoon half of the vegetable mixture into a shallow oven-proof dish. Lay the fish over. Spread with the rest of the vegetables, cover with foil and bake for 20 minutes.

Best eaten at room temperature or chilled straight from the fridge but also good hot. Serve with fresh white bread.

Sea Bass with Green Peppercorns

serves 4 £££

The last thing you'd think we need is another recipe for something cooked with cream and green peppercorns: steak, duck, chicken, venison, halibut, rabbit and game birds have all appeared regularly *au poivre vert* on more or less pretentious restaurant menus all over Britain for a decade or more. Sometimes you can see the point, most often not.

So, you can imagine the blasé arching of eyebrows when famous Basque chef Pedro Subiyana proffered *lubina a la pimienta verde* for one of the star courses of a press dinner in Madrid. Well ... it came, we saw, it conquered. Very simple and rich, here is a domestic adaptation of a prime example of the Basque reply to *nouvelle cuisine*.

½ oz butter
3 tablespoons pure olive oil
1 shallot – trimmed and finely chopped
4 7 oz fillets of sea bass – off the bone but with skin still on

2 oz canned green peppercorns – drained
2 fl oz Calvados
7 fl oz double cream
salt

Pre-heat oven to Gas 7/220°C/425°F. In an ovenproof skillet on a medium flame, heat the butter and oil. Add the shallot and let soften for a minute or two without colouring, then put in the sea bass fillets, skin side up. Tip the peppercorns over and around them.

Add the Calvados, let it warm through for a few seconds, then set light to the fumes and shake the pan until the flames die down. Sprinkle the cream evenly over the whole dish. Then shove it straight in the oven for exactly 7 minutes.

Take fish out of dish and arrange on warm plates or serving platter. Reduce and stir sauce until smooth and thick, season with salt, then spoon over the fish.

The delicacy of the fish and the pungent, velvety sauce are designed to stand on their own. Subiyana served it garnished only with a teeny puff-pastry fish, but at home this might be an occasion for nancy little side plates of vegetables – the odd mange-tout and baby carrot.

Pig's Trotters Stuffed with Chicken and Pistachio

serves 4 as a main dish, 8 as a starter £££

The trotters here just serve as a casing for a more delicate filling. Sliced thinly and served with salad, it is almost elegant.

4 pig's trotters
2 teaspoons salt
1 large carrot – peeled and cut in half lengthways
1 large onion – peeled and quartered
2 sticks celery – trimmed and sliced
small bunch parsley stalks
big sprig fresh thyme
2 bay leaves
6 allspice berries
1 teaspoon peppercorns
6 fl oz dry white wine
3 fl oz wine vinegar
12 oz raw chicken breast – finely minced or chopped in a food processor
4 spring onions – trimmed and very finely chopped

1 tablespoon finely chopped fresh tarragon
1 teaspoon grated lemon zest
2 tablespoons shelled unsalted pistachio nuts
1 egg – beaten
2 tablespoons double cream
freshly ground black pepper
vinaigrette:
8 tablespoons salad oil
2 tablespoons wine vinegar
1 teaspoon Dijon mustard
1 clove garlic – peeled and minced
salt and freshly ground black pepper
2 tablespoons finely chopped parsley

Singe trotters over naked flame, scrape off the burnt bristles, then rub all over with the salt. You are now going to splint them so that they do not curl too much out of shape during the initial cooking. Tie each trotter firmly between two strong wooden skewers, as if it were a tiny roasting joint. The string should pass round each trotter at least six times.

Put into a large pan with the carrot, onion, celery, parsley stalks, thyme, bay, allspice, peppercorns, white wine and wine vinegar. Cover well with water. Bring to the boil, cover tightly and simmer for 5 hours.

Take off heat. Scoop trotters out of stock (which should be kept for later) and leave until they are cool enough to handle. They will seem hopelessly ragged and falling apart, but persevere. Cut the strings and remove the skewers. Slit the trotters carefully along their length, through the 'palm' side, and open them out. Take out all the obvious bones then, squeezing along between your fingers, feel out all the other tiny bones and splinters which lurk. Discard them all.

In a bowl, mix the chicken breast, spring onions, tarragon, lemon zest, pistachio nuts, egg, cream and a few twists of black pepper.

Lay two of the trotters, end to end and skin down, on a boiled and wrung out piece of cheesecloth (or boiled pristine J-cloth). Pile chicken mixture along the centre. Lay the other two trotters, end to end and skin up, over the stuffing. Wrap the cloth around what should now resemble a fat sausage, and tie securely at both ends. Then tie string around again, exactly as if this were a joint for roasting. Simmer for another hour in the stock.

Take 'sausage' out of the liquid to cool. Chill in the fridge overnight.

Make vinaigrette by shaking oil, vinegar, mustard, garlic and seasoning together in a clean screw-top jar, then stirring in the parsley.

Unwrap 'sausage', slice thinly and serve with the vinaigrette handed separately. Also good with roasted red pepper vinaigrette (see page 135).

Ottoman Baked Lamb

serves 8 ££

My version of an Ottoman palace favourite, *hünkâr beğendi*, which is braised lamb served on a pile of hot aubergine purée thickened with cheese and bechamel. Here the large leg of lamb is tenderised in a yogurt marinade then baked rather than roasted, although it should take on a nice brown tomato-flavoured crust in the last 45 minutes of cooking. By itself it is good served with mashed potatoes, rice or noodles.

However rude and rustic this dish, I have a lingering affection for it because it was part of the menu that won me joint first prize in *The Guardian*/Mouton Cadet cookery competition 1982. Ask the butcher to remove the bones from the lamb if you feel daunted by them.

½ pint yoghurt	2 teaspoons fresh thyme leaves
4 heaped tablespoons tomato purée	1 teaspoon sugar
8 tablespoons rough red wine	1 teaspoon salt
4 tablespoons olive oil	1 teaspoon freshly ground black pepper
6 cloves garlic – peeled and minced	6 lb leg of lamb – trimmed of all fat and the two complicated bones at the body end removed
2 dry bay leaves – crumbled	

Beat yoghurt with tomato purée. Still beating, dribble in the wine and oil. Stir in the garlic, bay leaves, thyme, sugar, salt and pepper.

Make deep incisions all over the leg of lamb. Put in marinade. If you don't have a pottery, glass or stainless steel bowl large enough, use a washed plastic bag without any holes or a bucket. Cover and leave in fridge for 24 hours. Turn occasionally.

Take out of marinade (don't bother to shake off excess) and place in roasting pan. Cover with foil and put in pre-heated oven at Gas 6/200°C/400°F for 1¾ hours.

Take out of oven, pour off juices from tin and keep for later. Remove foil, take leg out of tin and put back in the oven straight on the bare shelf, with the tin on shelf below to catch dripping juices. Cook for another 45 minutes.

Remove lamb from oven, cover once more with foil and leave to stand in a warm place for 20 minutes before carving. Strain drips from tin together with those kept from the first period of baking and reduce down in a small saucepan to almost nothing.

Carve leg in thick slices and arrange on serving platter, on top of a flat bed of the aubergine purée, if you are using it. Spoon the reduced roasting juices over.

Aubergine Béchamel

makes about 1½ pints £

3 lb aubergines	2 oz flour
salt	¾ pint milk – heated to boiling
2 oz butter	2 oz grated Cheddar

The aubergines are given a good, smoky taste by charring under a grill or over a naked flame before peeling. Curiously, Cheddar is actually better than the authentic *kasar peyniri* in the purée. Alone it is a good accompaniment to chops and other simple lamb or beef grills.

Char aubergines on naked flame or under hot grill until soft and black all over (for a fuller explanation see page 153, Aubergine Dip). Peel under running water then leave to soak in slightly salty water for 30 minutes. They will look like grubby rags – don't worry.

Squeeze the rags in your fists to get out as much liquid as possible. Mash the aubergine with a fork or whizz in a food processor.

Melt butter in a saucepan. Add flour and cook together for a minute until the flour is a pale sandy colour, then pour in the boiling milk all at once and beat until the sauce is smooth and thick. Cook for 3 minutes, stirring all the time.

Stir in the aubergine purée and allow to heat through, then stir in the cheese. When it has melted, season with more salt, if necessary, and pour into a serving dish (making a bed for the lamb slices, if you are preparing the full dish). Serve hot.

Herb Cheeses

With the exception of Palet Perigordine and Sariette – both hard to find in this country – cheeses made with herbs tend to lack distinction. You have nothing to lose by making your own.

Choose a delicate base such as Lezay, Saint-Maure, Riblaire or, at best, Valencay. Wash and dry thoroughly your selection of fresh herbs, then chop finely and mix with a few twists of freshly ground black pepper. Cut any rind off the cheese, then press the cut edges into the herbs.

Wrap loosely in greaseproof paper and leave in a cool place for a few hours.

The more delicate, less woody herbs work best: chervil, tarragon, marjoram, chives. Thyme and savory, both strong and woody, are suitable exceptions.

SEPTEMBER

The first month with an autumnal 'r' in it heralds oysters', mussels' and scallops' return to the scene, as well as more game. Fruit and vegetables reach their peak of abundance so this is prime time for pickling, bottling and preserving.

VEGETABLES

In good years, with wet springs and warm, dryish summers, all the produce in New Covent Garden will be looking lovely. But if June and July were wet, followed by a hot, humid August rounded off with more rain, we will have what the trade calls a 'glutty period': produce coming in early, thick and fast, but with no staying power. Some years conditions are such that less hardy items are unsaleably rotten after a few hours in the wholesale market, let alone a day or two in the shops.

Although winter root vegetables, Brussels sprouts and leeks start to make more frequent appearances, most will tighten up only after a snap of cold. Cauliflower should be good and the Isle of Wight is now putting out some superb sweetcorn.

The Mediterranean fruit vegetables – aubergines, tomatoes, sweet peppers and courgettes – make some of the month's best eating. Braise any combination together with onions, garlic, olive oil and fresh basil for one of late summer's major treats.

Shopping list

Aubergines, avocados, **beetroot**, Belgian chicory, **broccoli** (calabrese), broad beans, Brussels sprouts, **cabbages (summer/autumn varieties**, Savoy), **carrots, cauliflowers, celery**, Chilli peppers, **Chinese leaves, courgettes, cucumbers, fennel, garlic, globe artichokes, green beans (French** and **runner)**, greens, herbs (especially **basil**, chives, fennel, marjoram, **mint, parsley, rosemary, sage**, tarragon, **thyme), kohlrabi** (new-season), **leeks** (new-season), **lettuce and other salad leaves, mange-touts, marrows and squashes,** mooli, mushrooms (cultivated and some wild), **okra, onions** (including small pickling varieties), **parsnips** (new-season), peas, **peppers** (capsicums), **potatoes** (second earlies including **pink fir apple), pumpkins, radishes**, spinach, spring onions, **swedes** (new-season), **sweetcorn**, sweet potatoes, **tomatoes** (including large **beef or marmande** and **plum** varieties), **turnips** (new-season), watercress

Some stores promote 'pickling packs' of onions, cabbages and fresh gherkins at this time of year. Pickling *cornichons* (gherkins) is a French national pastime in late summer. Fresh horse-radish root, now in season is one of this country's great treasures that hardly ever finds its way on to greengrocery shelves. If you grow your own, you will know its inimitable clean vigour; if you have to buy it in jars, you're missing out. Also look for pak choi, rocket, ceps and **chanterelles.**

FRUIT

Keep an eye out for the second crop of strawberries and raspberries from Kent and Hampshire. The plum season gets into full swing with delicious greengages, exquisite damsons and the stately

Victoria. September's grapes are usually of fine quality, with an influx of Greek Sultana, Italian Italia and French Alphonse. Melons are still good, with enormous watermelons beginning to dominate. Try eating sweet, ripe watermelon with feta cheese as part of an Eastern Mediterranean *meze* table.

The first English Cox's Orange Pippins should be through by the end of the month. Before, look for Tydeman's Early, Worcester Pearmain, Miller's Seedling and James Grieve in the rare outlets where you'd have any chance of finding them. New-season Bramley Seedlings have already appeared, but other good early cooking apples include Grenadier and Howgate Wonder. French Golden Delicious have a justified reputation for flavourlessness, but the new crop, which starts this month, is in a different league for crunch and taste.

Shopping list
Apples, **Asian pears** (nashi), bananas, **blackberries**, **blueberries**, coconuts, custard apples, **damsons**, **figs**, **grapes**, **greengages**, **ogen**, **cantaloup**, **honeydew**), **nectarines**, passion fruit, **peaches**, pears, **plums**, **pomegranates**, **raspberries**, **strawberries**, watermelon.

Of the imported pears, Italian Williams are particularly good.

FISH AND SEAFOOD

I urge all who still think they do not like oysters, and who have a little spare money burning a hole in their pockets, to head straight for a reputable oyster bar at their earliest convenience. Take your time with half a dozen 'native number ones' to start. Perhaps a squeeze of lemon and a twist of black pepper, then fork the meat on to your trembling tongue.

See . . . nothing slimy or mucoid about these – just a texture like silky chicken breast and the cold clean slap of the sea on your palate. Drink the remaining juice from the shell, then a swig of ice-cold Muscadet. By the third oyster you should be a convert.

Having been weaned on the best, you should be able to deal with the rest (mainly because they'll remind you of natives). So, on to Irish natives or French varieties of the same common, flat or plate oyster – Belons, Marennes or Gravettes d'Arcachon – or the other important type of European oyster, the Portuguese Cupped (usually just shortened to Portuguese), cultivated especially in France, where the best are called *fines de claires* or *spéciales claires*.

The numbered grading system for oysters in Europe runs from no 00000, for monsters, to No 4, which weigh around 1½ oz each in the shell.

Over the last few years, European native and Portuguese oyster beds have been intermittently ravaged by viruses, wiping out whole colonies. But the introduction of resistant Pacific varieties, similar to Portuguese, has kept supplies up.

It seems a shame to muck around with natives but Portuguese and Pacific oysters – available all year – are good for cooking. The frozen-food trade has cottoned on to this and now produces packs of the regal bivalve pitifully breaded for deep-frying. Perhaps it'll soon go the way of all scampi.

Clams are entering their best season and other molluscs to be welcomed back this month. This is also, on the whole, a very good month for many types of white, flat and oily fish.

Shopping list
Brill, clams, cockles, **cod**, **coley**, conger eel, crab, crawfish (spiny lobster), dab, **Dover sole**, **eel**, flounder, **grey mullet**, **gurnard**, **haddock**, **hake**, **halibut**, **herring**, huss, langoustines (Dublin Bay prawns or scampi), lemon sole, **ling**, **lobster**, mackerel, mock halibut (Greenland halibut), monkfish, **mussels**, **oysters** (natives and Pacific), **pilchards**, **plaice**, **prawns**, **red mullet**, salmon (farmed), scallops, **sea bass**, **sea bream**, **shrimps**, **skate**, **smelt**, **squid**, tuna, **turbot**, **whelks**, **whiting**, winkles, **witch**

MEAT, POULTRY AND GAME

The season opens for mallard, partridge and teal, ensuring that several more of Dingley Dell's life insurance companies will go bust. But these birds, along with hare and snipe, make better eating later in the year; the best game for September is pigeon and those monarchs of the glen and moor, venison and grouse.

Traditionally, which in this case means before widespread refrigeration, this was also the month in which pork returned to the table. Many of my Lincolnshire grandmother's best anecdotes begin, 'It was the first chilly snap of September and we were in the yard killing the pig . . . .'

Pork is much underrated. Treated properly, either cooked in fierce heat just beyond pink, so that it retains its juice, or long and fairly slowly so that it falls apart easily, it has a delicate flavour that flatters many loud ingredients. Try a braise of boned loin slices in lots of onions, garlic and tart plums, perked up with grated fresh root ginger and soy sauce.

One advantage of living in a society which is squeamish in its food tastes is that butchers sell off almost everything that is not a chop or a boned and rolled joint for next to nothing. Explore the fundamentals of liver, sweetbreads, kidneys, tongue, brains, trotters and tails.

Shopping list
Beef, **chicken**, **duck**, **grouse**, **guinea-fowl**, **hare**, lamb, mallard, partridge, **pigeon**, **pork, quail** (farmed), **rabbit**, snipe, teal, turkey, veal, **venison**

CHEESE

A fine English cheese for September is Appleby Farmhouse Cheshire, available at many specialist food shops. It is the only Cheshire still to be made in the traditional way from unpasteurised milk. The whole cheeses – from the 2¾ lb truckles to the largest 56 lb wheels – are then cloth-bound to allow steady maturation, rather than coated in wax, as is now more common, which at least partially arrests this process. Mrs Appleby says that the cheese should not be eaten before it is six to eight weeks old. The farm also produces an excellent Double Gloucester.

Seasonal Gallic pleasures include the powerful Boulette d'Avesnes and very vigorous Maroilles. Gentler times may be had with Carré de l'Est and Beaumont or, best of all, a good Brie de Meaux.

This is produced by 14 authorised makers in the *arrondissement* of Meaux in the province of Ile-de-France and is one of only 32 cheeses which is subject to the rigorous quality protection of *appellation d'origine* (similar to wine's *appellation contrôlée*). A ripe Brie de Meaux is supple of skin, with a rippled surface and light brown flecking. It smells of mushrooms, rather than pongs of ammonia, and does not run when cut but gently bulges. The taste is rich and nutty, offset in the mouth with bland rind (although this might be pared off if old and sharp). Excellent names to look for on the label are Rouzaire, Goussin, André Collet and St-Simeon – all of which should carry the *appellation* Haute-Brie on the box. Beware of imitations.

Lobster with White Beans
serves 4-6 £££

Hybrid Mediterranean first-course salad. Serve with warm, white baguette for mopping up the juice.

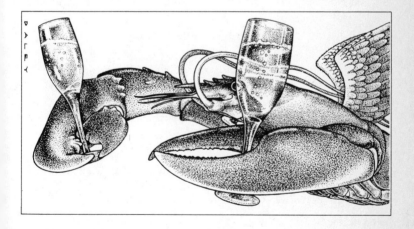

meat of 1 freshly boiled lobster – cut into large dice	freshly ground black pepper
1 large beef (marmande) tomato – skinned, de-seeded and cut into thin strips	optional 1 shallot – peeled and finely chopped
	optional lemon wedges to serve

8 oz dry white haricot beans –
  picked over, rinsed and soaked
  overnight
4 tablespoons best olive oil – plus
  optional 2 spoons extra for
  dressing
1 small onion – peeled and finely
  chopped
1 medium carrot – peeled and
  finely diced

½ clove garlic – peeled and
  minced
½ pint boiling water
1 whole dried hot red chilli
bundle parsley stalks
pinch salt
handful fresh basil leaves – torn
  into small pieces

Boil soaked beans in plenty of fresh water in a covered pan over high heat for 20 minutes. Drain.

Heat 4 tablespoons olive oil in a heavy pan. Add onion and carrot and sauté until the onion is soft and both vegetables have begun to colour. Add garlic and stir around for a minute or two. Turn heat to low.

Tip in the drained beans, the half pint of boiling water, chilli, parsley stalks and salt. Cover pan and simmer until the beans are tender (1-1½ hours), adding a splash more water from time to time if the pan gets too dry.

When ready, take off the heat and leave pan covered until completely cold. This takes several hours, even in the fridge.

Discard pepper and parsley stalks. Gently stir in the basil, lobster, tomato, black pepper, extra oil and shallot, if using. Leave to stand for at least another hour before serving, with lemon wedges if you like.

Sweetcorn and Chicken Chowder

serves 4 £

The corn's sweetness comes out strongly in this chunky chowder, so avoid using the variety known as Supersweet.

1 oz butter
1 clove garlic – peeled and minced
2 fresh sweetcorn cobs
4 tablespoons double cream

salt
freshly ground black pepper
optional Tabasco sauce

1 raw roasting chicken (about 2½ lb)

1 carrot – peeled and roughly sliced

2 medium onion – peeled, 1 quartered, the other finely chopped

1 stick celery – trimmed and roughly chopped

bouquet garni made from fresh parsley, thyme and bay leaf tied together

3 cloves

1 teaspoon whole black peppercorns

2 pints water

2 lean rashers smoked bacon – de-rinded and cut into thin strips

Cut legs, wings, skin and breasts off chicken carcass. Pull off and discard any lumps of fat. You are going to use everything except the legs and wings, which should be saved for another dish.

Put carrot, quartered onion and celery into a medium-sized saucepan along with the stripped chicken carcass, chicken skin, neck and heart (from the giblets), herbs, cloves and peppercorns.

Cover with the water and bring to the boil. Skim off any scum that rises, then lower heat, cover pan and leave to bubble gently for two hours. Lower in the chicken breasts for the last 30 minutes. Strain stock into a measuring jug. Rescue breasts and chop finely. Discard other debris.

Return strained stock to saucepan and reduce by rapid boiling until there is only 1 pint left.

Fry the bacon in the butter in another pan. Add the finely chopped onion and the garlic. Cook until onion is soft and just

beginning to colour. Pour in the reduced pint of stock and bring to the boil.

Cut corn nibs off central husk with a sharp knife. Add to the stock, bring back to the boil and cook for 7 minutes. Briefly liquidise or whizz up in a food processor (or pass through a mouli-légumes – hard work), then tip back into the saucepan. The soup should still have a coarse texture.

Add the chopped chicken breast and cream. Stir in salt, pepper and Tabasco, if you're using it, then heat to serving temperature (don't boil).

Oyster Gratin

serves 4-6 ££££

Shucking raw oysters is not easy. Ask your fishmonger to demonstrate and buy a proper knife with a stubby, thick blade and a finger-guard. Wear thick gloves and hold the oyster flat side up and hinge away from you, in the palm of your hand. Insert knife at an acute angle into the hinge to a depth of half an inch or so, then prise open by twisting the knife a little way. Tip the juice into a jug. Now run the blade of the knife along the inside of the flat shell to detach the muscle. Remove flat shell and flick out any stray shards of shell from the meat with the point of the knife. Then cut the meat out of the other shell.

Use Pacific or Portuguese oysters for this dish, which comes more or less straight out of a promotional pamphlet handed to me on a press trip to Normandy. We were supposed to be building up an acquaintance with the local produce – a limited range but of excellent quality – which led to a few gastronomic low points in hotels whose chefs decided to combine as many regional ingredients as possible in a single dish: for example, steaks stuffed with melted Camembert, flamed in Calvados, then swamped with cream.

freshly ground black pepper
24 raw, medium-sized oysters –
  shucked and drained (use the
  juice in fish soups or chowders)

5 fl oz thick crème fraîche (see
  page 230 or use double cream
  ripened with a little lemon
  juice)

This may sound a bit like that, but somehow everything comes together magically.

2 large dessert apples – peeled, cored and cut into thin slices	knobs of finest unsalted butter for frying

Fry apple slices with very little butter and a good sprinkling of pepper for 10 minutes or so over medium flame, until tender and just beginning to colour. Spread across bottom of flame-proof gratin dish.

Scatter on the oysters, cover with cream, sprinkle whole dish with more pepper and place dish under pre-heated grill until the top is golden brown. Serve immediately.

Grandmother Martin's Corn Bread

serves 4-6 £

Corn, rice and beans, are the domestic staple of America's Old South. Hominy is the result of soaking and hulling dried corn; when this is dried and ground, it becomes grits. Ground corn or corn meal is the basis of many fine dishes from dog bread (a crisp drop scone), through the deep-fried hush puppies, to the elegant spoon breads that are more like a soufflé.

This recipe is from John Taylor, an authority on Southern food who runs a cookery book shop called Hoppin' John in Charleston, South Carolina. This is his grandmother's corn bread, given here in the face of protests from his relatives, who hold that it is an old family secret. He insists that it can be found in many cookery books and family collections.

1 generous teaspoon bacon grease (made by rendering fatty bacon over a gentle flame)	1 scant teaspoon salt 1 scant teaspoon bicarbonate of soda
1 small egg – at room temperature	1 scant teaspoon baking powder
16 fl oz buttermilk – at room temperature	about 10 oz corn meal (maize flour)

Put the bacon grease in a 10in baking tin. Serious Southern cooks keep a heavy, round cast-iron skillet, which is never washed and so builds up a stick-resistant patina, especially for this dish.

Put the greased tin into an oven pre-heated to Gas 8/230°C/
450°F. Leave the tin to heat for at least 5 minutes.

In a large bowl, beat the egg with the buttermilk. Mix in the salt,
bicarb and baking powder. Mix in the corn meal to thicken,
although the batter will still be sloppy.

When the bacon fat in the tin is at the point of smoking, tip in
the batter and bake for about 15 minutes until the top is beginning
to brown. Tip out on to a wooden board to serve. The bottom and
the edges should be very dark

Eat hot or warm with lots of butter.

Common *or* Garden Corn Bread

serves 4-6   £

A less painstaking version, quoted in John F. Mariani's *Dictionary of
American Food and Drink.*

2 tablespoons butter	12 oz corn meal (maize flour)
1 egg	4 teaspoons baking powder
12 fl oz milk	1½ teaspoons salt

Heat butter in skillet at Gas 8/230°C/450°F. Pour in batter made
by beating the egg with the milk, then mixing in the other ingredients. Bake for 20-25 minutes.

Hoppin' John

serves 6   £

According to authority John Taylor 'this is pure soul food ...
strongly associated with Gullah traditions in the Low Country and
common fare on the old rice plantations around Charleston in the
eighteenth and nineteeth centuries'. Gullah is one of the black
English creole communities and languages of the Atlantic seaboard.

For true authenticity, the dried legume used should be the cow-
pea or black-eyed pea – a smaller member of the same family as the
black-eyed bean – known locally by names such as Jerusalem pea,

marble pea and Tonkin pea. The variety was introduced to America along with many other staples of the present day domestic cuisine by enslaved West Africans. If you can find cow-peas for the recipe below, cut the initial simmering time by about half an hour.

Cereals and pulses taken separately are incomplete sources of protein, lacking specific amino-acids, but in combination the deficiencies are cancelled out. This explains why these dishes, mainstays of societies where meat and other concentrated proteins have been comparatively difficult to come by, have been picked upon by Western vegetarians. But they should also be discovered for their glorious flavour.

Hoppin' John (nobody has a definitive explanation for the name) is eaten in Charleston and the surrounding areas as a good luck dish at New Year, with boiled greens and corn bread. It's also good with spinach salad.

8 oz dry black-eyed beans
2 pints water
1 raw smoked fore-end knuckle of
  bacon (about 1¼ lb)
1-2 whole dried hot red peppers

1 medium onion – peeled and
  chopped
8 oz long-grain rice
Tabasco sauce and black pepper to
  serve

Pick over beans. Wash thoroughly in plenty of cold water. Discard any that float.

Bring beans to boil in 2 pints fresh water in a large, heavy saucepan. Boil hard for 5 minutes, then add bacon knuckle, whole red pepper and onion. Lower heat and leave pot to simmer, covered, for about 1¾ hours until the beans are soft but not mushy.

Tip contents of pan into a colander over a measuring jug. You need ¾ pint of the cooking liquid, made up with water if necessary.

Skin the bacon knuckle and take the meat off the bone. Chop into small chunks.

Tip beans, measured 'pot likker' and meat back into the saucepan with the rice. Bring back to the boil. Cover pan and simmer for another 20 minutes until the rice is cooked and the liquid absorbed. Turn off the heat and leave covered pot to stand for another 15 minutes before serving. Sprinkle on your own requirements of Tabasco and pepper.

Stewing Okra

In the second half of the summer, peaches, watermelons, okra and tomatoes seem to take pride of place on the roadside stalls in the vast Carolina flatlands between the mountains and the Atlantic, known as the Low Country.

Okra is one of the many staples of southern cooking brought across to America by enslaved West Africans. Perhaps its most famous use is as one of the three essential thickeners (used alone or in combination) of Louisiana's gumbo soup/stews, of which the name is supposed to derive from African words such as the Bantu *gombo* and Umbundu *ochinggombo*.

Excellent pickled okra – hot Texas okra pickle is one of the essential edible souvenirs to bring back from a trip to the States –

also appears dipped in corn meal and deep-fried, and in various simple marriages with tomato. Here are two different versions.

Charleston, SC, Okra and Tomatoes

serves 4 £

This is a slight adaptation of a Charleston, South Carolina version served to accompany roast pork, rice with sieva beans (like tiny green butter beans) and corn bread.

2 very fatty rashers of smoked, streaky bacon – de-rinded and chopped small
1 medium onion – peeled and chopped
12 oz fresh okra – washed, de-stalked and cut into ½in lengths
2 cloves garlic – peeled and minced
1 lb tomatoes – peeled, seeded and roughly chopped
salt and cayenne pepper

In a heavy, well-used frying pan, cook bacon very gently to render out the fat. Turn up the heat and add the onion. Fry until just beginning to brown.

Add okra and garlic and continue to fry over medium-high heat, stirring from time to time, until it, too, is nicely flecked with brown (5-10 minutes). Add the tomatoes and cook until they are soft enough to break up easily. Season with salt and cayenne pepper.

Savannah, GA, Okra and Tomatoes

serves 8 £

Mrs Wilkes's Boarding House is a lunchtime institution in Savannah, Georgia. Every weekday for 40 years she has served up steaming dishes of home cooking to a communal table of paying guests. This is her dubious sounding but good-tasting tomato and okra gumbo.

2 lb fresh okra – washed, de-stalked and cut into ½in lengths

2 lb tinned tomatoes

½ teaspoon salt

1 tablespoon margarine (or substitute butter)

3 slices of bacon – de-rinded and chopped

Stew together in a covered pan over medium heat for 20 minutes.

Brunswick Stew

serves 4-6 £

Jane and Michael Stern's *Real American Food* is 'American cuisine as eaten by real folks every day', from Mary Mac's Green Tomato Chowchow to Winnemucca Coffee.

The section on the South has a recipe for Brunswick Stew, slightly adapted below, which the Sterns call 'domesticated' to distinguish it from the supposed original 'slave's make-do meal of stale bread, onions and a brace of fresh-killed squirrels'. Several Brunswicks in North Carolina and Virginia claim this, although I've only eaten it in Brunswick, Georgia, where – although a trashy version made of minced beef and chicken – it was the only item of note on at the local branch of the Western Sizzlin' steak-house. It is similar to the famous burgoo of Kentucky, although I can find no authorities prepared to back the possibility of linguistic connection.

I have left the squirrel option out of the ingredients. Toy instead with the idea of adding to the basic recipe rabbit or chicken giblets, finely chopped pork offcuts, celery, carrots, finely sliced cabbage, garlic, dried red pepper, potatoes and additional vegetables in season such as green beans or okra.

2 lb jointed and skinned rabbit or chicken (or mixture)

4 tablespoons cooking oil

2 onions – peeled and sliced

2×8 oz tins crushed tomatoes (or equivalent in skinned, de-seeded, finely chopped, fresh plum tomatoes)

½ teaspoon salt

½ teaspoon freshly ground pepper

1 tablespoon chopped parsley

1 bay leaf

sprig fresh thyme or pinch dried

8 fl oz water

12 oz kernels cut from sweetcorn cobs (or frozen)

6 oz frozen broad beans (or fresh when in season)

Brown meat in oil in a large pan. Remove meat and brown onions in remaining oil. Return meat to pan. Add all other ingredients except sweetcorn and broad beans. Bring to the boil. Cover. Reduce heat and leave to simmer for one hour.

At this stage you can either bone and hack up the meat or leave it on the bone. Add corn, broad beans and up to another 8 fl oz water, if stew is too thick. Simmer 30 minutes. Check seasoning.

Fruit Cobbler

serves 4-6 £

Rural Southern summer treat.

fruit:
1 lb peaches – stoned and sliced
12 oz blackberries – washed and hulled
2 teaspoons cornflour
8 oz sugar
big knob butter for buttering dish
cobbler:
8 oz plain flour plus more for rolling

1 level teaspoon salt
3 level teaspoons baking powder
2 oz butter
1 tablespoon sugar plus more for sprinkling
4 fl oz milk
1 fl oz double cream

Toss fruit gently but evenly in an even mixture of the cornflour and sugar. Stew together gently in a covered saucepan until the juices are running nicely and begin to thicken. Stir.

Butter a wide pie dish very generously. Pour fruit into dish. Sift flour with salt and baking powder. Rub in the butter evenly. Stir in the sugar. Make a well in the centre and pour in a mixture of the milk and cream. With a dozen confident strokes with a palette knife, cut the liquid into the dry ingredients to form a soft dough.

Knead dough lightly until smooth, then roll out on a floured surface to about ½in thickness. Stamp out scone-sized circles with a pastry cutter and sprinkle with sugar.

Make sure oven is pre-heated to Gas 7/220°C/425°F. Arrange scones quite closely on top of the stewed fruit in the dish, then bake until scones are lightly browned and fruit is bubbling (about 20 minutes). Serve with whipped cream or ice-cream.

Plum Crumble

serves 4-6 £

Fans of English puddings have been increasingly pandered to by smart restaurants over the last few years. Bread and butter pudding received its most glamorous promotion through Anton Mosimann, although his addition of apricot jam did not please purists. Prue Leith has been another influential apologist, serving up butterscotch tapioca and apple and sultana crumble.

Plums, rhubarb and apples make the most serious crumbles. Some of the best September cooking plums, if you can find them, are the beautifully tart, golden-fleshed Warwickshire Droopers.

crumble:
6 oz plain flour
pinch salt
4 oz butter
2 oz caster sugar
1 oz flaked almonds

filling:
2 lb cooking or eating plums
½ oz unsalted butter
1 tablespoon caster sugar (more or less depending on fruit)
3 tablespoons brandy
optional pinch cinnamon

Sift flour into a bowl with the salt. Rub in the butter until the mixture looks like home-made breadcrumbs (or whizz in a food-processor). Stir in the sugar and nuts.

Cut plums in half and remove stones. Heat butter in a heavy frying pan, add plums and sugar, then the brandy. Set light to the fumes and toss the fruit in the flames. When they have died down, stir in the cinnamon if you like, then tip the contents of the pan into a deep pie dish.

Sprinkle crumble mixture evenly over and bake for 30 minutes in oven pre-heated to Gas 6/200°C/400°F, until golden.

Serve hot or warm.

Egg Custard

makes about ¾ pint £

½ pint milk
1 tablespoon caster sugar plus
   more for sprinkling
1 vanilla pod

2 egg yolks
2 tablespoons double cream
optional sprinkle of brandy

Preferably using a non-stick saucepan, heat the milk with the sugar and vanilla pod. Bring mixture very slowly to the boil.

Beat yolks in a bowl with a wooden spoon, without allowing them to become too frothy.

Remove vanilla pod (which can be wiped and reused many times) from the milk. Pour milk on to the yolks in a steady stream, stirring all the time. Return to the pan when well mixed. Stir in the cream.

Stir over a gentle heat until the mixture is thick enough to coat the back of a spoon. Do *not* boil. Stir in the brandy, if you like. Sprinkle with caster sugar to prevent a skin forming.

If the custard curdles, strain it immediately into a cold saucepan and whisk vigorously.

OCTOBER

Although the last home-grown green beans and plums, and imported melons and peaches from southern Europe may still be around, autumn's sweet rot has taken firm hold. British mycophiles will spend weekends grubbing about in secret pine and beechwood locations looking for delicious edible funghi.

VEGETABLES

Although abundant in Britain, wild funghi rarely reach our markets and shops as they do all over Europe. But in late September and early October fine funghi, such as trompettes de la mort and pale orangey chanterelles with their whiff of apricots, may be found by those in the know. Most wild species need no more than quick sautéeing in butter with a little finely chopped onion, shallot or garlic and seasoning, to show at their best.

    Pumpkin tends to be dismissed here as boring. Try young, firm specimens cut into cubes and sautéed in a little butter with salt and plenty of black pepper. Add fresh nibs of sweetcorn cut from the cob, cook for a couple of minutes more, then stir in a tablespoon or so of double cream.

Shopping list

Aubergines, **avocados**, **beetroot**, Belgian chicory, **broccoli** (calabrese), **Brussels sprouts**, **cabbages** (including **green autumn varieties, red, white** and **Savoy**), **carrots**, **cauliflowers**, **celeriac**, **celery**, chilli peppers, **Chinese leaves**, **courgettes**, **cucumbers**, **fennel**, **garlic**, **globe artichokes**, **green beans** (French and **runner**), greens, herbs (especially basil, **mint**, **parsley**, rosemary, **sage**, tarragon and thyme), **kohlrabi**, **leeks**, lettuce and other salad leaves, mangetouts, **marrows** and **squashes**, mushrooms (including wild varieties), **okra**, onions (including **pickling**, **mild Spanish** and **strong red** varieties), parsnips, peas, **peppers** (capsicums) **potatoes**, **pumpkin**, radishes, salsify, scorzonera, spinach, spring onions, **swedes**, **sweetcorn**, **sweet potatoes**, tomatoes, **turnips**, watercress

Specialities to look for in some stores include short, bulbous Parisian carrots, chard, horse-radish, ceps, **chanterelles** and **black and white truffles**.

FRUIT AND NUTS

Fresh walnuts are an early autumn treat, with a mild, creamy flavour and crisp, moist texture. Crack them open like ordinary walnuts, then peel off the bitter, inner brown skins from the kernels. This is a fiddly process, well suited to the end of long, relaxed meals. Fresh walnuts go well with muscat-flavoured grapes, such as some of the intensely sweet Italia variety around at the moment (the yellower the sweeter).

Mediterranean pomegranates, also in season now, present other problems to the eater. Having cut or broken them into quarters, should you just bite in and risk decimating your tastebuds on the bitter yellow pith partitions between the clusters of jewel-like seeds? I cop out by simply squeezing the halved fruit like an orange and drinking the sour/sweet nectar.

With fresh black figs, cut twice through from the stem end so that the quarters are still joined at the bottom. Open the four petals and gently mouth the honeyed flesh away from inside the skin.

Cox – star of the modern English apple season – will be with us by the end of the month.

Shopping list

Apples, **Asian pears** (nashi), bananas, **blackberries**, coconuts, cranberries, custard apples, **damsons**, **dates**, **figs**, grapefruit, **grapes**, **hazelnuts** (including **Kentish cobs**) lemons, limes, **mangoes**, melons, nectarines, peaches, **pears**, **pomegranates**, **quinces**, **satsumas**, **walnuts**

Crab apples and **medlars** are in season for those lucky enough to have access to the bushes or trees – too perishable and unprepossessing in appearance for the retail food chain it seems.

FISH AND SEAFOOD

Mussels, back at their best, can be as useful as truffles in perfuming fish dishes. Take neat one-portion fillets of any white or flat fish and arrange on buttered greaseproof paper or foil with very fine slivers of onion or leeks and other vegetables such as fennel, carrot and tomato. Add a leaf or two of suitable fresh herbs, seasoning and as few as two, well scrubbed, de-bearded raw mussels in their shells. Seal the paper, making a tight seam but allowing plenty of room inside the packets. Bake on a metal sheet in a hot oven for up to 15 minutes. Cut open the packets at table. The mussels will have opened and their fragrant liquor permeated the whole dish.

This month sees peak season for bloaters, lightly cured herring with their guts left in to give them a subtle gamy flavour.

Shopping list

Brill, **carp**, clams, cockles, **cod**, **coley**, **conger eel**, crab, dab, **Dover sole**, **eel**, flounder, **grey mullet**, **gurnard**, haddock, **hake**, **halibut**, **herring**, **huss**, langoustines (Dublin Bay prawns or scampi), lemon sole, **ling**, lobster, mackerel, mock halibut (Greenland halibut), monkfish, **mussels**, oysters, **pilchards**, **plaice**, pollack, **prawns**, scallops, **sea bass**, **sea bream**, **shrimps**, skate, smelts, **sprats** (**fresh and smoked**), **squid**, tuna, **turbot**, whelks, whiting, winkles, **witch**

MEAT, POULTRY AND GAME

Game newly in season includes pheasant and woodcock, although both will make better eating next month. Grouse is at its very best, with stiff competition from partridge and wood pigeon.

There should be no mystique about cooking prime quality game birds. Enjoy their succulence and flavour simply by spatchcock-grilling or barbecuing them as you would a whole spring chicken. Cut all the way along the backbone, flatten out the bird by pushing down on the breast, season both sides well with salt and pepper, brush with a little olive oil, then cook under a pre-heated grill, or on a glowing barbecue, for 10-25 minutes – turning once or twice – until it is done. Serve with a dollop of plain or herbed butter, wedges of lemon and some crisp salad.

Shopping list
Beef, **chicken**, **duck**, goose, **grouse**, **guinea-fowl**, **hare**, lamb, mallard, **partridge**, pheasant, **pigeon**, **pork**, **quail**, **rabbit**, snipe, teal, turkey, veal, **venison**, woodcock

CHEESES

Fine cheeses, eating well this month include Caerphilly, Sariette – a white, cow's milk cheese covered with the herb savory – and smelly Epoisses from Burgundy with its shiny brick-coloured rind.

Notices will now be going up in cheese shop windows all over France, 'Le Vâcherin est arrivé'. This Franco-Swiss queen of the winter cheeseboards, made with very rich milk, comes encircled by a strip of sappy wood in a box. The bottom of the cheese sticks to the box and the top rind is an undulating orangey mattress. All this makes for extreme difficulty when serving.

Cheese guru Michael Day explains the flashy way: 'Support the box at about 60° from horizontal. Cut a neat isosceles triangle from the top rind and let the cheese run gently on to a plate, helping it along with a spoon if necessary.' This should get easier with the more relaxed cheeses which come later in the season.

Although recent years have seen some Vacherin bans due to listeriosis, an occasionally fatal strain of food poisoning, checking procedures are now strict.

Spanish Clams

serves 2 £

One of the most delicious things I have ever eaten was a Catalan seafood mélange – *zarzuela de pescado* – as reported by Claudia Roden in her *Mediterranean Cookery*. The following is a much simpler use of the techniques she quotes, to produce a rich coating for one of the most flavoursome bivalves.

sofrito:
1 small onion – peeled and grated
scant tablespoon olive oil
1 medium-sized tomato – peeled, de-seeded and finely chopped
salt
4 tablespoons dry white wine
picada:
   1 thin slice white bread – crusts removed, fried until golden brown in olive oil, then drained on absorbent paper

3 blanched almonds – toasted and finely chopped
1 clove garlic – peeled
1 tablespoon very finely chopped parsley
assembly:
24 small live clams – scrubbed
1 tablespoon brandy
salt and cayenne pepper

In a small non-stick saucepan, gently fry the onion in the oil until soft and beginning to colour. Add tomato and salt and cook to dry out the tomato flesh a bit. Splash in the wine and simmer, stirring until the sauce is thick but still sloppy.

Crumble bread, then pound in a pestle and mortar together with the almonds and garlic. Stir in the parsley.

Heat clams in a large, heavy, dry, covered frying pan, over a medium flame. Hold the lid on as you toss the pan gently to help them cook evenly. When all the clams are open, pour in the brandy and set light to the fumes. Pour in the *sofrito*, cover pan again and let simmer over a lower flame for 3 minutes. Stir in the *picada*, sprinkle in some cayenne and extra salt, if necessary, then cover again and let heat through for another minute.

Serve with good white bread to mop up the juice.

Damson Sauce

serves 3-4 £

For a particular breed of home cook who might be called the broo-
dies, the end of the damson season means preserves, wine and a
freezer full of purée. The rest of us find that we have an energy
problem. You know the picture: you get home with a couple of
pounds of the sour little black plums. But you feel tired and the
idea of jelly-making defeats you. So you leave the brown paper bags
in the salad box of the fridge. For the next three days, they nag at
your conscience, but then you forget about them until you next go
to stow a lettuce. The bags have dissolved in black sludge and
everything is sprouting grey-green fur.

Tut tut! Next time, buy only half a pound and rescue them for
this tastebud-jolting relish, excellent with fatty lamb or pork chops.

8 oz damsons – stoned
4 tablespoons dry sherry
1 oz sugar
½ level teaspoon salt
2 tablespoons groundnut oil
1 teaspoon peeled and minced
   garlic

1 teaspoon peeled and grated fresh
   root ginger
finely chopped fresh hot green
   chilli pepper (as much as you
   might enjoy)

Bring fruit to the boil with the sherry. Cover pan and cook for 5
minutes or so until soft. Liquidise, or sieve, and pour back into the
pan with the sugar and salt. Reduce to a jammy consistency.

Heat the oil in another pan until almost smoking. Add the garlic,
ginger and chilli. Push this around for a second or two until it has
given up its surface moisture but not quite begun to colour. Add
the fruit purée and stir briskly until hot and glossy.

Mushroom Risotto with Beans

serves 4 ££

A good dish for any type of vegetarian, depending on whether you
use the Parmesan.

2 tablespoons olive oil

1 lb mushrooms (any fresh, firm species will do, such as field, brown-cap, Shiitake, button as a last resort) – wiped clean and cut into big pieces

2 cloves garlic – peeled and crushed

½ teaspoon chopped fresh sage or small pinch dried

1 teaspoon salt

freshly ground black pepper

8 oz white risotto rice (arborio, ordinary long grain will not work)

½ pint red wine

½ pint water

4 oz fresh French beans – washed, trimmed and chopped into¼in lengths, then rinsed in boiling water to blanch

optional freshly grated Parmesan – generous ½ tbsp per serving

Heat the oil in a heavy based saucepan. Throw in the mushrooms, garlic, sage, salt and pepper. As they cook, the mushrooms will give off quite a lot of juice. Continue boiling, stirring from time to time, over a medium-high flame until this juice reduces away again. Stir in rice, then wine.

Turn down the heat until the liquid settles down to a friendly simmer. Stir gently until the wine is all absorbed – about 5-10 minutes – then pour in the water and beans and stir while bringing back up to a simmer. Continue to stir gently while the mixture cooks for another 10-15 minutes. The risotto is ready when the rice is *al dente* – cooked through but still with a slight resistance to the bite – and the texture of the whole dish is quite soupy and creamy without being mushy.

Serve in bowls, sprinkled with the Parmesan if you like, and accompanied perhaps by a tomato salad.

Paella with Artichokes and Rabbit

serves 6 £

This recipe, adapted from one demonstrated at the Alambique cookery school in Madrid, gives some idea of the subtle, earthy flavour of the classic Valencian paella; the adaptation is slight, but enough to have forfeited any claim to authenticity. Note the temperate use of garlic and seasonings. One lesson the school tries to drum desperately hard into its pupils is that authentic paellas are made either with meats or with seafood, never a mixture. Original versions, apparently, were flavoured with artichokes and snails (or rosemary when they couldn't get snails).

The most important ingredient is the rice, with its thick and stubby grains, grown in the marshy flatlands around the extraordinary city of Valencia. This can be bought as paella rice from Spanish delicatessens; no other will do. The essential utensil is a wide, slope-walled, shallow, sturdy paella pan (called a *paella*). For these quantities a 15in diameter one will do, which just about fits a gas hob; much larger and you also have to buy a special double-ringed butane-gas burner. I include this recipe in the hope that some of you will have bought such pans back from Spanish holidays or will feel inspired to go out and buy one from a delicatessen here. If you haven't got one already, remember next time.

5 fl oz good olive oil
big pinch salt plus more for
  seasoning
1½ lb chicken – skinned and cut
  into joints
1 lb rabbit – skinned and cut into
  serving pieces
8 oz fresh flat green beans – cut
  into stubby pieces
8 oz trimmed raw artichoke hearts
  – cut into large chunks
4 oz peeled and de-seeded
  chopped tomato
1 garlic clove – peeled and finely
  chopped

sprig fresh rosemary
½ teaspoon paprika
1½-2 pints water
big pinch saffron threads – lightly
  toasted in a dry pan, then
  crumbled
8 oz slightly undercooked and
  drained borlotti, white haricot,
  butter or flageolet beans
  (frankly, I use tinned)
freshly ground black pepper
1 lb paella rice

Heat oil in paella over a steady, moderate flame, making sure the pan is absolutely flat. When it is quite hot, sprinkle in a pinch of salt and the well dried pieces of chicken and rabbit. Sauté, turning from time to time until they are a rich, golden brown.

Add the green beans, artichokes, tomato, garlic and rosemary. Sauté for a few minutes. Stir in the paprika and immediately after, the water, saffron and almost cooked beans.

Bring to the boil and allow to simmer for about an hour, until the meat is tender. Season.

Pour on the rice in the shape of a cross covering the whole pan. Turn the heat up to fairly high for the first 10 minutes after adding the rice, then down to a simmer until it is fully cooked – about 20 minutes in all. As the pan is not covered and even slightly different packets of rice absorb different amounts of water, you may need to splash on a little more as you go.

Remove from heat and let stand for 10 minutes before serving.

Pork Adobo

serves 4 £

Unlikely sounding dark, tangy Filipino stew.

2 lb lean pork meat – cut into bite-sized cubes

6 tablespoons soy sauce

6 tablespoons distilled malt vinegar

2 tablespoons vegetable oil

1 head garlic (about 12 large cloves) – each clove peeled and quartered

1 teaspoon freshly ground black pepper

1 lb medium-sized waxy potatoes – peeled and quartered

Sprinkle pork cubes with the soy sauce and vinegar in a pottery, glass or stainless steel bowl and leave to marinate for an hour.

Heat the oil in a large, heavy, lidded saucepan or fire-proof casserole. Add the garlic and stir for a minute or two, then spoon in the meat. Turn this in the oil until it has lost its raw look, but do *not* let it brown. Add the pepper, potatoes, remaining marinade and water to cover. Bring to the boil, reduce heat so it is just bubbling gently, put on the lid and cook for 30 minutes.

Remove the lid. Increase the heat and continue cooking for about another 20-30 minutes, stirring from time to time to prevent the bottom sticking and burning, until the meat is tender and the sauce is thick and syrupy. Serve with white bread or plain boiled rice and salad.

Making Gratins

What all proper gratins have in common is a browned top. They are generally homey, comforting dishes. Cauliflower cheese, shepherd's pie and Lancashire hot-pot are all gratins, as long as their potentially pallid and uninteresting surfaces have been transformed into savoury crusts of gold flecked with darker brown.

The word gratin comes from the old French *grater*, to grate, referring to dishes treated with 'raspings of bread' and cooked 'between two fires so as to produce a light crust'. But the dictionary definition has broadened over the centuries: the browned crust can now be achieved by baking the dish in the oven at suitable temperatures or by thrusting it under a hot grill at the last moment – and may be made of cheese, breadcrumbs, a sauce, greased potatoes or any combination of these. That is what to expect of something *au gratin* or *gratinée* in a cookery book or on a traditional restaurant menu.

Nouvelle cuisine has, as with many old terms and methods, bent gratins to its own ends. One of the most fashionable restaurant sweet courses of the last few years has been the gratin of fruits – usually a pretty arrangement of fruit slivers under a sheet of sabayon sauce (a refined relative of zabaglione), shown to a fierce grill to char the surface just before serving.

Of traditional gratins, some of the most classic are the family of dishes starring thinly sliced potato.

Grimod's Gratin

serves 4-6 £

A hearty composite gratin, like lasagna or moussaka, of the type that cookery books used to label 'family suppers'. It is adapted from a peculiar eighteenth-century gourmand, Grimod de la Reynière's, *potage à la camerani*.

3 oz butter plus a little for greasing	salt and freshly ground black pepper

6 oz peeled and diced carrot
4 oz peeled and diced turnip
4 oz peeled and diced parsnip
8 oz trimmed and sliced leek
4 oz trimmed and chopped celery
1 lb chopped raw chicken livers – cleaned

big pinch ground cinnamon
big pinch ground allspice
12 oz dry macaroni
6 oz block Parmesan – freshly grated

Melt the butter in a large, heavy saucepan. Add all the vegetables and cook, partly covered, for about 30 minutes, stirring from time to time. Add the livers, a lot of black pepper, a little salt, the allspice and cinnamon about 10 minutes before the end of cooking. The vegetables should be almost tender and the liver cooked through. Boil off any excess liquid.

Boil the pasta in salted water until *al dente*. Drain. Butter a large heavy casserole and tip in half the pasta. Spoon in half the liver mixture, then half the cheese, the rest of the pasta, the rest of the liver, and finally the rest of the cheese – smoothing each layer flat as you go. Bake, uncovered, at Gas 6/200°C/400°F for no longer than 20 minutes, until the crust is pale gold. Serve hot with green salad.

Gratin Dauphinois

serves 6-8 £

Cooks fight about what makes the authentic version of this dish – unrinsed floury potatoes for the starch to hold the dish together or rinsed waxy potatoes for a lighter texture; milk, cream, crème fraîche, or a combination for the liquid. There are other debates about whether to use egg yolk or a little flour to thicken the mix; whether cheese is essential or nutmeg heresy. Most agree on the use of butter and garlic – Edouard de Pomiane, writing in the 1930s, has 4 cloves of garlic to 1½ lb potatoes. This is a very rich, luxurious version to be served in mean portions, either as a course by itself or alongside plain roasts or grills.

If making this dish in smaller quantities, stick to the same proportion of cream to potatoes, for example ½ pint to 1 lb; for larger quantities, use less cream – 1¼ pints to 3 lb.

1½ lb peeled waxy yellow
  potatoes
butter for greasing dish
1-2 cloves garlic – peeled and
  minced

salt and freshly ground black
  pepper
small pinch freshly grated nutmeg
scant ¾ pint double cream

Thinly slice potatoes as regularly as possible (a mandoline or the
fine-slicing disc of a food processor helps). Butter a gratin dish and
sprinkle with some of the garlic.

Arrange potatoes in layers, sprinkling with garlic, salt, pepper
and tiny amounts of nutmeg, and dribbling each layer with cream
to cover. Finish top layer with cream.

Bake at Gas 3/160°C/325°F for 2 hours.

Gratin Provençal

serves 6-8 £

4 tablespoons olive oil
6 oz onions – peeled and very
  thinly sliced
1 lb large tomatoes (beef or
  marmande) – skinned and thinly
  sliced
1½ lb peeled floury potatoes – cut
  into thinnish slices
1 small tin anchovy fillets in oil –
  finely chopped

2 cloves garlic – peeled and
  minced
½ tablespoon finely chopped fresh
  basil leaves
½ teaspoon finely chopped fresh
  thyme leaves
freshly ground black pepper
2 heaped tablespoons freshly
  grated Parmesan

Rub a flame-proof gratin dish with a little of the olive oil. Scatter
some of the onions over the bottom, then some tomato slices, then
some potato followed by a seasoning layer of some of the anchovy,
garlic, basil, thyme, pepper and a sprinkling of olive oil.

Continue layering – onion, tomato, potato, seasoning, olive oil –
until those ingredients are all used up. Finish with a layer of potato.
Cover the gratin dish closely with foil and bake at Gas 6/200°C/
400°F for 45 minutes. Remove foil, sprinkle on the Parmesan and
return to the oven for another 10 minutes or so until the cheese has
browned.

Pecan Pie

serves 6 ££

The pecan, pronouced variously in the States, but 'p'*kahn*' more often than not in the Old South, is a variety of native American hickory nut. The word comes directly from original Indian names.

Sociologist John Egerton's weighty volume, *Southern Food*, traces the history of pecan pie – undoubtedly the South's favourite dessert – back to a pie of molasses which was popular in the early nineteenth century. This was pretty much like our own treacle tart.

Every serious Southern home-cook has his or her own combination of ingredients. Experiment with one more egg, more or less sugar, syrup, vanilla, butter and different darknesses of sugar and proportions of molasses or maple syrup to make up some of the volume. The bourbon is, to some extent, optional.

Karo corn syrup is the *sine qua non* of American recipes. If you can get it, use it instead of the golden syrup mentioned in the recipe below.

pastry:
7 oz flour
big pinch salt
4 oz butter (or lard or margarine or any combination)
about 3 tablespoons cold water
filling:
scant 2 oz butter
3 oz demerara sugar

2 eggs (size 2) – beaten well together
½ teaspoon salt
½ teaspoon vanilla essence
2 tablespoons bourbon
8 oz golden syrup
7 oz pecan kernels (broken are fine)

Make the pastry by rubbing the flour and salt with the fat until the texture resembles fine breadcrumbs (or whizzing it all briefly in a food processor), then mixing in the water until the dough holds together.

Wrap in clingfilm and chill for 30 minutes, then roll out to line a 9in pie dish. Prick the bottom, cover with clingfilm and chill again until needed.

Make the filling by beating the softened butter with the sugar. When well mixed and creamy, gradually add the beaten eggs.

Mix in all the other ingredients, pour into the unbaked pie crust and bake at Gas 4/180°C/350°F for 30 minutes, then at Gas 2/ 150°C/300°F for another 30 minutes or until the filling is set.

Serve warm or cold with vanilla ice-cream or whipped double cream.

Walnut Tart

serves 4-6 ££

London chef Simon Hopkinson at his restaurant, Bibendum, uses a similar but slightly cakier walnut filling, as follows, I marginally prefer it to the recipe above. You can, of course, use pecans here instead.

pastry:
4 oz plain flour
pinch salt
2 oz butter
2 oz caster sugar
2 egg yolks
filling:
2 oz softened butter

7 oz caster sugar
3 eggs
7½ fl oz golden syrup
1 tablespoon flour
1 teaspoon salt
1 teaspoon vanilla essence
6 oz shelled walnut halves

With pastry this rich, it is better to use a good-processor. Whizz up the flour, salt, butter and sugar. Then, with the machine running, plop in the yolks. The mixture should come together into a crumbly dough. Take out and press together gently in your hands. Wrap in clingfilm and chill for 30 minutes, then roll out and line a 9in flan tin. This is very short pastry. Don't worry if it tears and falls apart, just plasticine over the gaps with offcuts of dough and press down firmly. Prick the bottom and bake blind for 10 minutes at Gas 6/200°C/400°F.

For the filling, beat butter, sugar and eggs together. Stir in the golden syrup until well incorporated, then the flour, salt and vanilla essence.

Scatter the pie case with walnuts, pour the syrup mixture over and bake for 1½ hours in the middle of an oven pre-heated to Gas 4/180°C/350°F.

Serve warm with whipped cream.

Candied Pumpkin

serves 6 £

The most specifically autumnal of Turkish desserts. The pumpkin pieces stay relatively firm and take on a beautiful waxy gloss. Use the dense-fleshed golden Jamaican pumpkins to be found in Caribbean stores, if the ordinary variety seems loose and watery.

3 lb pumpkin – peeled, seeded and cut into large chunky strips (the size of a Mars Bar cut lengthways in half)
8 oz sugar

6 tablespoons water plus more if necessary
4 oz shelled walnuts – coarsely chopped

Layer pumpkin and sugar in a heavy saucepan. Add water. Put on very low flame, covered tightly, for 50 minutes or so until the pumpkin is tender. You may need to splash on more water from time to time, or you may need to reduce an eventual excess of liquid by boiling hard, with the pan uncovered, at the end of cooking time – it all depends on the pumpkin. Leave to cool in the pan with the syrup.

Tip on to a serving dish with the pan juices. Sprinkle over the walnuts and chill. Serve cold with whipped cream.

Noah's Pudding

serves 6-8 £

One version of a popular Turkish pudding said to have been prepared on the Ark to use up remaining provisions. The wheat – available in most good health-food stores – makes the pudding set into a loose jelly when it is puréed.

9 oz whole grains of wheat
3 oz dry chickpeas
3 oz dry white beans
3½ pints water plus soaking waters

2 oz dried figs
2 oz dried apricots
2 oz chopped hazelnuts
2 oz whole blanched almonds
2 oz seedless raisins

10 oz sugar   2 tablespoons pine kernels
1 teaspoon rose-water   seeds from 1 large pomegranate

Soak the wheat, chickpeas and white beans overnight, well covered with cold water, in separate bowls. Strain each and discard the soaking water.

In a large pan, boil the soaked wheat in 3½ pints of fresh water for 3 hours. Leave the wheat in the water that remains. Separately, in two other pans, boil the chickpeas and white beans until tender. Strain, but keep back the liquid in case you need more later.

Coarsely chop the figs and apricots. Put the chopped fig and apricot to soften in a little water.

Purée half the cooked wheat with enough of the cooking liquid to lubricate the process, in a liquidiser or food processor. Pour back into the pan with the rest of the wheat. Add the chickpeas, white beans, hazelnuts, almonds, raisins and the drained, chopped figs and apricot.

Stir in the sugar and bring slowly to the boil. Keep at a lively simmer for 20 minutes, adding more of the reserved liquid if the mixture seems to be getting gluey. Add the rose-water 5 minutes before the end.

Pour the mixture into individual glass dessert bowls, making sure the nuts, fruit and pulses are evenly divided. Let it cool for several hours before decorating with the pine kernels and pomegranate seeds.

Chill. Serve cold.

NOVEMBER

If November has a barren ring, a walk around many good provincial markets at this time of year reveals an unexpected profusion of fine produce: wet walnuts, red pomegranates, fat partridges, glassy savoys, creamy sweetbreads, glistening scallops, fragrant quinces. This is a month for slow cooking and mellow flavours, for game, nuts and root vegetables, and for comfort food after the shock of having an hour's light knocked off the end of the day. Hallowe'en ushers in the baked potato and sausage season.

VEGETABLES

Sprouts, carrots, parsnips and turnips – winter's staples – are now in plentiful supply. As frost gets the last of the Lincolnshire cauliflowers, Jersey and French will fill the gap.

Beetroot is good gently baked in its skin (loosely wrapped in foil), served with butter or sour cream and plenty of black pepper as an accompanying vegetable to plain roasts, grills or meaty white fish. Simply boiled, it slices into purplish salads with ingredients such as eggs, potatoes, onion, garlic, chives, pickled or smoked fish, or fruit such as apple or orange. Parsnips make fine soggy chips, and purée well, although liberal doses of butter and/or cream are essential; toasted sesame seeds are a successful complementary flavour.

Big turnips roast well like potatoes in thick pre-blanched slices round the joint for the last half hour or so of cooking time. Small new ones need only slowish shallow frying in butter, perhaps with Claudia Roden's happy addition of skinned and quartered fresh dates and a fair sprinkling of salt.

Try red cabbage not only the traditional ways – braised long and slow with onion, apple, dried vine fruit, wine and spices – but also as cooked by chef Jeremy Ashpool at the King's Head in Cuckfield, Sussex, cut into very fine slivers, then sautéed briefly with cumin, coriander seed, garlic and fresh ginger.

Shopping list

Aubergines, **avocados**, **beetroot**, **Brussels sprouts**, **cabbages (red**, **Savoy**, **white** and **winter green** varieties), **Belgian chicory**, broccoli (calabrese), **carrots**, **cauliflowers**, **celeriac**, **celery**, chilli peppers, Chinese leaves, courgettes, cucumbers, curly kale, **fennel**, **garlic**, **globe artichokes**, green beans (French), greens, herbs (mint, parsley, rosemary, sage, thyme), Jerusalem artichokes, **kohlrabi**, **leeks**, lettuce and some salad leaves, marrows and squashes, mushrooms (cultivated), **okra**, **onions** (including pickling, mild Spanish, and strong red varieties), **parsnips**, peppers (capsicums), **potatoes**, **pumpkin**, **salsify**, **scorzonera**, **shallots**, spinach, **swedes**, sweetcorn, **sweet potatoes**, **turnips**, watercress

Look for the dense golden-fleshed Jamaican and small British-grown Japanese varieties of pumpkin as well as the large, sometimes watery ones. If you have access to fresh **horse-radish** root – hardly ever available from retail outlets – this is a good time to be using it. Also look for **bamboo shoots**, cardoon, **chard, Chinese artichokes**, chanterelles and black and white truffles.

FRUIT AND NUTS

Apart from apples and pears, we've just about had it with British-grown fruit for another year. In my opinion, the most flavoursome, easily obtainable English apple of all – now in the shops – is the Egremont Russet. Almonds and chestnuts join fresh walnuts, hazelnuts and the closely related filberts as one of autumn's main consolations.

Easy-peel citrus fruits such as clementines and satsumas are beginning to put in an appearance. Otherwise – this is a good time of year to become better acquainted with some of the less familiar seasonal imports, such as the sharon fruit, persimmon and custard apple.

Make good use of the short British-grown and imported quince season for compôtes, preserves and baked, braised or stewed savoury dishes. In the area around Konya in central Anatolia, they stuff partially hollowed out quinces with spiced rice, onions and minced lamb.

Shopping list
Almonds, **apples** (UK – Egremont Russet, Cox's Orange Pippin, Bramley Seedling; import – Laxton, Golden and Red Delicious, North American Reds), **Asian pears** (nashi), bananas, **Brazil nuts**, **chestnuts**, **clementines**, coconuts, cranberries, **custard apples**, **dates** (fresh), **figs**, **filberts**, grapefruit, **grapes** (white Almeria and black Napoleon from Italy), guavas, **hazelnuts**, **kumquats**, lemons, limes, **mangoes**, melons (ogen, cantaloup, yellow honeydew), **oranges** (new-season Navellinas from Spania), pawpaws (papaya), **pears** (UK – Comice, Conference; import – William), **persimmons**, **pineapples**, **pomegranates**, **quinces**, **satsumas**, **sharon fruit**, **walnuts**

As well as the new-season Yarden River and Red Blush grapefruit from Jaffa, look for sweet red varieties air-freighted from Florida. Muscat grapes are the most heavily scented of the later varieties, expensive, but worth searching out from high-class greengrocers. In addition to the last of the fresh **figs**, start looking for this season's freshly-dried figs imported from Iran and Turkey, also **prunes**.

FISH AND SEAFOOD

Having said goodbye to the summer crustacea, this is a good month for rediscovering the British seaside-prom heritage of cockles, whelks and winkles, still perfectly good doused with pepper and vinegar. Early cross-Channel shoppers to Ostend might try Flemish *warme wullocks* (whelk stew) sold from stalls along the harbour walls.

Huss is a neglected fish – perhaps the legacy of being the cheapest thing on chip shop boards (often retitled rock salmon); its cartilaginous nature makes it good for cold weather stews. Other as yet socially deprived seasonal fish worth getting to know are grey mullet (its lowly status with many fishmongers being because they associate with 'ethnic' cuisines) and eel (although London still has its queues outside places which sell it jellied with parsley liquor).

Shopping list
Brill, **carp**, clams, cockles, **cod**, **coley**, **conger eel**, crab, dab, **Dover sole**, **eel**, flounder, **grey mullet**, **gurnard**, **haddock**, **hake**, **halibut**, **herring**, **huss**, langoustines (Dublin Bay prawns or scampi), lemon sole, **ling**, lobster, **mackerel**, mock halibut (Greenland halibut) monkfish, **mussels**, **oysters** (native and Pacific), **plaice**, prawns, scallops, **sea bass**, **sea bream**, **skate**, **smelts**, **sprats** (fresh and smoked), tuna, **turbot**, whelks, **whiting**, winkles, **witch**

MEAT, GAME AND POULTRY

This is the best month for most game, including pheasant, partridge, snipe, woodcock and species of wild duck. As grouse get tougher toward the end of their season (10 December), they are happier casseroled than roasted.

Pheasant easily dries out if roasted, even if covered in bits of bacon and smeared with butter. Instead, try browning in butter in a flame-proof casserole. Add finely sliced onion and chopped apple, flame with Calvados, season, cover, then leave over a low flame – turning the bird or birds once or twice – until cooked through. Remove from pot to carve and stir double cream or créme fraîche into the debris to make a coarse sauce.

If you are intending something less usual for Christmas, now is the time to sate your more conservative nearest and dearest on the dry white body of the economical turkey bird. After a week or so of roasted breast joint on Sunday, stewed thighs Monday, rissoles Tuesday, curry Wednesday, cold turkey Thursday, turkey escalopes Friday and turkey tetrazini Saturday, you'll have them begging for goose or whatever you decree by 25 December.

Get the festive fowl out of the way with an American Thanksgiving supper on the last Thursday of November. This is based around roast turkey, cranberry sauce and pumpkin pie, although the first, held in 1621, is supposed to have included unspecified game birds, popcorn, oysters, eel, leeks and plums.

Shopping list
beef, **chicken**, **duck**, **goose**, grouse, **guinea-fowl**, **hare**, lamb, **mallard**, **partridge**, **pheasant**, **pigeon**, **pork**, quail, **rabbit**, **snipe**, **teal**, **turkey**, veal, **venison**, woodcock

CHEESE

An excellent cheese for the season from Yorkshire is Ribblesdale. Fine French varieties include Saint-Nectaire (look for the lozenge shaped mark on the curved surface to check you have a good one), Saint-Florentin, Saint-Marcellin and Rigotte.

Turkish Battered Mussels

serves 4 £

The Balīk Pazarī, fish market, and adjoining Çiçek Pasajī, flower alley, in the Galatasaray district of Istanbul's old commercial and diplomatic area, have some of the city's best street food. The star attractions are the fried mussel stalls, where raw shelled mussels strung on small wooden skewers are dipped in a simple beer batter and deep-fried, then served as they are with a dribble of garlicky *tarator* sauce or in a split chunk of fresh white bread with a squeeze of lemon.

Here is an anglicised version, to be served with the *tarator*, recipe following.

Opening live mussels is a fag. Some fishmongers shell them and sell just the meat, usually floating in brine, but you have to trust that he has done this pretty shortly before you buy. Otherwise, scrub the shells (discarding any that float or feel over-heavy for their size) and pull off the beards. Then, holding the creature with its flat edge outwards in a gloved hand, insert a sharp knife into the hinge and along the side. Twist open. Cut meat away from each shell, severing the small white tendons at the hinge end. Slip the meat on to a clean cloth or kitchen paper to dry.

24 large live mussels – shelled	2 oz plain flour
2 egg yolks (size 2) – beaten lightly together	oil for deep-frying salt
5 fl oz lager	

Pat mussels dry. Mix yolks very lightly together with the lager. When the foam subsides, tip in all the flour at once and cut through the mixture with a knife a dozen times or so. The batter should still be very lumpy.

Have the oil over a medium flame at a low boil (about 160°C/325°F). Dip the mussels one-by-one into the batter, shake off excess, and drop into the oil. Work fast. Let them cook for about 3 minutes until golden brown, then take out with a slotted spoon and put to drain for a minute or two on paper towels. Sprinkle with salt.

Either arrange on a serving plate as they are, or quickly push two or three on to each of several small wooden skewers. Serve with lemon wedges and/or tarator sauce. Eat hot.

Tarator Sauce

serves 4-6 £

Very medieval, pale, thick nut and garlic sauce. Popular all over the Middle East for serving with baked or boiled fish, vegetables and some fried foods.

3in slice day-old French bread – crusts removed	2-3 oz pine kernels
2-3 fat cloves garlic – peeled	3 tablespoons or so olive oil
½ teaspoon salt	1 tablespoon or so lemon juice

Soak bread in water then squeeze dry. Pound garlic to a pulp with the salt in a pestle and mortar. Add the pine kernels and pulverise. Crumble the bread into the mixture and pound until well incorporated. Add olive oil, a drop at a time, pounding to form a thick paste (you may need to add drops of lemon juice to thin the mixture as you go). Stir in the rest of the lemon juice.

Truffle Tortilla

serves 4 as a meal, 8 as a snack *££-£££££*

This simplest of uses for the valuable black subterranean funghus is also the one which I think best shows off its elusive flavour. Suitable for vegetarians.

1½ lb waxy potatoes
salt
big knob best unsalted butter or
　generous splash bland olive oil
　for frying

1 fresh black truffle (as much as
　you can afford, the size of a
　walnut will do)
freshly ground black pepper
5 eggs – beaten

Cover scrubbed but unpeeled potatoes with cold salted water. Bring to the boil. Lower heat, cover pan and leave at a lively simmer until cooked. Take out of water and leave until thoroughly cold. Pull off skin and slice potatoes quite thickly.

Heat butter or oil over medium-low flame in a heavy, preferably cast-iron frying pan (this should either be non-stick or used sufficiently to have developed a non-stick patina). Scrub truffle hard to remove all mud and grit. Dry. Slice very thinly, skin and all, or grate coarsely into the warm fat. Sprinkle generously with salt and pepper. Heat gently for five minutes or so, stirring occasionally; you are getting it to develop its flavour without letting the truffle harden or cook.

Now add the potato slices to the pan, turning them so each is well basted in fat and truffle pieces. Pour over the beaten eggs then work over the potato slices with your spatula to ensure that they are separate and coated in egg. The temperature should be such that the egg does not sizzle at all; turn it down if necessary. Cover frying pan and leave to cook for about 30 minutes or longer until the egg is set on the top. The bottom of the tortilla should be pale golden brown.

When cooked, put the lid back on and leave for at least another 20 minutes off the flame. Then turn out on to a serving platter and eat warm – not hot nor cold – in wedges, or cut into bite-sized cubes.

Circassian Chicken

serves 6-8 ££

Be careful when making this Middle Eastern chicken with nut paste – a tiny step up the evolutionary scale from the *tarator* sauce on page 221; just one rancid walnut can turn the whole thing inedibly bitter. Of course, you can use chicken meat from anywhere on the bird but I think just thighs, the leg minus the drumstick, gives the dish a silkier texture and fuller flavour. Some butchers and super-markets sell packs of thighs.

6 chicken thighs
2 carrots – peeled and coarsely sliced
2 small onions – peeled and coarsely chopped, plus 2 teaspoons finely chopped peeled onion
1 teaspoon black peppercorns
6 parsley stalks – bruised
big sprig fresh thyme
2 bay leaves

8 oz shelled walnuts
2 cloves garlic – peeled and minced
½ teaspoon salt
½ teaspoon cayenne pepper
½ teaspoon paprika
few twists freshly ground black pepper
2 tablespoons bland oil mixed with 1 teaspoon paprika

Cover the chicken thighs with cold water in a saucepan. Add carrot, coarsely chopped onion, peppercorns, parsley, thyme and bay-leaves. Bring to the boil, cover and boil for 30 minutes. Take out of stock to cool. Reserve stock.

Skin and bone chicken thighs. Chop roughly.

Whizz nuts in a processor until finely chopped. Mix in the finely chopped onion, garlic and seasonings. Whizz again, adding up to ½ pint of the reserved chicken stock to make a smooth, pale sauce. Tip this over the chopped chicken and stir thoroughly. Pile into a smooth mound on a serving dish. Dribble over the paprika-coloured oil. Chill.

Serve by itself, with pitta bread, or as part of a *meze* table.

Mini Pizza Crusts

serves 6 £

Small pizzas make a good light meal with salad. Quite a lot of the fun is in assembling your own toppings. Don't feel bound by the usual formula of thick tomato sauce on the bottom, mozzarella on the top. Try the naked discs spread just with tapenade (see page 36) or Circassian Chicken (on page 223) before baking.

If you do want to use a tomato sauce base, reduce a tin of chopped tomatoes to a thick pulp with red wine, minced garlic and/or finely chopped onions sautéed in olive oil, bay leaves, thyme, dried oregano, fresh basil or crushed fennel seed (especially if topping with sausage meat or fish), a splash of fruity olive oil and salt and freshly ground black pepper.

Spread this on to the unbaked discs, then ponder the merits of topping with anchovies, different varieties of mushroom, black olives, capers, mozzarella, more basil, different Italian cheeses, different hams or cured sausages, fresh sausage meat or minced beef, chilli peppers, sweet peppers – roasted or raw – aubergines, courgette, shellfish, tinned tuna and parsley or other herbs.

Toppings that work well in combinations without tomato sauce and cheese include cooked and well drained spinach, cinnamon, white truffles, tinned tuna, peas, cooked artichoke hearts, shellfish, pine kernels, raisins and some herbs. If you are not using tomato sauce, brush the disc with olive oil before assembling other ingredients on top; they may also need brushing with oil to prevent drying up.

8 oz plain flour	1 mean tablespoon olive oil
1 teaspoon salt	4-5 fl oz hand-hot water.
mean ½ oz fresh yeast (or scant ¼ oz dried plus big pinch sugar)	

Mix flour and salt. Crumble the fresh yeast into a little of the water, or beat the dried yeast and sugar into some of the water as directed on packet. Leave yeast until it froths (about 10 minutes). Pour yeast liquid into a well in the flour. Add the olive oil, then mix together, gradually drawing in the flour and adding as much more of the water as you need, until you have a stiffish dough.

Knead for about 10 minutes, as you would for pasta (see page 58) until the dough is smooth and elastic. Leave in a clean, loosely covered bowl standing in a warm place until the dough doubles in size. This may take up to 3 hours.

Knock the risen dough back by punching its surface lightly. Knead again for a minute or two.

Pre-heat oven to Gas 7/220°C/425°F. Lightly oil two flat baking trays. Form the knocked back dough into 12 balls and roll out into ¼in thick discs, pressing up the edges so that these are thicker than the rest of the disc. Put on the greased sheets, covered loosely, to prove a little more.

Fill as required, to within ¼in of the edges. Bake for 15-20 minutes.

Roasted Hare with Garlic and Wild Mushrooms

serves 2-4 ££

One of the best dishes cooked at the finals of the first *Independent* cookery competition was this rare roasted hare. Although its creator, Christopher Martyn, an epidemiologist from Winchester, missed first place by a whisker, he took consolation later in hearing that Jane Grigson, one of the guest judges, now used the recipe at home herself.

1 hare	6 black peppercorns
olive oil (not too strong or fruity)	at least 2 fat cloves garlic per person – unpeeled
1 small onion – peeled and thickly sliced	1 tablespoon or so dried funghi (such as porcini)
1 small carrot – peeled and thickly sliced	splash Madeira
few parsley stalks	sea salt
few slices of celery – trimmed	few small cubes cold butter

Have the butcher draw, skin and joint the hare. You need the whole saddle but keep the legs for other dishes – game pies, rissoles etc. The remaining pieces of the carcass are used for the stock.

Carefully cut off the outer membranes of the saddle. Smear it all over with olive oil. Pre-heat the oven as hot as it will go. Brown the hare remnants with a little olive oil in a heavy pan over high heat. Add the onion, carrot, parsley stalks, celery and peppercorns and cover with water. Bring to the boil, then leave to bubble for 30-45 minutes.

Fry the whole, unpeeled garlic cloves in a little hot olive oil for 2-3 minutes. Add a ladleful of water, or clear stock, cover and leave to simmer quietly for 30-45 minutes until soft. Splash the dried funghi with hot water and leave for up to 15 minutes.

Put the oiled saddle in a roasting pan into the top of the hot oven for, at most, 12 minutes. Then turn the heat off, prop open the door and put the hare to rest in the warmth at the bottom of the oven.

Strain the reducing stock into a clean saucepan and reduce further to about a quarter of a pint. Add the drained funghi and the splash of Madeira and leave to bubble away. Cut the four long muscles from the saddle (two larger on top, two smaller underneath), then cut each lengthways into thin slices. Lay these ribbons in slightly overlapping rows to one side of warmed dinner plates and crumble over a little sea salt.

Whisk the cubes of cold butter into the reduced stock to make a glossy sauce and spoon on to the other side of each plate. Garnish with the braised garlic cloves. Serve immediately.

Clapham Peasant Stew

serves 2 £

Hearty autumn fare for modern hunter-gatherers. You can also chuck in any slightly dodgy game, poultry, off-cuts of pork, smoked meats and sausages. Adding vinegar at the end kills off any rank flavours. Cinnamon also sometimes adds quite a nice touch.

4 bone-in rabbit joints (about 1 lb)
4 tablespoons olive oil

2 tablespoons freshly peeled and minced garlic (about 10 cloves)
1 bay leaf

2 cloves – crushed	1 teaspoon salt
8 oz dry green lentils	optional 1-2 tablespoons wine or
freshly ground black pepper	cider vinegar
24 fl oz (just under 1¼ pints)	
water	

Brown the rabbit in the oil in a heavy, flameproof casserole. Lower the heat and throw in the garlic. When the garlic is cooked, translucent and just beginning to brown, add – in order, stirring between each addition – the bay leaf, cloves, lentils, black pepper and the measured water.

Bring to the boil, then simmer for 40 minutes or until the lentils are tender. When ready, stir in the salt and optional vinegar. Serve in big sloppy portions accompanied by a winter salad of grated carrot, raisins and Belgian chicory.

Fresh Pasta Pie

serve 8-10 £

An Ottoman court showpiece snack, now the speciality of many a small café in Turkey. It has a softer, more satisfying texture than Greek phyllo-pastry pies such as *spanakopitta;* its blandness makes it perfect autumnal comfort food.

To drink with it, try chilled buttermilk, or *ayran:* 50/50 plain yoghurt and iced water whisked together with a little salt, then garnished with half a hot green chilli pepper, which adds its sappy, crisp flavour to the mix, even if you don't actually eat it. Perhaps most authentic would be a tulip-shaped glass of strong black tea sweetened to taste.

For a full explanation of the pasta techniques, see page 58.

dough:	*assembly:*
14 oz flour	cornflour or potato starch for
1 teaspoon salt	rolling
3 eggs (size 3) – beaten	4 oz salted butter or more –
thoroughly together	melted
4 tablespoons water	8 oz feta cheese – crumbled

1 whole egg beaten together with 1 egg yolk

2 fistfuls of flat-leaf parsley leaves – coarsely chopped

few twists freshly ground black pepper

2-4 fl oz milk

large pan of boiling water

large basin of ice-cold water

For the dough, sift dry ingredients. Make well in centre. Pour in eggs and gradually incorporate with flour, adding as much of the 4 tablespoons of water as necessary to form a firm dough.

Knead for about 10 minutes until dough is smooth and elastic. Rest dough for an hour, covered in clingfilm.

Divide the ball of dough into six balls of equal size. Divide five of these in half. Roll each ball into the thinnest possible sheets, first with an ordinary wooden rolling pin and then with a length of dowelling the thickness of a broom-handle, rolling up the pastry round the broom-handle, then without exerting any downward pressure, rocking the handle back and forth while edging your hands apart from the centre to the ends of the handle. Use generous quantities of cornflour or potato starch to flour the board and handle to prevent sticking. One sheet will be much larger than the other ten.

Brush a large, deep roasting pan with melted butter, then lay the large sheet in with its edges overhanging the sides of the tin all round. Brush the whole surface with melted butter.

Mash the cheese, egg, parsley and black pepper together with enough of the milk to make a loose mixture. Do not go overboard with the pepper. Put aside for the moment.

Dip one of the smaller sheets first into the boiling water for 40-50 seconds, then quickly in and out of the cold water, where it will take on a slippery texture like well used chamois leather. Carefully remove from the cold water, drain and pat dry. Wrinkle this sheet over the bottom of the pan to fit the tin. Brush with melted butter.

Repeat this process with all the other sheets, pausing only to spread the cheese, egg, parsley and pepper mixture between the fifth and sixth sheets. When all the small sheets have been used, brush the top of the whole pie with butter and fold the overhanging edges of the larger bottom sheet over the top of the pie to seal. Brush over the seal with butter.

Bake uncovered at Gas 5/190°C/375°F for 45 minutes, when the top should be golden. The pie can be served hot or tepid. Leave it in the roasting tin until you are ready to serve, then turn out on to a platter so that the seams are underneath. Cut into thick wedges and eat with your own addition of more freshly ground black pepper.

Quince Cheese
makes about 2 lb £

A dry Portuguese preserve capturing the fragrance and acidity of quinces in a thick red paste, adapted from Edite Vieira's *The Taste of Portugal*.

2 lb quinces	1 lb 10 oz white sugar
boiling water	

Rub all the fluff from the quinces' skins, wash them, then peel, core and cut into quarters. Put in a saucepan and pour in enough boiling water just to half cover them. Put over a medium flame to cook, covered, for 10-12 minutes until just tender. Drain well. (Edite Vieira advises you to keep the peel, cores and cooking water, boil together to extract all the flavour and pectin, then strain and boil again for 10-12 minutes with an equal volume of sugar to make a splendid quince jelly.)

Mash and sieve the flesh until completely smooth. Melt the sugar in a heavy pan, as soon as it is tacky – but before it starts to cara-melise – take off the heat and stir in the fruit pulp with a wooden spoon. When well mixed, return to a gentle heat and cook until the mixture is as dry as possible without actually burning.

Take off the heat and beat with your spoon to cool the mixture. Pour into shallow trays to set. Place trays in the lowest possible oven for several hours until it hardens and a sugar crust forms on top.

When cool, if thick enough, cut into strips (spoon out if not) and eat in sparing portions with crème fraîche, whipped double cream or hard white cheese such as Caerphilly. Or pack in airtight con-tainers, where it will keep for weeks.

Crème Fraîche

makes 7 pint £

The fat content of the original cream dictates the luxuriousness of this thick, slightly tart cream, used all over France as we would use double cream. Some cooks add a much greater proportion of souring agent than in the recipe below – up to one part in every two of the 'ordinary' cream. Some use sour cream instead of buttermilk.

1 pint whipping or double cream   1½ tablespoons buttermilk

Heat together over a gentle flame until the mixture feels still slightly cool to a dipped finger. Leave overnight in a vacuum flask or covered in a warm place – such as an airing cupboard. Stir, then keep in a covered bowl in the fridge. It will ripen and thicken over a few days.

Pear and Prune Tart

serves 6-8 £

For years, my favourite sweet course. The frangipane, flavoured with alcohol, is a soft, scented layer to take the whole flan into another class. Calvados is good for apples, kirsch for plums and peaches, Poire William *eau de vie* for pears, but, of them all, nothing perfumes a frangipane like *vielle prunes eau de vie*. Another beauty is the simplicity of the method and speed of assembly if you use a food processor. This recipe is adapted from a Normandy apple flan in Anne Willan's *Observer French Cookery School*.

pastry:
6½ oz plain flour
½ teaspoon salt
3½ oz unsalted butter
1 egg yolk – beaten
2-2½ tablespoons cold water
frangipane:
3½ oz unsalted butter – softened
3½ oz caster sugar

1 egg and 1 extra yolk – beaten together
2 teaspoons *vieille prune eau de vie*
3½ oz ground almonds
2 level tablespoons flour
assembly:
3 large ripe, but still firm, dessert pears (eg Williams)

6 large pre-soaked prunes (or the sort that don't need pre-soaking)

5 tablespoons tart but unassertive fruit jelly (red or white currant,

or rowan-berry are good by themselves; or stir a couple of teaspoons of lemon juice into quince, guava or similar)

Make the pastry by hand by sifting flour and salt, rubbing in the fat, mixing in the yolk with enough water to form a short dough. Or, using a food processor's metal blade, whizz flour, salt and butter together briefly, then, with the machine running, pour in the yolk followed by enough of the water so that the pastry comes together in a ball. Wrap in clingfilm and chill for 30 minutes.

Roll out and line an 11in diameter flan tin. Prick bottom with fork, blind bake at Gas 6/200°C/400°F for 10 minutes, with the bottom covered by a circle of greaseproof and a layer of dried beans, then for 5 minutes without the paper and beans. It should just have cooked enough to have lost any translucent patches. Leave to cool (do not chill in the fridge).

Make the fragipane by hand by creaming butter, gradually beating in sugar, then gradually beating in egg and finally stirring in the other ingredients. Or, without washing out the bowl, whizz butter and sugar together until light and creamy, then, with the machine running, trickle in the egg and yolk drop by drop. Turn machine off, add other ingredients then whizz very briefly to mix. It doesn't affect the final result too much if this frangipane curdles.

Pour frangipane into cool blind-baked pastry case and smooth over the surface.

Peel and core pears. Cut each in half lengthways, then hold in shape on the cut surface while you slice very thinly across the fruit. Push firmly at a slant down the fruit with the palm of your hand to flatten each sliced pear half, allowing the slices to slip over each other a little (like fanning a hand of cards), until each half pear is as long as the radius of the flan. Pick up each flattened row of slices on the blade of a wide knife and lay with the narrowest slices at the centre of the flan and the other end out by the crust. Arrange the six halves in this manner, like the spokes of a wheel.

Slice the prunes and scatter over the uncovered frangipane.

Bake toward the bottom of the oven at Gas 6/200°C/400°F for 15 minutes, then turn heat down to Gas 4/180°C/350°F, move tin to middle of oven and continue cooking for another 15-20 minutes until the pastry and any bare patches of frangipane are browned and the frangipane is set.

Let pie cool to room temperature. Then melt fruit jelly in a small saucepan over a low flame and brush over the whole surface of the flan to glaze.

Serve at room temperature with crème fraîche or whipped double cream.

Apple and Walnut Cake

serves 4 £

This is the dish that won Linda Sue Park the first *Independent* cookery competition. My first inkling that she would walk off with the prize was when I caught guest judge Raymond Blanc, in a corner, wolfing down seconds. Instead of apples, you could use any hard fruit – pears, say, or quinces.

topping:
2 oz butter
4 oz soft dark brown sugar
big pinch cinnamon
pinch ground nutmeg
2 oz shelled walnuts – broken into large pieces
1 lb Cox's apples – peeled, cored, quartered and cut into ½in chunks
grated zest of half a lemon

batter:
4 oz butter
4 oz caster sugar plus extra ½ tablespoon
2 eggs – separated
4 oz plain flour
up to 2 fl oz milk (if necessary)
cream:
5 oz soured cream
2½in cubes crystallised ginger – finely chopped

Cut the 2 oz butter into small cubes and scatter over the bottom of a pie, gratin or baking dish at least 1½in deep. Scatter the sugar, spices and walnuts over. Add the apples. Sprinkle with the lemon zest.

Make the batter by creaming together the butter and sugar, then mixing in the egg yolks and flour. If stiff, loosen with a little milk.

Whisk the egg whites to firm peaks with the extra ½ tablespoon sugar, then fold into the flour mixture.

Mix the soured cream with the ginger and put to chill.

Spread batter roughly over the apples.

Linda Sue would normally cook this for 40 minutes at Gas 4/180°C/350°F, but on the day of the competition had it in a much hotter oven (about Gas 9/240°C/475°F) for just a little over 15 minutes. This successfully caramelised the topping, browned the batter and took the dish into another class.

Loosen with a palette knife, turn out on to a serving platter (putting back any bits which stick) and serve hot or warm with the cold ginger cream.

DECEMBER

As the Christmas and New Year rituals come round again, it is not last January that feels a long way off, but the intervening months of plums and peaches, strawberries and sea trout. TV advertising hits with its annual exhortations to buy the same old ginger wine, frozen breast joints and mass-produced mince-pies. But the real choice of produce is much wider and stranger than at any other time of the year. Producers and wholesalers keep back a massive bulk of choice items for the festive rush, from Stiltons to oysters and smoked salmon, and importers pull out all the stops to make the humblest corner-shop into an Aladdin's cave of unseasonal exotica.

VEGETABLES

British greengrocers seem increasingly given over to Christmas staples — Brussels sprouts, parsnips, big, floury potatoes. There are plenty of ways to ring the changes. Shred raw, washed Brussels sprouts through the fine slicing disc of the food processor, then stir-fry in a little butter, with seasoning and freshly grated nutmeg until they are flecked with golden brown but still crunchy. Try the same technique with slightly wider shreds of Savoy cabbage or greens, stir-fried with a little bland vegetable oil, then stirred through with grated orange zest and a little sesame oil.

There is also a wealth of fine produce for non-festive meals, from subtle salsify for elegant gratins to the last of the year's Mediterranean globe artichokes for serving simply with melted butter and lemon juice. Try curly kale, as served by Ros Hunter of the Village Restaurant in Ramsbottom, Lancashire, blanched and shredded, then stirred through with soured cream and fat, seedless raisins.

Shopping list
Aubergines, **avocados, beetroot, Belgian chicory, Brussels sprouts, Brussels tops, cabbages (Savoy, red, white** and **winter green** vari-

eties such as Celtic), broccoli (calabrese), **carrots**, cauliflowers, **celeriac**, celery, chilli peppers, cucumbers, **curly kale**, **fennel**, **garlic**, globe artichokes, green beans (French), **greens**, herbs (parsley, sage and thyme), **Jerusalem artichokes**, **kohlrabi**, **leeks**, lettuce and some salad leaves, marrows and squashes, mushrooms (cultivated), **onions** (including **strong red**, mild **Spanish** and small pickling varieties), parsnips, **potatoes**, **pumpkin**, **salsify**, **scorzonera**, **shallots**, spinach, **swedes**, sweetcorn, **sweet potatoes**, **turnips**, watercress

Rare seasonal specialities worth trying to come across by fair means or foul include the little tuber **Chinese artichokes**, English horse-radish, **English seakale**, French or Spanish **fresh black truffles**, **arrowhead**, **bamboo shoots**, water chestnuts, cardoon and **chard**.

FRUIT AND NUTS

Exotic seasonal imports such as slithery fresh lychees and tart orange kumquats come into their own at this end of the year. As well as eating kumquats as they are, marinating them in alcoholic sugar syrup or making preserves with them, chef Jeremy Ashpool has the cleverest use I've seen: stewed until soft with water, wine vinegar, bay leaves, a little honey and seasonings, to use as a fresh relish garnishing any meat main course.

As well as the British crops of apples and pears – many still in prime condition – the Christmas trade brings in a host of further-flung and totally unseasonal fruits, including peaches and strawberries. Fresh cranberries from America make a bright red sauce for sharpening up the festive fowl. Their subtle tartness has also made them a fashionable restaurant addition to many dishes, from Anton Mosimann's escalopes of salmon trout with cranberries to Raymond Blanc's roast woodcock with a St Emilion sauce garnished with bread mousse and cranberries.

Shopping list
Almonds, apples (UK – Egremont Russet, Cox's Orange Pippin, Bramley Seedling; import – North American Reds), **apricots (dried)**, **Asian pears** (nashi), bananas, **Brazil nuts**, chestnuts, **clementines**, coconuts, cranberries, **custard apples**, dates (fresh and dried), **figs** (fresh and **dried**), grapefruit (including the less tart

sweetie from Jaffa), **grapes** (Italian Italia, Spanish Napoleon and Almeria), guavas, **kumquats**, lemons, limes, **lychees**, **mangoes** (Brazilian and Kenyan), **oranges** (Navellinas followed by the bigger Navels from Spain and Morocco), **ortaniques**, pawpaws (papaya), **pears** (UK – Comice and Conference), **persimmons**, **pineapples** (from Uganda, Ghana and the Ivory Coast), **pomegranates, pomelos, rhubarb** (early forced from Yorkshire), **satsumas, sharon fruit,** star fruit (carambola), **walnuts**

FISH AND SEAFOOD

A large baked turbot, steamed sea bass or pan of poached lobsters would make a glorious alternative Christmas dinner for non-meat eaters. Or set up a barbecue in a sheltered part of the garden and grill a dozen langoustines per portion, basting with melted butter stirred through with fennel seeds.

The Christmas market accounts for the vast majority of the country's smoked salmon trade. Tastes vary, but I prefer it made from fresh, not frozen, fish cured in nothing but salt or brine. It should be moist inside and have a very mild flavour of the wood chippings over which it was smoked. A reliable mark to look for on packs is the Scottish Salmon Smokers' Association Quality Seal.

Other special smoked fish for the season are hot-smoked eel, shown off best in the same way as smoked salmon, with just a twist of black pepper, and cold-smoked halibut – a Flemish obsession – served in thin slices with a squeeze of lemon, black pepper and brown bread and butter. Lemon is unnecessary with the best specimens of any smoked fish and horseradish 'just blows good eel apart', according to one smoker.

Shopping list
Brill, **carp**, clams, cockles, **cod, coley, conger eel**, crab, dab, **Dover sole, eel,** flounder, **grey mullet, gurnard, haddock, hake, halibut, herring, huss,** langoustines (Dublin Bay prawns or scampi), **lemon sole, ling,** lobster, **mackerel,** mock halibut (Greenland halibut), monkfish, **mussels, oysters (native and Pacific) plaice,** scallops, **sea bass, sea bream, skate, smelts, sprats (fresh and smoked),** tuna, **turbot,** whelks, **whiting,** winkles, **witch**

Imports of carp step up for seasonal Jewish and Eastern European dishes. Pike may be available in specialist outlets. Many oyster farmers, especially in northern France, keep the bulk of their stock for the Christmas season.

If your criterion for Yuletide pleasure is quality rather than quantity, caviar might fit the bill. As well as the various grades of sturgeon eggs, there is Keta salmon roe – big, orange sacs filled with clean-tasting fishy juice – excellent with blinis and soured cream.

MEAT, GAME AND POULTRY

A big fat goose provides the warm-up to the Queen's speech on 25 December in more households every year. Tough old birds can be avoided by fingering the carcass before you buy; a young fresh goose has clean white skin, soft and dry to the touch. The major branches of most supermarket chains usually stock fresh geese, at least in the week immediately preceeding Christmas. A 10-11 lb bird can serve 4-6 people.

Christmas is when most traditionally cured hams are sold. Nothing beats the dry-salted, properly matured varieties bought on the bone.

Pheasant is now at its best. Hens are generally thought to have the best flavour, but cocks are bigger. Use the final week or so of grouse in stews and pies.

Shopping list
Beef, **chicken**, **duck**, **goose**, grouse (until 10 December), **guinea-fowl**, **hare**, **mallard**, partridge, **pheasant**, **pigeon**, **pork**, quail, **rabbit**, snipe, teal, **turkey**, veal, **venison**, woodcock

CHEESE

Stilton is the seasonal king of cheese. If you are buying a whole Stilton, make sure it is satisfactorily blued by asking the cheesemonger to iron it (insert a hollow metal spike which draws out a bore of cheese for checking). The only non-pasteurised one still produced is Colston Basset, which has a milky white body, dense, blotchy royal-blue veining and a robust un-salty taste of old carpets. An excellent pasteurised one, such as Long Clawson, may have a yellower body, meaner violet-grey veining and a softer saltier flavour.

Some households, who let nothing else but Boursin, Lymeswold and Primula cheese spread across the threshold for the rest of the year, seek out a hunk of good mature Cheddar for the Christmas board. Another revelatory British cheese is Tiverdale, the fat winter cheese made by the Bonchester Dairy.

Creamy, rich, spoonable Vâcherin Mont d'Or is the queen of seasonal imports. Try it seasoned with a few twists of black pepper. Otherwise there are excellent non-pasteurised Camemberts, such as Moulin de Carel, with its bumpy irregular rind the colour of thick cream flecked with cinnamon, its smell of sweet peppery hay and its full, complex flavour with a winey, almost oniony edge, or rich, creamy, silky textured non-pasteurised Bries such as St-Simeon. Even the best pasteurised Camemberts and Bries, being effectively dead with no potential for proper maturity, are no match for well kept, ripe, non-pasteurised varieties.

Fresh goat's milk cheeses stop being made in winter. Pack any stragglers you can find whole into sterilised preserving jars with pure olive oil (not better), onion, whole cloves of garlic and sprigs of fresh herbs to preserve them for a month or two.

Roast Goose

serves 4-5 £££££

I have two dream Christmas meals. The first would be simply roasted partridge, its pan juices scented with whole slivers of fresh black truffle, served with bread sauce and Château Latour '61. The alternative, starting with a dozen raw oysters and finishing with a luxurious ice-cream, centres on this most satisfactory way of cooking your Christmas goose, quoted from a Swabian source by Susan Campbell in her *English Cookery New and Old*. The simplicity of the stuffing makes a good foil to the rich meat and festive trimmings. I have very slightly adapted the recipe here.

Although potatoes star in the stuffing, they still make a good accompanying vegetable to this dish. Try them crisply roasted in fat rendered from the extraneous white fat removed from the raw goose, or puréed with lots of butter and pepper, or slowly sautéed in larger cubes until golden brown with pieces of apple and par-boiled cloves of garlic. A more extravagant suggestion, but also the most delicious and festive tubers I have eaten, are potatoes as pre-pared by John King, head chef of the Ritz Club; turned (cut into regular 2in pieces the shape of elongated barrels), par-boiled, sau-téed in a little fat until well-coloured, then warmed through in a mahogany coloured meat glaze flavoured with truffle juice.

1½ lb potatoes – peeled and cut into small cubes	chopped fresh marjoram and sage to taste
6 oz salt pork or bacon (quite fatty) – de-rinded and finely chopped	salt
	freshly ground black pepper
1 medium-sized onion – chopped	11 lb goose
4 tablespoons chopped parsley	butter

Boil diced potato for 10 minutes in salted water. Drain. Sauté the pork or bacon, at first gently to render out some of the fat, then over a slightly higher flame to crisp. Remove with a slotted spoon and set aside. In this same fat, sauté the onion until soft and golden. Return pork or bacon to pan, add potatoes and herbs. Season. Leave to cool before stuffing the bird.

Pull out excess fat from inside the back end of the bird's cavity. To make carving the breast easier, you could also remove the wish-bone by scraping along it with the tip of a sharp knife inside the bird without breaking the skin. Sever the ends of the wishbone from the shoulder joint first.

Fill the cavity with the stuffing, but only loosely. If the mixture is packed in tightly, the bird will not cook properly. Truss. Sprinkle the skin with salt and rub all over with a generous amount of but-ter.

Roast on a rack above a roasting tray at pre-heated Gas 7/220°C/425°F for 45 minutes, then reduce to Gas 3/160°C/325°F and con-tinue cooking for 2-2½ hours, basting every 20 minutes or so. The bird is done when the juices run clear from the thickest part of the thigh when pricked with a skewer.

Wild Rice

serves 4-6 ££££

Whether you're having turkey, goose, baked turbot or some splendid vegetarian concoction for the main festive event, consider
whether you can really deal with the same old traditional accompaniments. Mashed and roast potatoes, which almost invariably turn
up on Christmas plates, are all very well, but how about a change?

Bake whole sweet potatoes at Gas 6/200°C/400°F for an hour,
then mash the middles with sherry, butter, salt and freshly ground
black pepper. Or peel them, par-boil, then cut into thick slices and
sauté in butter with seasonings and a sprinkling of brown sugar.

Or cook wild rice – long, black grains, not a proper rice at all –
making up the liquid with strong meat, or other appropriate, stock.
Stir in reconstituted dried wild mushrooms at the beginning of
cooking and, if you are cooking turkey or goose, a few fried and
chopped poultry livers, hearts or whatever at the end. Another
favourite wild rice recipe, suitable for accompanying all kinds of
centrepieces, is as follows:

8 oz wild rice
2 tablespoon bland oil
3 fat cloves garlic – peeled and
  minced
1 level tablespoon grated fresh
  peeled root ginger
2 hot green fresh chilli peppers –
  finely sliced
2 pints water

salt and freshly ground black
  pepper
pinch freshly grated lemon zest
8 oz fresh oyster mushrooms –
  evenly chopped into medium
  dice
2 tablespoons finely chopped fresh
  green coriander leaves

Pick over rice and rinse. Heat oil in a heavy saucepan and in it sizzle
the garlic, ginger and peppers for a minute or two. Add the rice and
stir until well coated. Pour in the water. Add seasoning and lemon
zest. Bring to the boil, turn to a lively simmer, cover and leave to
cook for about 50 minutes.

If you are roasting a bird, collect the pan juices and stir into the
rice now. With the lid off, boil any remaining liquid away until the
rice is merely moist and glossy. Take off the heat and stir in the raw
oyster mushrooms and green coriander.

Let it stand for a few minutes before serving.

Cranberry Parfait

serves 8-12 £

Here is a brilliantly simple but luxurious alternative to Christmas pudding, a dessert invented by mistake by chef David Cavalier.

A lighter and more voluminous variation is to make hard, dry meringues with the whites from at least some of the eggs, leave them to cool, then break them into smallish pieces and fold into the mixture below before freezing. If you do this, you should cut the amount of sugar in the cranberry purée by the weight you use in the meringue.

1 lb fresh cranberries	8 egg yolks
5 fl oz water	1 pint double cream
8 oz caster sugar	juice of half a lemon

Reserve a few cranberries. Put the rest in a saucepan with the water and half the sugar. Cook until tender. In a liquidiser or food-processor, blend to a purée and pass through a sieve.

Whisk egg yolks and the rest of the sugar in a bowl over a pan of simmering water until a ribbon of the mixture trailed over the surface holds its shape for at least five seconds. Whip the cream.

Fold the purée into the thick yolk mixture, then the whipped cream. Season to taste with the lemon juice and throw in the few reserved whole cranberries. Pour into a terrine mould or lined loaf tin and leave to set in the freezer for 4-6 hours.

Remove from freezer 10 minutes before needed. Serve in ½in slices with cold egg custard sauce or single cream.

Hazelnut Praline Ice-Cream

serves 4-6 £

Funfair toffee apples at the Kursaal in Southend were my introduction to the idea that food could be more than something you wolfed down before trying to find excuses for not doing your homework. The contrast of dense, crisp, tangy fruit and clear, dark-tasting, brittle shell had nothing to do with being good for you or making you big and strong. The notion of food as pleasure had taken hold. Other milestones were ice-cream made with cream (instead of Mr Whippy's sweetened and aerated vegetable oil shaving cream) and, much later, toasted nuts. This recipe brings the high points of all these together. The question is whether the human tongue can cope with having such a ball.

First make your praline (praline is caramel stirred through with nuts – usually toasted almonds – then broken up into a crunchy powder):

4 oz whole shelled hazelnuts	bland oil for greasing baking sheet
4 oz white sugar	

Spread nuts on a baking tray and place in the oven heated as high as it will go for about 5 minutes. The papery skins should now be easy to rub off with a cloth and the nuts should be coloured to a golden brown.

Melt sugar in a heavy pan. Cook until it is a pale gold colour then throw in the peeled hazelnuts and cook for about a minute. The addition of the nuts will bring the temperature down enough to stop the caramel burning.

Pour mixture immediately on to a lightly oiled baking sheet and leave to cool for about 20 minutes. When cold, crush praline with a rolling pin. It will keep in an airtight jar for a week or more. Excellent sprinkled on all sorts of puddings.

6 egg yolks	8 fl oz double cream
2 oz caster sugar	2 tablespoons brandy
4 oz hazelnut praline plus more for texture	crushed ice or cold water for cooling
½ pint milk	

Whisk yolks together with sugar and 2 oz praline until mixture is firm and the whisk leaves a trail. Pour milk and cream into a saucepan and bring to the boil. Pour this over the whisked mixture. Return to the pan with the brandy. Stir over a gentle heat until the mixture thickens enough to coat the back of a spoon.

Cool the mixture quickly, by placing the pan over crushed ice or a bowl of very cold water and stirring constantly. When cold, stir in the remaining praline powder to taste. Either put to churn in your ice-cream maker, or pour into shallow freezing containers until half-frozen. Turn out into a cold bowl and beat until smooth (or whizz in food processor). Pour back into containers and freeze until firm.

Cynical Party-Giving

As soon as the last grand crescendo of moans about Christmas starts up, with one camp muttering about the true message being lost in cynical commercialism and the other winging about hypocrisy and wasted time and money, you know that this is party season. Aside from more or less formal meals and proper parties, perhaps you have thought of asking over a dozen or so people on a semi-spontaneous basis, to wassail for an hour or two sometime during the month. Here, then, are four quick-party scenarios, all in line with the essential food and drink rules for party-giving – minimum choice, far too rich and difficult to eat comfortably. The kedgeree and onion tart both need plates and forks. Just napkins will do for the others. Each plan below includes details of both food and drink.

Croustades and Bloody Marys

serves 120 *£££ (mozzarella) – ££££ (crab and aubergine)*

Preparing enough fried-bread croustade cases is a relatively fast operation with two deep mince-pie tins of 12 holes each. These can be made up to 2 hours in advance. Add interest to the mozzarella filling by experimenting with chopped fresh oregano, cayenne pepper and anchovies. The quantities below assume you will be making all mozzarella or all crab and aubergine; halve the filling quantities if you're making half and half. The fino sherry in the Bloody Marys is a stolen idea to give the drink some 'nose'.

FOOD

cases: up to ½ pint good olive oil
60 thin slices white bread (about
    3 loaves)

mozzarella filling:
5 oz capers in brine – drained
2 lb mozzarella – coarsely
 chopped
10 oz large button mushrooms –
 cut lengthways into thin slices
freshly ground black pepper

crab and aubergine filling:
2 lb aubergine – skinned and
 roughly diced
3 tablespoons olive oil
4 cloves garlic – peeled and
 minced
1 lb skinned, seeded and roughly
 diced tomato flesh
1 lb white crab meat
juice of 2 lemons
salt and black pepper

Cut a circle of bread from each slice, using a 3½in pastry cutter. With fingers dipped in olive oil, pat both sides of each circle, leaving a thin film. Press into the holes in the mince-pie tins.

For mozzarella filling, bake at pre-heated Gas 6/200°C/400°F for 5 minutes until beginning to crisp. Turn out on to wire rack. Line up the cases on two baking sheets and fill each with 5-6 capers, about ½ oz mozzarella, then top with a slice of mushroom dipped in olive oil. Twist over some black pepper. Put back in the oven for 10-15 minutes until golden and bubbling. Eat immediately.

For crab filling, bake at pre-heated Gas 6/200°C/400°F for 10 minutes until golden brown. Turn out on to wire rack. Line up cases on two baking sheets. Sauté the aubergine in olive oil over a medium flame with the garlic. When well browned, stir in the tomato, crab, lemon juice and seasoning to taste. Turn heat up to evaporate all juices then spoon mixture into the croustade cases. Put back in the oven for 5 minutes. Eat immediately.

DRINK

6 fl oz Worcestershire sauce
1 tablespoon Tabasco sauce or
 more
1 tablespoon celery salt
4 fl oz freshly squeezed lemon
 juice
6 fl oz freshly squeezed orange
 juice
1 tablespoon horse-radish sauce
 (not creamed)

2 teaspoons freshly grated orange
 zest
3 teaspoons freshly ground black
 pepper
8 pints tomato juice – chilled
4 fl oz fino sherry – chilled
¾ pint vodka – chilled
celery sticks to garnish
40 ice-cubes

Shake all non-alcoholic ingredients together except tomato juice. This is your seasoning mix. Pour half into one enormous jug with half the tomato juice and ice cubes. Add sherry and vodka to the other half, pour into another slightly more enormous jug with the rest of the tomato juice and ice cubes. Put a stick of celery in each of 12 long tumblers. Stir jugs well before pouring.

Kedgeree and Mango Bellinis

serves 12 £££££

Purists will raise their eyebrows at the now hackneyed idea of salmon in kedgeree. Don't invite any purists.

FOOD

stock:

36 fl oz (just over 1¾ pints) water	6 bruised parsley stalks
3 tablespoons lemon juice	20 mixed peppercorns (black, white, pink, green)
12 fl oz dry white wine	3 oz carrot – peeled and grated
2 bay leaves	3 oz celery – trimmed and grated

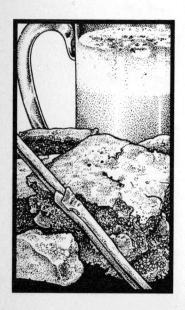

3 oz onion – peeled and chopped
3 sprigs fresh thyme
3 big sprigs fresh tarragon
3 teaspoons salt
assembly:
3 lb raw fresh salmon steaks
6 oz butter
3 tablespoons hot curry powder

1½ lb long grain rice
9 eggs – hard-boiled, shelled, then
  coarsely chopped
3 oz parsley leaves – very finely
  chopped
salt and freshly ground black
  pepper
lemon wedges to serve

Put all ingredients for poaching stock in a heavy, lidded casserole. Bring to the boil, then simmer for 5 minutes. Immerse salmon steaks, bring back to simmering point, cover and cook for 3-5 minutes. Gently lift fish out of stock and put aside until cool enough to handle. Strain the stock, discarding debris.

Rinse casserole and return to a medium flame with butter and curry powder. Sizzle together for 30 seconds, add dry rice and mix until well coated. Stir in a measured 36 fl oz – just over 1¾ pints – of the stock. Bring to the boil, then lower heat, cover and leave to cook undisturbed for 15 minutes. Turn heat off but leave covered and undisturbed for another 5-10 minutes.

Skin, bone and flake salmon. Fork egg, parsley, fish and seasoning into the rice. This dish will keep covered in a slow oven – (no more than Gas 2/150°C/250°F) – for up to 30 minutes.

Serve piled on a vast platter with lemon wedges.

DRINK

10 mangoes – chilled
6 passion fruit – chilled
at least 3 bottles workaday
  champagne – chilled

at least 3 pints tonic or soda water
  – chilled

Make sure all ingredients and jugs are well chilled. Halve mangoes lengthways, just grazing one side of the fibrous stone. Slice along the other side of the stone to remove it. Rescue band of flesh from top and sides of stone and dice. Score the flesh of the fruit's two halves, by cutting right through it as far as the skin, first diagonally one way, then diagonally the other way. Turn the skins inside out. All the flesh should now be standing out from the inside of the skin in proud lozenges. Cut these off the skin and straight into a liquidiser or food processor goblet. Whizz until smooth. You may be able to purée three or four mangoes at a time. Pour purée into jugs in the fridge while you process the rest.

Add pulp scooped from the passion fruit to the last batch before liquidising, then strain off the pips. Add this passion fruit-scented batch equally to the other jugs. Chill.

Two mangoes make about ¾ pint purée, which mixes with one bottle of champagne or a pint of soft fizz. Prepare jugs of alcoholic and non-alcoholic. Pour into champagne flutes, or long tumblers, to serve.

Onion Tart and Calvados

serves 12 ££

The tart is adapted from Anne Willan's classic *French Regional Cooking*. Any rich 'proper' quiche-type flan will do.

FOOD

pastry:
1½ lb plain flour – sifted
3 teaspoons salt
15 oz butter
1 teaspoon caraway seeds
6 tablespoons cold water
filling:
3 oz butter

3 lb onions – peeled and very
    thinly sliced (use the fine disc of
    a food-processor)
salt and freshly ground black
    pepper
big pinch freshly grated nutmeg
9 eggs
2 pints double cream or crème
    fraîche

Blend flour, salt and butter for a few seconds in the food processor until the texture of fine breadcrumbs, or rub in by hand. Stir in caraway seeds. Add water with the machine running and wait for the dough to form a ball (or make a dough by hand). Wrap in cling-film and put in the fridge for 30 minutes.

Roll out and line three 10in tart tins. Prick the bottoms all over and bake blind, using discs of greaseproof paper and dry beans to keep the bottoms from rising, for 20 minutes at Gas 5/190°C/375°F. Remove paper and beans and return to oven for another 5 minutes. Cool.

For filling, melt butter in large, heavy frying pan. Add onions, salt and pepper, cover and cook over a low flame, stirring occasionally for 20-30 minutes or until very soft but not brown. Spread out evenly over the baked shells.

Beat eggs with cream, salt, pepper and nutmeg. Pour over the onions. Bake at Gas 5/190°C/375°F for 30 minutes until golden (not longer, or the filling will curdle). Serve warm.

DRINK

The Calvados should be kept in the freezer so that it is thick and icy. Grappa, marc, schnappes, or other clean fruit *eaux de vie* might be substitutes. Serve in small, chilled tumblers. Big jugs of chilled apple juice garnished with fresh mint leaves are the non-alcoholic alternative.

Gingerbread and Egg Nog

serves 12 ££

The gingerbread is an adaptation of one by cake expert Barbara Maher, her lily gilded only with the addition of stem ginger. Mince pies such as Josceline Dimbleby's – pastry spiked with orange zest and with the addition of cream cheese to moisten the filling – make a good alternative. The egg nog is a traditional one from the Southern states of America.

FOOD

6 oz butter – softened, plus more
    for greasing
6 oz muscovado sugar

3 fl oz medium sherry
1 lb plain flour
2 teaspoons cream of tartar
2 heaped tablespoons ground
    ginger
3 teaspoons ground cinnamon
3 teaspoons ground nutmeg

6 fl oz black treacle
6 fl oz golden syrup
6 fl oz milk – warmed

4 eggs (size 2) – well beaten
juice and zest of 2 large oranges
8 oz preserved stem ginger –
    drained and roughly chopped
2 teaspoons bicarbonate of soda
2 tablespoons warm water

Beat butter and sugar together until thick and fluffy. Mix in treacle, syrup, milk and sherry. Sift flour with cream of tartar, ground ginger, cinnamon and nutmeg.

Mix alternate spoonfuls of flour mixture and egg into creamed ingredients. Add orange juice and zest plus chopped stem giner. Dissolve bicarb in warm water and blend into the mixture.

Pour into two buttered 12in×8in×1½in cake tins and bake for 35-40 minutes at Gas 4/180°C/350°F. Cool in tin. Cut into squares. Serve heaped on large platter.

DRINK

18 eggs (size 2)
3 oz plus 9 tablespoons caster
  sugar
¾ pint bourbon

¼ pint dark rum
3 pints single cream
freshly grated nutmeg

Separate eggs. Beat whites with the 3 oz sugar until they hold soft, moist peaks. Put yolks in large serving bowl and beat with the other 9 tablespoons of sugar until creamy. Whisk in the bourbon and rum, then the cream.

Fold in the egg whites fairly thoroughly, but leaving a distinct, cream coloured, foamy layer. Sprinkle with nutmeg. Serve in big tumblers.

There is no related non-alcoholic alternative. Fall back on angostura bitters and tonic, fizzy water or orange juice.

GLOSSARY

The majority of this glossary is given over to vegetables, because these are the cookery ingredients that most of us stand more chance of being able to buy at reasonably high quality through supermarkets, local specialist shops and markets. Fruit generally needs less preparation and so needs less explanation. The state of fish retailing in this country is such that to dwell on the raw materials at any length would just rub salt into the wound (see introduction); meat has already figured hugely in the recipes; and cheese unfortunately suffers an even worse fate than fish, decent standards only being upheld by a dozen or so specialist shops nationwide.

Finally, this is a personal selection rather than an attempt to be comprehensive.

Key to seasonal availability boxes

The symbols or space below the month initial refers to that particular month. A space means nothing is available.

For example

ASPARAGUS	J F M A M J J A S O N D
	· · ○ ● ★ ★ ○ · · · · ·
	☆

Key to symbols:
★ = best UK-grown season
☆ = UK-grown available
● = best import season
○ = import available
· = marginally available

VEGETABLES

ARROWHEAD: see Eastern Exotics

ARTICHOKES: see Globe Artichokes and Jerusalem Artichokes

ARUGULA: see European Exotics/Rocket

ASPARAGUS   J F M A M J J A S O N D
                                               · · ○ ● ★ ★ ○ · · · · ·
                                                       ☆

The budded stem or spear from a large member of the lily family. Old names for it include 'sparrow-grass'. It is still called 'grass' by the trade. Short British season, mostly English (from East Anglia and southern counties, with some from the Midlands and Scotland's east coast). Imports available year-round, although hardly ever as superb, from Spain, France, USA, Chile and Australia. Finger-thick, green varieties have the best flavour; the bland, very thick, white varieties popular in France are rarely available here. Pencil-thin stems, called sprue, tend to be cheaper, taste good and are also suitable for stir-frying, soups etc. Wild asparagus is very small, can be eaten raw and has a fine, sweet flavour. Very little gets into this country, available only in specialist shops (or buy it in season on spring trips to the Continent).

Buy healthy looking firm, smooth, clean spears. Check buds are still tight.

Frozen can be okay for soups, purées, gratins and so on. Tinned is a dubious out of season treat, not comparable with fresh, but slummily enjoyable in its own right. Eat cold, straight out of the tin as a midnight snack (especially when the worse for drink), or drain well, pile on thick toast, cover with grated Swiss cheese and cayenne pepper, then grill until the cheese is golden and the asparagus heated through.

See also pp. 117-18 (preparation etc); pp. 118-19, 130 (recipes).

AUBERGINES   J F M A M J J A S O N D
                                               · · ○ ○ ○ ● ● ● ● ● ○ ○
                                                           ★ ★

As well as the now familiar purple/black long, bulbous fruit (called eggplant in America), other specialist varieties are imported, mostly for the Asian market – from the tiny pea-aubergine used in Thai cookery to the small, spherical white aubergines used in the cuisines of China and India. All are part of the nightshade family. Ordinary aubergines are better from warmer climes such as Cyprus, the Canaries, Italy and Spain. Dutch and British-grown often lack distinction.

Buy smooth, firm, glossy specimens without brown patches.

Recipes used to insist on de-gorging before cooking – that is, slicing, salting then rinsing and squeezing to remove bitter juices. This is not necessary for most specimens, especially the younger, fresher ones, but does help cut the vegetable's fat absorbency if it is to be fried. Whether to peel or not depends on the dish, although large quantities of tough skin in a ratatouille or whatever can be off-putting. I usually half-peel by cutting off alternate strips of skin lengthways down the vegetable.

Better fried or sautéed than steamed, boiled, casseroled or stewed, when it can become pappy.

Frozen is never satisfactory.

See also pp. 153-4 (roasting and grilling); pp. 131, 140-1, 153-4, 180-1 (recipes).

AVOCADO PEARS
J F M A M J J A S O N D
● ● ● ● ○ ○ ○ ○ ● ●

The four main varieties available here are thinnish skinned, green, relatively large Ettinger, Fuerte and Nabal, and the small, rough-skinned, dark purple Hass, which has the nuttiest, most buttery flavour. Nabal and Ettinger can be bland and watery. The main crop of Israeli Hass are available here from January to May, followed by American imports. Excellent Israeli Fuerte are around from November to March. With imports from Kenya, the Americas and elsewhere, avocados are readily available all year round, but many of these are disappointing. The tiny, unseeded cocktail avocados can be eaten whole, skin and all, or peeled and cut up in a salad.

Retailers rarely have avocados at the perfect stage of ripeness. The essential thing is never even to try eating a hard, unripe avocado; when ripe, they yield all over to gentle pressure. Very soft ones are okay for sloppy dips. Blackened, discoloured and stringy fruit can be off-putting.

Buy them hard 2-4 days in advance and wrap in newspaper with a ripe apple or banana (which give off ripening gases), then keep at room temperature until required. Ripe, soft fruit will keep perfectly well whole in a not too cold fridge for 4-5 days.

Forget lemon juice for keeping a cut half of avocado from discolouring while you build up an appetite for it. Leave in the stone and smear the whole cut surface and stone liberally with olive oil. Then wrap closely with clingfilm and keep in the fridge. It will remain perfectly green and good for 12 hours or more.

I have never found a successful recipe for cooked avocado.

See also pp. 93-5 (recipes).

BABY CORN: see Eastern Exotics

BAMBOO SHOOTS: see Eastern Exotics

BASIL: see Herbs

BATAVIA: see Lettuce and Other Salad Leaves

BAY LEAVES: see Herbs

BEANS: see Green Beans; Broad Beans

BEANSPROUTS: see Eastern Exotics

BEEF TOMATOES: see Tomatoes

BEETROOT   J F M A M J J A S O N D
                                              ★ ★ ★ ☆ ☆ ☆ ★ ★ ★ ★ ★ ★

British grown. If you're only used to the pickled sort, fresh can be a revelation raw, boiled or baked. Check for undamaged skins before boiling,
as the colour and flavour can leach out. When cooked, the skin will rub off
easily.
    See also p. 216 (recipe suggestion).

BELGIAN CHICORY   J F M A M J J A S O N D
                                              ● ● ● ☆ ☆ ☆ ☆ ☆ ☆ ☆ ● ●

Also called witloof (and endive in Europe and USA). Tight, conical heads
(called 'chicons') or bitter white leaves, forced in darkness to keep them
pale, tipped with pale yellow. The best is imported from Belgium, the
Netherlands and Italy, and is sold wrapped in purple tissue paper to protect it from the light.
    Eaten raw as a salad ingredient or can be braised.
    See also p. 51 (recipe suggestion); p. 38-9 (recipe).

BELL PEPPERS: see Capsicums

BLACK SALSIFY: see Scorzonera

BLACK TRUFFLE: see Funghi

BOLETUS EDULIS: see Funghi

BROAD BEANS   J F M A M J J A S O N D
                                              ○ ★ ★ ★ ☆ ☆

Mostly British. Very small, young ones can be cooked whole and eaten pod and all. Usually, just the bean is eaten. The tougher older ones are best slipped out of their grey, leathery jackets and excellent puréed. The vegetable has a particular affinity with fresh dill and savory. Frozen can be reasonably good.

See also pp. 113-15 (recipes).

BROCCOLI	J	F	M	A	M	J	J	A	S	O	N	D
Calabrese	○	○	○	○	○	★	★	★	★	★	★	☆
Cape Broccoli			★	★	★							
Purple Sprouting			★	★	★							

Calabrese is ordinary green broccoli, available year round with imports.

The best of the lot is purple sprouting broccoli, as special as asparagus, and available here only during its short UK season. There is also a rarer white variety.

When buying sprouting broccoli, avoid limp looking specimens and pick over your purchase carefully when you get it home, cutting off tough ends and coarse leaves. For long perfect specimens, tie in bundles and boil or steam as for asparagus so that the stems are tender and the flowering heads just cooked, then serve with a dipping sauce of melted butter stirred through with a little lemon juice and black pepper, or home-made hollandaise. Otherwise, just steam or boil for 3-4 minutes so that the leaves remain bright green and the flowering heads haven't reached beyond a purpley-copper colour, then serve as a vegatable, perhaps dribbled with a little butter.

Frozen calabrese can be okay.

See also p. 38 (recipe suggestion).

BRUSSELS SPROUTS	J	F	M	A	M	J	J	A	S	O	N	D
	★	★	★						☆	★	★	★

British grown. Frozen Brussels Sprouts never retain a good texture.

See also p. 72; p. 235 (recipe suggestion).

BRUSSELS TOPS: see Cabbages

CABBAGES	J	F	M	A	M	J	J	A	S	O	N	D
Green (all varieties)	★	★	★	★	★	★	★	★	★	★	★	★
Red	★	☆	☆	☆						★	★	★
Savoy	★	★							★	★	★	★
Spring Greens	★	★	★	★	☆	☆	☆	☆	☆		★	★
Tops	★	★										★
White	●	●	★	☆	☆	☆				★	★	★
	★	★								●	●	●

British grown with some Dutch imports of winter whites.

All are varieties of brassica of which the leaves are eaten, either fully developed and separate or still packed together in tight globes. Green are just ordinary cabbages, with Savoy being a particularly good winter variety. Red and white are hard balls of very closely packed leaves suitable for shredding into salads (especially white in coleslaw) as well as cooking.

Spring greens – actually now available all year, so perhaps more properly just called greens – are unhearted cabbages. Collards is another name. Tops are the loose leaves from young plants (especially Brussels and turnips). For greens and tops, buy much more than it looks as if you will need, then use only healthy leaves, cutting off all the tough, stringy stalks. Cook, covered, for a few minutes in briskly boiling salted water, drain, then toss in a frying pan with hot butter or good olive oil in which, perhaps, you have softened some finely chopped garlic. Season with lots of black pepper and maybe a little grated lemon zest.

Very good greens can be cooked like spinach – just washed then wilted in their own juices with a knob of butter.

See also pp. 51, 217 and 235 (recipe suggestions).

CALABASH: see Western Exotics/Dudi

CALABRESE: see Broccoli

CAPE BROCCOLI: see Broccoli

CAPSICUMS

J F M A M J J A S O N D

Peppers, sweet peppers or, in America, bell peppers. British in the summer, supplemented with Dutch imports. Better from Mediterranean. Year round supply maintained from Canary Islands, Israel, Kenya and others.

Of all the available colours, red, yellow and the new Day-Glo orange are fully ripe and can be deliciously sweet. Apart from green, the others – in which the colour really is only skin deep – are gimmicks.

Tinned pepper strips – sometimes roasted, sometimes not – can be superb. Frozen are never exciting. Dried, especially some of the sun-dried whole varieties from Spain and the Balkans, can be excellent.

See also pp. 150-3 (roasting or grilling and recipes).

CARDOON: see European Exotics

CARROTS

J F M A M J J A S O N D

Mostly British, supplemented with imports from Europe and America. The tiny young ones sold with their feathery tops still attached are particularly delectable. One novelty variety available sometimes in spring is the round Parisian carrot.

Carrots are one of the few products for which organically grown varieties taste appreciably better than non-organic. Frozen and tinned are both hopeless.

See also pp. 44 and 83-4 (recipes).

CAULIFLOWER

Mostly British with some winter imports from Britanny and other supplements from France and Spain when necessary. Cape broccoli is a purple-headed cauliflower cooked in exactly the same way as cauliflower. Another spring variety, with a green turreted head, is Romanesco. I've never found frozen any good.

See also p. 38 (recipe suggestion).

CELERIAC

Perhaps the most under-used of our root vegetables: a large, bulbous, thick-skinned, knobbly root. Mostly British grown with some European and Israeli imports. Check for pulpy frost-bitten patches when buying after a cold snap.

Always pared thickly before cooking. Keep cut raw celeriac in acidulated water to prevent discoloration. Usually boiled or steamed in pieces, then tossed in butter or white sauce. Excellent briefly blanched then grated or cut into julienne strips for salads (especially with a thick, mustardy dressing), also par-boiled then sautéed. Best of all puréed by itself or with other root vegetables with butter and/or cream.

Very thin slices of celeriac fried until golden and crunchy like potato crisps (deep fry for a long time at medium-high temperature as the vegetable will give out a lot of water before it starts to brown) make a great winter garnish.

See also p. 42 (recipes).

CELERY

British-grown with Spanish and Israeli imports in winter and spring.
Frozen and tinned not worth buying.
See also pp. 167 and 134-5 (recipes).

CEPS: see Funghi

CHANTERELLES: see Funghi

CHARD: see European Exotics

CHAYOTE: see Western Exotics

CHERRY TOMATOES: see Tomatoes

CHERVIL: see Herbs

CHICORY: see Belgian Chicory or Salad Leaves

CHILLI PEPPERS

J F M A M J J A S O N D
☆ ☆ ☆ ☆ ☆ ☆ ☆ ☆ ☆ ☆ ☆ ☆

Imports. Widely available in supermarkets.

Few of the world's many fascinating varieties of hot green or red chilli pepper reach our shops. We get green ones, either tiny or small, and perfectly serviceable in a whole range of Chinese, Indian, South East Asian, Middle Eastern, Afro-Caribbean and Latin American dishes. What we are missing is the surprising subtlety in the differences of flavour underneath the common denominator of a certain degree of heat.

Of the few speciality types sometimes available, the Caribbean bonnet-peppers (like minute Tam o'Shanters) are searingly wonderful.

Be careful when chopping; the juices can be a virulent skin and eye irritant. Accepted wisdom is to remove the supposedly hotter seeds and internal pith, but this surely depends on how much heat you like.

See also p. 167-8 (recipe).

CHINESE ARTICHOKES: see European Exotics

CHINESE FLOWERING CABBAGE: see Eastern Exotics/Pak Choi

CHINESE KEYS: see Eastern Exotics/Galangale

CHINESE LEAF VEGETABLES: see Eastern Exotics/Pak Choi

CHINESE LEAVES

J F M A M J J A S O N D
☆ ○ ○ ☆ ★ ★ ★ ★ ★ ★ ☆ ☆
○   ○ ○ ○   ○ ○

Officially called Chinese leaf by the British growers' association. Pale, weighty cylinders of leaves that can be eaten raw in salads or cooked, but either way are pretty uninspiring.

CHINESE MUSTARD GREENS: see Eastern Exotics/Pak Choi

CHINESE PARSLEY: see Herbs/Coriander

CHIVES: see Herbs

CHOI SUM: see Eastern Exotics/Pak Choi

CHRISTOPHENE: see Western Exotics/Chayote

CILANTRO: see Herbs/Coriander

COLLARDS: see Cabbages

CORIANDER: see Herbs

CORN ON THE COB: see Sweetcorn

CORN SALAD: see Lettuce and Other Salad Leaves

COURGETTES

J F M A M J J A S O N D
○ ○ ○ ● ● ★ ★ ★ ★ ★ ○ ○

Zucchini in America. British and Mediterranean imports. For the best flavour, must be absolutely hard when bought. No need to peel, although you should rub hard, scrub or run the back of a knife along them to get rid of any tiny bristles. The youngest, smallest and freshest are the most delicious.

Courgette flowers are sometimes available. These are big yellow affairs attached to an embryonic vegetable. They are washed carefully, then stuffed with anything from ricotta cheese and spinach to minced fish or poultry then lightly braised.

Frozen are hopeless.

See also pp. 154-5 (recipes).

CROSNES: see European Exotics/Chinese Artichokes

CUCUMBERS

J F M A M J J A S O N D
○ ☆ ● ● ★ ★ ★ ★ ☆ ○ ○
☆ ★

British plus the Netherlands, Spain and Canaries. Excellent imports of small young varieties from Cyprus in the spring.

See also p. 133 (recipe suggestion); pp. 111-13 and 121 (recipes).

CURLY ENDIVE: see Lettuce and Other Salad Leaves

CURLY KALE   J F M A M J J A S O N D
                                              ★ ★ ★ ☆ ☆   ☆ ★

Dark green, unhearted brassica with curly foliate. British grown. Cook like spring greens.

See also p. 236 (recipe suggestion).

DAIKON: see Eastern Exotics/Mooli

DASHEEN: see Western Exotics/Yams

DILL: see Herbs

DUDI: see Western Exotics

DWARF BEANS: see Green Beans

EASTERN EXOTICS (INDIA, CHINA, SOUTH-EAST ASIA)

The less familiar fresh vegetables of exotic origin are sold mainly in stores serving specific ethnic communities. Also see: Chilli Peppers; Chinese Leaves; Ginger; Mange-tout Peas; Okra.

                                              J F M A M J J A S O N D
Arrowhead   ● ●   ●

Imports. Sold in Chinese stores. A firm, white bulb with papery brown skin, resembling a tulip bulb. Used in braised dishes, stir-fries or treated like a waxy potato, it takes on a creamy texture and faintly nutty flavour.

                                              J F M A M J J A S O N D
Baby Corn   · · · · · · · · · · · ·

Imports, mainly from Thailand. Widely available in up-market supermarkets. Novelty vegetable ingredient in South-East Asian stir-fries. Excellent griddled in a dry wok or pan until evenly browned. This gets rid of any slight ammoniac overtones.

See also p. 157-8 (recipe).

J F M A M J J A S O N D
Bamboo Shoots ● ● ● ●   ● ●

Imports. Sold in Chinese stores. Dense tapering cylinders, the young shoots of bamboo with a delectable tight texture and mild fresh flavour. Used chopped or in slivers to add a special waxy crunch to many Chinese preparations. Also available tinned, which must be rinsed well and even then does not lose a boiled metallic taste.

J F M A M J J A S O N D
Beansprouts ☆ ☆ ☆ ☆ ☆ ☆ ☆ ☆ ☆ ☆ ☆ ☆

British and European imports. Commonly available in supermarket cellophane packs. These sprouts of the mung bean should be bought white and full of sap, not yellowing and floppy. Use raw in salads or quickly cooked in stir-fries. Tinned beansprouts are a sour, crunchless pastiche.

J F M A M J J A S O N D
Galangale · · · · · · · · · · · ·

Imports from China, Thailand and others. The rhizome greater galangale is available from Chinese and South-East Asian stores and used in curries, marinades and sauces in those cuisines to impart a delicate, gingery note. The hotter root galangale, also called Chinese keys, is only available from specialist Thai shops and is used in similar ways. Habitués of Thai restaurants will recognise galangale as one of the essential flavourings in tom yam, a soup. Dried and powdered also available.

J F M A M J J A S O N D
Lemon Grass · · · · · · · · · · · ·

Imported from Thailand. Fresh lemon grass, which adds the scent of lemons to many South Indian, Thai and Sri Lankan soups, curries, sauces, salads, grills and other dishes, is now available in some supermarkets as well as speciality stores. The dried version needs soaking before use.

J F M A M J J A S O N D
Methi · · · · · · · · · · · ·

British. Sold in bunches in Indian and Middle Eastern stores. The cloverlike green leaves of the fenugreek plant, spicily aromatic with an edge of bitterness, are popular all over India and the Middle East, eaten raw in salads and cooked in all kinds of vegetable and meat dishes. Dried is all right in stews, curries and braises.

J F M A M J J A S O N D
Mooli ☆ ☆ ☆ ☆ ☆ ☆ ☆ ☆ ☆ ☆ ☆ ☆

British and imports. Widely available in supermarkets, this long, tapering white radish – called daikon in Japan – is used raw, grated or cut into slivers in salads or to garnish Japanese and Korean dishes. Shredded and soaked in iced water, it is the essential bland, crisp accompaniment to any presentation of Japanese raw fish. Also used cooked in Indian dishes. Use to add a radishy note to salads.

See also p. 44-5 (recipe).

J F M A M J J A S O N D
· · · · · · ☆ ☆ ☆ · · ·

Pak Choi

British and Dutch imports. Available in some supermarkets as well as from Chinese stores. A Chinese green leaf vegetable with thick fleshy white stems, it is only the best known of many leaves, all more or less similar to chard, spinach or sprouting broccoli, that are used in Chinese cooking. Most are steamed, stir-fried or blanched then simply sauced and eaten as an accompanying vegetable; some are also good in soups. Some are sold when flowering, some have a distinctive taste, for example Gaai-Choi's (Chinese Mustard Greens) strong tang of mustard. Perhaps the choicest of all is Choi-Sum or Chinese Flowering Cabbage.

Slice the stems of pak choi and sauté for a minute or two in bland oil; cook the leaves briefly like spinach, then mix stem and leaves together and serve hot, dribbled with oyster sauce.

J F M A M J J A S O N D
●   ●

Water Chestnuts

Import. Sold in Chinese shops. We're all used to tinned water chestnuts in dishes from the local takeaway, so why not try fresh during their short season to see what we've been missing? Eat raw or cook in anything that would benefit from its extraordinary, fabulous, brittle crunchy texture – stir-fries, kebabs, salads, stuffings and so on.

EDDOE: see Western Exotics

EGGPLANT: see Aubergine

ENDIVE: see Belgian Chicory; Lettuce and Other Salad Leaves

ESCAROLE: see Lettuce and Other Salad Leaves

EUROPEAN EXOTICS (BRITAIN, CONTINENTAL EUROPE, THE MEDITERRANEAN)

Misfits from closer to home. The delights that have to be searched out in specialist greengrocers while most of the British retail trade – still in pursuit of the fork-lift-truck-friendly, perfectly shiny, perfectly regular, perfectly tasteless Dutch tomato – continues to ignore them. Also see Salsify; Scorzonera; Funghi.

J F M A M J J A S O N D

Cardoon ○ ○   ·   ·   ○ ○

Import. Buy from specialist greengrocers or Spanish shops. Popular all over southern Europe. This celery-like stem of a relative of the thistle can be well trimmed, strung and eaten raw in salads, or cooked (usually braised).

J F M A M J J A S O N D

Chard ● ● ○ ○ · ·   ○ ● ●

Imported from Cyprus and Spain. Available from some supermarkets and high street greengrocers. Chard – variously called Swiss chard, seakale beet, spinach beet and many variations – has fleshy white stems and beautiful dark leaves, which can be cooked separately like spinach with a seasoning of nutmeg. Cut the stalks into stubby lengths, removing the fine skin and stringy bits. Cook in boiling water until tender, cover with a good white sauce stirred through with generous quantities of grated Swiss cheese, and bake in a medium-hot oven until the surface is golden. This goes well with simple grilled meats and fish.

J F M A M J J A S O N D

Chinese Artichokes ○ ○   ·   ● ●

British and imports. Try supposedly high class greengrocers. These little, pale, segmented tubers – also called crosnes – are excellent sautéed or quickly braised in stock as an accompaniment to roasts and grills. The French love 'em.

J F M A M J J A S O N D

Horse-Radish ☆   ☆ ☆ ☆

British. Try specialist greengrocers. Nothing matches the exhilarating, tear-jerking piquancy of the fresh root. Good grated into all sorts of things as well as the essential condiment for roast beef and the stronger smoked fish.

The prepared jars of sauce or horse-radish cream never have the same pungency. For a severe test of your mettle, try the green Japanese horse-radish available as a powder or in tubes, to be mixed with soy as a dip for raw fish.

J F M A M J J A S O N D
○ ○ ○ ☆ ☆ ☆ ☆

Rocket

British and imports. Fashionable in America, where they call it arugula. Some supermarkets now sell expensive, fancy little packs, although this peppery leaf is best eaten lightly dressed in salad quantities to accompany grilled fish, as in the Eastern Mediterranean. Available here in proper-sized bunches quite cheaply from Cypriot, Greek and Turkish shops in spring.

J F M A M J J A S O N D
· ☆ ★ ☆ ☆

Samphire

British and imported, also known as marsh samphire or glasswort. Available from a few fishmongers in season, also from fish stalls in Norfolk and Suffolk. Rinse, trim off the wiry roots, boil or steam until tender, then serve hot with melted butter. The thin fleshy stems can also be successfully picked in brine. Rock samphire, or sea fennel, is more strongly aromatic and lends itself to being pickled in vinegar.

J F M A M J J A S O N D
★ ★ ★   ★

Seakale

British and French imports. Only available very occasionally from highest quality specialist greengrocers. A native national treasure, it is a scandal that these mild-tasting, pale, fleshy stalks are not more widely retailed. Try growing them yourself. Rinse well and eat the tenderest specimens raw in salads. Mature stalks should be steamed or boiled for about 15 minutes until tender, then served with melted butter and lemon juice, hollandaise or cheese sauce.

J F M A M J J A S O N D
● ●   ● ●
★ ★   ★ ★

Shallots

British and imports. Buy from decent greengrocers and some supermarkets. Small varieties of onion providing a clean, sweet, oniony flavour without the brutal aroma. Much used in classical French cookery. Good raw or cooked. Jane Grigson says that if cooked it should merely be stewed in fat or other ingredients to soften, never browned or it takes on a bitter taste.

Sorrel

J F M A M J J A S O N D
· ☆ ☆ · · · ·

British and French imports. Acidic green leaves resembling spinach and cooked in the same way. Available infrequently in supermarkets and in over-priced little packs. Try specialist retailers or grow it yourself – it needs hardly any care. Sorrel adds a distinctive sharp note to soups, purées and sauces.

See also p. 136 (recipe).

FENNEL (BULB OR FLORENCE)

J F M A M J J A S O N D
● ● ○ ○ ○ ○ ○ ● ● ● ● ●
            ☆ ☆ ☆ ☆

The best is imported from Italy and Spain. Some British, Dutch and Belgian. Buy firm, very hard, white bulbs without much foliage. Don't buy if the foliage is deep green.

Good thinly sliced in salads, if you like bright, aniseedy flavours, or braised or in simple gratins.

See also pp. 38 and 100 (recipe suggestions).

FENNEL: see Herbs

FENUGREEK: see Eastern Exotics/Methi

FEUILLE DE CHENE: see Lettuce and Other Salad Leaves

FLAT BEANS: see Green Beans

FLAT-LEAF PARSLEY: see Herbs/Parsley

FRENCH BEANS: see Green Beans

FRISÉE: see Lettuce and Other Salad Leaves

FUNGHI

Some formerly strange varieties have now joined ordinary mushrooms in being available year round in supermarkets from British and European cultivation. Others are distinctly seasonal and available from only specialist greengrocers. Some can be picked wild in this country but these are mostly left to the private enthusiast – another native food resource ignored by the trade. Even slight errors in identification can be fatal. See also mushrooms and p. 200.

J F M A M J J A S O N D
Ceps
             • • ○

Import. The proper cep is *Boletus edulis*, called porcini in Italy, a plump-stemmed, fat-headed toadstool with vertical tubes instead of gills underneath the cap. The most prized of all above-ground funghi in European, especially French and Italian, cookery. Fry in olive oil, grill, bake or use in stews, soups, casseroles, braises, sauces and stuffings. Dried ceps can have an excellent flavour.

J F M A M J J A S O N D
Chanterelles
             • • • ○ •

Import. Sometimes used synonymously with girolles, although I have seen the two words on various market stalls all over France labelling slightly different varieties. The chanterelle is a beautiful orangey-yellow capped, up-turned trumpet with pale gills, which smells faintly of apricots. The girolle is similar in all respects except smaller and with a dull grey-brown cap. Authorities I've spoken to all disagree. These are justley one (or two) of the most popular funghi in French cookery. Sautéed in butter with a little chopped shallot for the best results. Also available dried, tinned and in jars – all decent.

J F M A M J J A S O N D
Morels
          ○ ○

Import. When mushroom lovers dream of spring, it is only for the morels. They are odd brown little things with distinctive fleshy droopy caps patterned with raised honeycomb ridges. Clean fresh ones by pouring boiling water over them and leaving for 40 minutes so all the grit drops out. Best stewed in butter for a few minutes, with their juices then thickened with crème fraîche or double cream and sharpened with a heavy-bodied white wine (such as a vin jaune from the Jura or an Alsatian Gewürztraminer). Dried, canned and jarred morels can also be excellent.

See also p. 100 (recipe suggestion).

J F M A M J J A S O N D
Oyster Mushrooms
         ☆ ☆ ☆ ☆ ☆ ☆ ☆ ☆ ☆ ☆ ☆ ☆
         ○ ○ ○ ○ ○ ○ ○ ○ ○ ○ ○ ○

British and Dutch import (cultivated). Called pleurotte in France. Wobbly, smooth, grey-topped, oyster-shaped funghus with a good mild flavour. Sauté in oil or butter, eat raw in salads, grill or bake.

See also page 241 (recipe).

Shiitake

J F M A M J J A S O N D
. . . .

Dutch import (cultivated) with some British, but very small quantities. Excellent meaty cap useable in any dish to replace ordinary mushrooms for a far superior flavour. Widely used in Chinese and Japanese cookery; recently fashionable in America. Japanese dried ones can be excellent.

Truffles (Black)

J F M A M J J A S O N D
● ● ○   ● ● ●

Import. If you can't get the fresh, black Perigord beast out from one of this country's pitifully few purveyors, consider using the excellent vacuum-packed ones that are now imported in little jars from Spain. The scent and flavour of truffle is sexy, rank, foxy, sweaty, scrotal, musty and elusive; if you're not going to put enough in a dish, there's no benefit in putting any in at all. Once you've experienced the subterranean funghus at its headiest, you'd have to have a shaved tongue not to understand what all the expense and fuss is about.

See also pp. 37-8 and 222-3 (recipes).

Truffles (White)

J F M A M J J A S O N D
          ● ● ●

Import. This Piedmontese speciality imported from Alba in Italy has a more powerful, almost cheesy, peppery flavour and aroma, best enjoyed grated over simple risotto, fresh pasta or omelettes. Not usually cooked.

GAAI CHOI: see Eastern Exotics/Pak Choi

GALANGALE: see Eastern Exotics

GARLIC

J F M A M J J A S O N D
● ● ○ ○ ○ ○ ● ● ● ● ● ●
      ☆ ★ ★ ★ ☆

The best is imported from Spain, Italy and France. Some British. The firmer and fresher the better. Look especially, at the height of the autumn and winter import seasons, for large heads of fat cloves encased in purply-pink skin. Fresh, mild, green garlic, popular around the Mediterranean – especially in Spain – is not available here through the retail trade.

Garlic salt and granules always have an unpleasant metallic edge. The pastes sold in tubes are hardly better. Some of the jars of paste mixed with olive oil are less offensive. Whole cloves preserved in oil or vinegar can be fine.

See also p. 100 (recipe).

GINGER   J F M A M J J A S O N D

☆ ☆ ☆ ☆ ☆ ☆ ☆ ☆ ☆ ☆ ☆ ☆

Imported from all over the world including Australia, Brazil, Costa Rica, Egypt, Fiji, Iran, Hawaii and Taiwan and widely available. Fresh root ginger is a knobbly, beige-skinned root. Buy as plump and smooth as you can. Avoid wrinkled, hard and dry specimens. Staple lemony/hot flavouring in Chinese, Japanese, Indian and South-East Asian cooking. Peel then grate. Usually fried briefly, often with garlic and chilli peppers, to set the initial flavouring of a dish.

Dry powdered ginger is not comparable in any way. Crystallised and preserved in syrup, ginger becomes a tangy sweetmeat, also used to flavour puddings. Japanese pickled ginger is a distinctive treat in its own right, an essential condiment with raw fish.

GIROLLES: see Funghi/Chanterelles

GLASSWORT: see European Exotics/Samphire

GLOBE ARTICHOKES   J F M A M J J A S O N D

○ ○ ● ★ ★ ● ● ● ○

● ● ☆

Ball of thick grey-green "leaves" enclosing inedible choke of infant seedhead on thick, stemmed, absolutely edible base. Reltive of the thistle. Some British but mainly superior Mediterranean imports. Two main varieties – red (darker and with purplish edges to the leaves) and green. Also keep an eye out for the superb tiny varieties, around 2in long.

Look for firm leaves, quite tightly packed, with some stem attached. Avoid sad, wrinkled specimens and browning edges. Watch for misty white mould. Even healthy ones should be cooked within a day or two of purchase.

This is a vegetable that discolours easily when raw. Use stainless steel implements to trim, rub cut surfaces with lemon juice if not cooking immediately. Acidulate cooking water.

For larger ones, trim ends of leaves with kitchen scissors (up to half way down), score heavily round stem, ½in down from base, then pull stem off with a sharp twist (to pull tough fibres out from the base with the stem). Then put into boiling salted water, acidulated with lemon juice and also containing a splash of olive oil to further protect against discoloration, cover pan and cook until leaves come away easily. This usually takes about 40 minutes.

Drain well and eat hot or warm with dipping sauces of melted butter and lemon juice, hollandaise or similar rich concoctions. Or eat cold with vinaigrette, mayonnaise or similar. Pull off the leaves, one by one, dipping the fleshy bottoms in the sauce and scraping them between your front teeth to remove the meat. Discard the rest of the leaves. Scrape away the choke when you get down to it, then eat the succulent base with a knife and fork (this is the best bit).

Fancy stuffed presentations require you to scrape out the choke from between the leaves of the cooked artichoke, then fill the cavity with a variety of mixtures from sautéed, chopped mushrooms plus a whole poached egg topped with hollandaise and finished off under the grill, to Jane Grigson's magical purée of broad beans, butter, cream and chopped savory.

Alternatively, you can cut away all the leaves and choke from the raw artichoke with a sharp knife, then cook the trimmed base by boiling, steaming, roasting, baking or cutting into slices and grilling or frying. Especially good for eating hot if boiled in meat, poultry or vegetable stock or broth. Puréed and stirred into hollandaise, béchamel or velouté, cooked aritchokes make a fine sauce for simply cooked fish or lamb.

The tiny varieties have no appreciable choke and so just need the ends of their leaves trimming before being boiled, steamed, casseroled, stewed or baked whole, or being quartered or sliced raw and then fried, griddled, grilled or roasted. The whole thing is eaten. Delicious in chunky salads dressed with mayonnaise or for pizza toppings and so on.

Frozen tiny artichokes can be okay to eat by themselves if sautéed from frozen rather than boiled or steamed. Tinned artichoke hearts are almost acceptable in caseroles, salads, as pizza toppings and so on, as long as they are well rinsed. You never quite get rid of a slight boiled, metallic taste.

See also pp. 115 and 206-7 (recipes).

'GRASS': see Asparagus

GREEN BEANS	J	F	M	A	M	J	J	A	S	O	N	D
French or Dwarf	•	•	•	•	•	★	★	★	★	○	○	○
						☆	☆	☆	☆	☆		
Runner and Flat	○	○	○	○	○	○	★	★	★	★		

Kenyan and other imported French (dwarf or shoelace) beans seem to be available year round. The other decent imports are large flat green beans from North Africa and the Canaries in late winter/early spring. Otherwise mostly British, some hot-house in winter and spring. Frozen are serviceable.

GREENS: see Cabbages

HERBS

Many fresh herbs are now grown year-round in this country for the retail and restaurant trade. These are supplemented by imports, especially from Israel and the Mediterranean. Most main branches of supermarkets will have a range (often badly washed and trimmed and crammed into tiny polystyrene trays), otherwise try speciality greengrocers. Below are a few of the most common and best tasting with a few basic ideas for use. The only herbs that have a valid separate life dried, best used in stews and other long-cooked wet dishes or where specifically required (for example, see page 76) are bay, mint, oregano, rosemary, sage and thyme. All the rest are cop-outs.

	J	F	M	A	M	J	J	A	S	O	N	D
Basil	·	·	·	○	○	★	★	★	★	○	·	·
	☆	☆	●	●	●	●	☆					

King of herbs, with a lush strong flavour that goes well with tomatoes. Widely used in Mediterranean (especially Provençal and Italian) and Indian dishes.

	J	F	M	A	M	J	J	A	S	O	N	D
Bay Leaves	○	○	○	○	○	○	○	○	○	○	○	○

Essential component of French bouquet garni. Widely used to flavour stocks, sauces, stews and so on. Lends an aromatic note when skewered with other ingredients on to kebabs of fish or meat before grilling.

	J	F	M	A	M	J	J	A	S	O	N	D
Chervil	·	·	·	☆	★	☆	☆	·	·	·	·	·
				○	●	○	○					

Very delicate feathery leaves with a faint musty, aniseedy flavour. One of the *fines herbes* of the classical French kitchen and excellent with fish and egg dishes. Scarcer in the shops than the others, perhaps because it has a shorter shelf-life.

	J	F	M	A	M	J	J	A	S	O	N	D
Chives	○	○	○	☆	☆	☆	☆	☆	☆	☆	☆	☆
	☆	☆	☆	○	○	○	○	○	○	○	○	○

Gently oniony, thin green grass. Snip over almost anything.

	J	F	M	A	M	J	J	A	S	O	N	D
Coriander	☆	☆	☆	☆	☆	☆	☆	☆	☆	☆	☆	☆
	○	○	○	○	○	○	○	○	○	○	○	○

Sold in decent bunches only in some Indian, Chinese and Cypriot stores; although widely available in supermarkets, they sell it in pathetic little packs, insufficient to flavour a sparrow. Also called Chinese parsley (it can resemble flat-leaf parsley, see below) and, in Latin American cookery, cilantro. Fresh green coriander is the plant of the spice, coriander seed, although its flavour is entirely different and the two are not interchangeable in recipes. Its distinctive, fresh, pungent, sweaty flavour is an essential part of Indian, South-East Asian, Middle-Eastern and South and Central American cuisines.

See also pp. 94-5 (recipe).

J F M A M J J A S O N D

Dill   · · · ☆ ★ ★ ☆ · · · ·
        ○ ● ● ○ ○

Fronds of slender leaves with a fresh, mild lemony-aniseedy flavour. Good with spring vegetables (especially broad beans and cucumber), fish (especially salmon). Used as the curing agent to turn raw salmon into gravadlax. A favourite herb of northern and eastern Europe and Scandinavia. Do not confuse with seed.

See also p. 121 (recipe).

J F M A M J J A S O N D

Fennel   · · · · ☆ ☆ ★ ★ ☆ · · ·
          ○ ○ ● ● ○

Similar to dill but slightly coarser in appearance and more assertive in flavour. Good with fish. Popular around Mediterranean. Do not confuse with seed.

J F M A M J J A S O N D

Marjoram/Oregano   · · · · ☆ ☆ ★ ★ ☆ · · ·
                    ○ ○ ● ● ○

Close relatives. Fine peppery fragrance good with many vegetables, tomato-based dishes, egg dishes, red meat and plain fish. Essential to Mediterranean cuisines especially Italian and Greek.

J F M A M J J A S O N D

Mint   · · ○ ☆ ★ ★ ★ ★ ★ ☆ ·
        ○ ● ● ● ● ● ○

One of the few herbs used with confidence in most British kitchens. As well as ordinary spearmint, there are dozens of varieties with other overtones; pineapple, apple, lemon, mint and so on.

Parsley

J F M A M J J A S O N D
☆ ☆ ☆ ☆ ★ ★ ★ ★ ★ ★ ★ ☆
○ ○ ○ ○   ○

The curly sort is the most used herb in British cookery. The Mediterranean flat-leaf sort (available here in summer), has a fuller flavour. Also see coriander, above.

See also p. 167 (recipe).

Rosemary

J F M A M J J A S O N D
• • • ○ ☆ ★ ★ ★ ★ ☆ ☆ •
               ○

Tough dark-green needles with strong distinctive perfume. Excellent with lamb and other meats. Remove from dishes before serving. Makes a pretty, but inedible garnish.

Sage

J F M A M J J A S O N D
• • • ○ ○ ☆ ★ ★ ★ ★ ☆ ☆
            ○ ● ● ● ○ ○ ○

Furry grey-green leaves associated in British cookery with pork and stuffings. Also good with poultry. A bit of a brute – use sparingly.

Savory

J F M A M J J A S O N D
• • • • • • • • • • • •

Winter and summer varieties both give a mild, warm, peppery fragrance. Perfect with broad beans and as a subtle stand-in where thyme would also be suitable.

Tarragon

J F M A M J J A S O N D
• • ○ ○ ○ ★ ★ ☆ ☆ ○ • •
          ☆ ● ● ○ ○

Fine, fresh, lemony-aniseedy flavour. One of classical French cuisines *fines herbes*. Great with chicken, fish, eggs dishes, cream sauces and some vegetables.

Thyme

J F M A M J J A S O N D
• • • ○ ○ ● ★ ★ ★ ☆ ○ ○
         ☆ ● ● ● ○

Powerfully aromatic herb, good with meats, some vegetable, grills, roasts, tomato-based dishes, stews, cheese dishes and so on. Well-used around the Mediterranean.

HORSE-RADISH: see European Exotics

JERUSALEM ARTICHOKES   J F M A M J J A S O N D
                            ★ ★ ★   ☆ ★

Smallish, thin skinned, light brown, more or less knobbly tubers. Absolutely no relation of globe artichoke. British grown.

Avoid soft, small and broken ones. The knobblier they are, the more difficult to peel. Look out also for the little round holes which indicate that slugs have already snacked.

This root vegetable discolours easily when raw. If peeling, use stainless implements and cook in acidulated water.

Either scrape off the skin and the twiddlier knobs, then bring to the boil from cold in salted water acidulated with lemon juice, cover pan and cook until tender (about 15 minutes – a skewer should glide in easily). Or boil in their skins then pull off the skins when cool enough to handle. Can also be steamed, roasted or baked (peeled or unpeeled), or puréed for vegetable sauces or soups. The ultimate way of cooking them is to par-boil them peeled, drain well, then sauté slowly until a golden brown crust forms.

Eat hot, whole as accompanying vegetable, or in casseroles, stews and the like. Also good gratinéed with cheese sauce or similar. Or dress with vinaigrette and eat tepid or cold in salads.

See also pp. 40-1 (recipe).

KOHLRABI   J F M A M J J A S O N D
                            ★ ★   ★ ★ ★ ★ ★

British grown. Strange white, purple or pale-green skinned, round vegetble – half root and half bloated stem. The smaller the better. Tinies can be grated raw or cut into matchstick strips then dressed with vinaigrette or mayonnaise. Otherwise steam or boil, then peel and use like turnips.

LADY'S FINGERS: see Okra

LAMB'S LETTUCE: see Lettuce and Other Salad Leaves

LEEKS   J F M A M J J A S O N D
                            ★ ★ ★ ★ ☆   ☆ ★ ★ ★ ★ ★

Mostly British with some European imports. Wash carefully to remove ingrained dirt by splitting in half almost to the root-end and shuffling the leaves under running water.

See also p. 72 (recipe suggestion); pp. 37-8 and 82-3 (recipes).

LEMON GRASS: see Eastern Exotics

LETTUCE AND OTHER SALAD LEAVES

J F M A M J J A S O N D

· · · ● ★ ★ ★ ★ ☆ · ·

○ ○ ○ ☆   ○ ○ ○

British. See also Watercress plus imports. The traditional British garden lettuce – butterhead, round or cabbage lettuce – is at last being shouldered out in favour of a wide range of salads, although I retain a lingering affection for its floppy, mild, gently soporific leaves.

The small, tight-hearted Little Gem has an excellent flavour. The almost flavourless, crisp-hearted Iceberg keeps well in the fridge (just take off a slice as required) for a few days. It's fine in hamburgers and tuna sandwiches, but otherwise a bit relentless. Of other crisp lettuces Cos – particular the sweetest strain, Romaine – has an infinitely superior flavour to Webb's.

Of the more exotic leaves that have begun to take over the supermarket shelves, several are members of the chicory or endive family, all bitter to some extent. Examples include the deep purply-red, white-veined radicchio; the frizzy-leafed, light yellow-hearted frisée or curly endive; and the broad-leafed green, tinged with red, escarole.

The shape of the bronzed red, milder tasting feuille de chêne or oakleaf lettuce is obvious. Batavia, which may be green, red or halfway between, is a lettuce closely resembling escarole. Then there are modern hybrids such as the frothy lollo rosso, which is like a curly leafed, almost tasteless escarole. The othe rmost commonly available of the new-wave salad leaves is lamb's lettuce, corn salad or mâche which has small, dark green, tongue-shaped leaves, a soft texture and a mild, almost meaty taste.

Nasturtium flowers add a good peppery note to salads and are available in late spring and summer from some retailers.

MACHE: see Lettuce and Other Salad Leaves

MANGE-TOUT PEAS

J F M A M J J A S O N D

· · ○ ○ ○ ● ★ ★ ★ ○ · ·

               ★

British and world-wide imports. Flat-podded with vestigial peas. The whole thing is eaten. Popular in Chinese and South-East Asian cuisines.

Freshness is all. Do not buy large, marked, wilted or floppy ones.

Top, tail and string, then steam, cook briefly in boiling, salted water, or stir-fry in very hot, bland oil. Eat hot, when cooked and flexible but still retaining some crunch in the mouth.

Similar is the more rarely available sugar-snap pea, in which the pods are round and the peas more developed. Once again, the whole thing is eaten.

Although frozen mange-touts cannot retain a crisp texture, their flavour is often very good – sometimes better than fresh specimens that have effectively spent longer getting from the plant to your plate.

MARJORAM: see Herbs

MARROWS AND SQUASHES

J F M A M J J A S O N D
● ● ● ● ○ ○ ○ ★ ★ ☆ ☆
☆ ☆ ☆ ☆ · ☆ ☆ ○ ○ ○ ○ ○

British marrows which would win the village show tend to be watery, coarse textured and taste very mild. They are suitable only for stuffing with mince and rice for re-runs of school dinners or boiling up into unpleasant preserves for giving away to enemies. Small, however, is beautiful . . . small and dense . . . when they can be cubed and sautéed or steamed, tossed in butter and served as a reasonable vegetable.

British-grown summer squashes are mostly the small, spherical, thin-skinned Tender and True, and the pie-shaped Patty Pan (best eaten small and young).

Far more exciting are all the imported varieties (many from the Mediterranean and USA), from the flying-saucer shaped 'turban' and elongated, chrome yellow 'crookneck' to the dense, orange-fleshed 'butternut' and smooth cylindrical 'spaghetti marrow', or 'vegetable spaghetti', with its flesh made up of spaghetti-like strands. Some are grown in autumn and winter, some in summer. Some have thin skins, some thick. The full list of names would run into treble figures.

Treat thin-skinned varieties like courgettes. Thick skinned, dense varities should be peeled and sautéed, steamed or boiled, then tossed with butter or other dressing, or mashed with butter and seasoning, to eat as a vegetable. Boil spaghetti squash whole for 30-40 minutes until it feels soft, then cut in half and eat the strands dressed with butter and cheese or a pasta sauce. Boil the apple-sized Little Gem whole and remove seeds after cooking.

The biggest treat is butternut squash, cut in half lengthways, seeds removed, then brushed with butter and seasoning (perhaps including brown sugar) and baked at Gas 6/200°C/400°F for about an hour. Eat the flesh, garnished with chives and more butter, straight from the skin like an avocado, or mash with butter.

See also p. 69 (recipe).

MARSH SAMPHIRE: see European Exotics/Samphire

METHI: see Eastern Exotics

MINT: see Herbs

MOOLI: see Eastern Exotics

MORELS: see Funghi

MUSHROOMS, CULTIVATED

J	F	M	A	M	J	J	A	S	O	N	D
☆	☆	☆	☆	☆	☆	☆	☆	☆	☆	☆	☆

See also Funghi

British with some imports. Mainly available as white buttons, sometimes as more open 'cups', sometimes as fully open 'flats'. The distinctive brown cap variety has the most flavour.

Frozen usually have an unpleasant spongy texture, although very small ones are sometimes alright sautéed in butter from frozen. Dried sometimes have a surprisingly good flavour in stews and so on. Tinned have a distinctive flavour which you either like or not.

See also pp. 135-6 and 205-6 (recipes).

NASTURTIUM FLOWERS: see Lettuce and Other Salad Leaves

NEW POTATOES: see Potatoes

OAKLEAF LETTUCE: see Lettuce and Other Salad Leaves

OKRA

J	F	M	A	M	J	J	A	S	O	N	D
●	●	●	●	●	●	●	●	●	●	●	○

Imported from Cyprus, Egypt, Kenya, Mexico and Zambia, and used widely in Indian, Middle Eastern, African and American cuisines.

Okra pods or lady's fingers have a downy skin and excude a thick, slimy juice when cut or cooked. In over-stewed or carelessly prepared dishes, the combination can be disgusting. Avoid outsize pods, which may be stringy, or stale ones that are very soft or dull in colour and going black at the tip and edges, rather than bright green all over.

Wash well, then cut off the hard conical stem caps, without slicing into the seed chamber, to cook whole. Or slice thinly or thickly for fried or lightly braised dishes.

Tinned have a distinctively tinned taste and soft, gelatinous texture that some people adore.

See also pp. 77-8 and 195-6 (recipes).

ONIONS

	J	F	M	A	M	J	J	A	S	O	N	D
Brown cooking	★	★	☆	☆	☆	☆	☆	★	★	★	★
	○	○	○	○	○	○	○	○			
Pickling								★	★	★	☆
Spanish									●	●	●

Strong Red   • • •
See also Spring Onions, Herbs/Chives, European Exotics/Shallots.
British and imports from as far away as Hungary, Poland and Chile. For
some reason, very few retailers sell top-grade ordinary cooking onions
(look at the label – it will usually say 'grade II'). The large mild Spanish
onions are used raw in salads.

Dried onions have a devoted following in the States, where, for
example, they are crumbled into salads and sandwich fillings.

See also pp. 248-9 (recipe).

OREGANO: see Herbs

OYSTER MUSHROOMS: see Funghi

PAK CHOI: see Eastern Exotics

PARSLEY: see Herbs

PARSNIPS   J F M A M J J A S O N D
                                              ★ ★ ★ ★   ★ ★ ★ ★ ★

British grown.
See also pp. 72 and 216-7 (recipe suggestions); pp. 82-3 (recipe).

PEAS   J F M A M J J A S O N D
                                              ☆ ★ ☆ ☆ ☆
                                              ○ ○ ○ ○ ○ ○

British with imports from France, Cyprus, Kenya, Tanzania and Zambia.
As a nation we tend to eat our peas tinned or frozen. Unless the fresh
ones really are fresh, they can be disappointing. Pod, then tip into boiling
salted water with a sprig of fresh mint and cook, lid off, for 10-15 minutes
(less if really young and fresh). Gardeners get the best flavour.

Frozen and tinned can be jolly nice, but one taste of the real thing and
you'll know what you've been missing.

See also pp. 156-7 (recipe).

PEPPERS: see Capsicums; Chilli Peppers

PICKLING ONIONS: see Onions

PIEDMONTESE TRUFFLES: see Funghi/White Truffles

PLEUROTTES: see Funghi/Oyster Mushrooms

PLUM TOMATOES: see Tomatoes

PORCINI: see Funghi/Ceps

POTATOES	J	F	M	A	M	J	J	A	S	O	N	D
New	○	○	○	○	★	★	★	☆				
							○					
Old	★	★	★	☆	☆	·			☆	★	★	★

British, with the only notable imports being early new potatoes; most come from North Africa and the Mediterranean but the best are fabulous Jersey Royals. The other truly exquisite variety that is reasonably widely available during its short late summer and autumn season is the pink fir apple. This is long and small, best used in salads.

As with apples, there are hundreds of varieties, each with its particular character. And, although the same half dozen or so comparatively reliable sorts tend to crop up in the shops, there seems to be more choice than a few years ago.

Of the new potatoes, Maris Bard is the commonest – white and boring, Home Guard ditto, Ulster Sceptre okay, Pentland Javelin fine, Epicure excellent (but not widely available). Dreary potatoes from later in the season are Wilja, Estima, Pentland Crown, Pentland Dell, Pentland Hawk and Cara.

Decent waxy main-crop potatoes for roasting, sautéeing, thin chips, home-made crisps or game chips, boiling to serve in pieces, and cutting up into casseroles, braises and stews, include the red-skinned Desiree and Romano. Decent floury potatoes for baking, mashing and thick British-style chips inclujde the workday Maris Piper, Pentland Squire and excellent King Edward.

Frozen, vacuum-packed and tinned new potatoes are disgusting. Dried mash powder or granules have their uses although never match the real thing.

See also pp. 32 and 133 (recipe suggestions); pp. 42, 55-6, 77-9, 210 and 211 (recipes).

PUMPKINS	J	F	M	A	M	J	J	A	S	O	N	D
	○	○	○	○					★	★	★	★

British imports of the familiar large orange-skinned variety hollowed out for Hallowe'en lanterns. Also look for the denser-fleshed Jamaican type in specialist shops.

See also pp. 200-1 (recipe suggestion); p. 214 (recipe).

PURPLE SPROUTING BROCCOLI: see Broccoli

RADICCHIO: see Lettuce and Other Salad Leaves

RADISHES   J F M A M J J A S O N D
                                  · · ★ ★ ★ ★ ★ ★ ☆ · ·

British and imported. Buy when very hard and crisp, preferably in bunches
with the leaves still on. For maximum crunch, soak in iced water for 2-3
hours before trimming and serving.

RED CABBAGE: see Cabbage

RED ONIONS: see Onions

ROCKET: see European Exotics

ROCK SAMPHIRE: see European Exotics/Samphire

ROOT CELERY: see Celeriac

ROSEMARY: see Herbs

RUNNER BEANS: see Green Beans

SAGE: see Herbs

SALSIFY   J F M A M J J A S O N D
                                  ● ● ● ● ○   ○ ● ●
                                  ★ ★ ★ ☆   ☆ ★ ★

Sometimes called 'vegetable oyster'. A long, slender, pale skinned root
vegetable. Most of the best in the shops is imported from Belgium and
France although there is a small British crop. It and the dark skinned scorzonera are interchangeable in recipes.

Look for firm, smooth, regular, tapered roots and handle them carefully.
They almost invariably come covered in dirty sand and so must be
thoroughly scrubbed. Damage results in the vegetable "bleeding". Use
stainless implements and acidulated water to keep cut vegetable from discolouring and when boiling. Better to peel after cooking.

Eat hot or warm as a vegetable, plain, tossed in butter or covered in
sauce. Good in gratins, casseroles and so on. Par-boiled lengths lend themselves to frying. Can also be used cooked and cold in salads.

Tinned and frozen salsify isn't bad in gratins and casseroles.

See also p. 38 (recipe suggestion).

SAMPHIRE: see European Exotics

SAVORY: see Herbs

SAVOY CABBAGE: see Cabbages

SCORZONERA   J F M A M J J A S O N D
                                          • •   ○ • •
                                          ☆ ☆   ☆ ☆ ☆

Also called "black salsify". Mostly imported from Belgium and the
Netherlands, minute British production. Looks like salsify, but dark-
skinned. Interchangeable with salsify in any recipe.

SEA FENNEL: see European Exotics/Samphire

SEAKALE: see European Exotics

SEAKALE BEET: see European Exotics/Chard

SHALLOTS: see European Exotics

SHIITAKE MUSHROOMS: see Funghi

SPANISH ONIONS: see Onions

SPARROW GRASS: see Asparagus

SPINACH   J F M A M J J A S O N D
                                          • • ★ ★ ★ ○ ○ ☆ ☆ ☆ ☆
                                                              ○ ○

Mainly UK with European and Mediterranean imports.

Buy perky-looking leaves and much more than it looks as if you need, as
they melt away to nothing in the pan. Check for a spongy appearance or
dark green slime around the edges. Leaves in cellophane supermarket
packs are particularly prone to rotting.

Pick over leaves very carefully, pulling off coarse stalks and discarding
yellowing, wilted, damaged or half-eaten ones. Wash by swishing around
energetically in at least three changes of cold, fresh water. Either tear into
shreds before cooking or chop when cooked if you are not using the whole
leaves.

Either plunge into generous quantities of boiling, salted water for 2-3
minutes this gets rid of potentially tooth-enamel-eating acids, then remove, drain thoroughly – sqeezing to remove as much liquid as possible –
and finish by tossing in butter or whatever. Or put leaves wet from
washing straight into a dry saucepan over a low-medium flame, cover, and
leave to wilt in their own juices, which takes 5-6 minutes. Then toss in
butter and squeeze thoroughly with the back of a slotted spoon as you
serve.

Spinach is very apt to be watery, which ruins it. Pressing out extraneous liquid is important.

This vegetable has a special affinity with butter, cream and minute quantities of nutmeg. Slovenly cooks might consider cooking the leaves as above hours in advance of serving, then reheating them gently in butter with seasonings, or puréeing them and heating through in double cream. Spinach makes good soups.

Very young, fresh leaves can be served raw as a salad (especially good scattered with hot bread croûtons and crisp, diced bacon).

Leave tinned spinach to Popeye, unless, like the eponymous proprietress of Nirmal's Indian restaurant in Sheffield, you can be bothered to cook it for three days with gradually more complex spicing. Frozen spinach can be okay – the whole leaf sort rather than the finely chopped.

SPINACH BEET: see European Exotics/Chard

SPRING GREENS: see Cabbages

SPRING ONIONS	J F M A M J J A S O N D
	· · ★ ★ ★ ★ ★ ☆ ☆ ☆ · ·

Mostly British. Essential component of Chinese cookery.

My latest discovery is that by griddling them in a heavy, dry frying pan over a fierce flame until blackened in wide stripes down the sides, you end up with something exceptionally delicious, with a faint taste of brown sugar. Eat without any dressing except a mean sprinkling of salt.

See also pp. 99-100 and 157-8 (recipes).

SPROUTING BROCCOLI: see Broccoli

SPROUTS: see Brussels Sprouts or Oriental Exotics

SPRUE: see Asparagus

SQUASHES: see Marrows and Squashes

SUGAR-SNAP PEAS: see Mange-tout Peas

SWEDES	J F M A M J J A S O N D
	★ ★ ★ ★ ☆ ☆ ★ ★ ★ ★

British grown, who else would bother? Best used conservatively in Cornish pasties.

SWEETCORN

J F M A M J J A S O N D
○   ○ ○ ● ☆ ☆ ● ○ ○
☆ ● ☆

See also Eastern Exotics/Baby Corn

A sort of maize, sometimes called corn on the cob. British plus imports.

The grains should be plump and pale, the cob full. Can be bought in its leaf-sheath with silky tassel still attached, or trimmed and packed.

Freshness if of prime importance to flavour. In some parts of America, they don't even pick the stuff until the rest of dinner is prepared and the pot's already boiling.

Boil whole in already boiling salted water for 5-8 minutes until just tender. Can also be brushed with oil and griddled or barbecued for 10-15 minutes or brushed with butter and baked wrapped in foil for 30-40 minutes at Gas 6/200°C/400°F. Eat hot or warm in your fingers with plenty of salt, pepper and more butter.

Otherwise, cut the raw corn off the cob and boil for 3-5 minutes, drain immediately, toss in butter and serve. Also good for soups.

Tinned and frozen cannot be dismissed.

See also pp. 188-90 (recipe).

SWEET PEPPERS: see Capsicums

SWISS CHARD: see European Exotics/Chard

TARO: see Western Exotics/Yams

TARRAGON: see Herbs

THYME: see Herbs

TOMATOES

J F M A M J J A S O N D
· · · ☆ ☆ ★ ★ ★ ★ ☆ · ·
● ● ● ● ● ● ○

British and multifarious imports. The ordinary salad tomato can be a dull, watery little beast, especially winter imports from Israel and almost any imports from the Netherlands. In spring and early summer, the tastiest come from the Canaries, Spain and the Channel Islands. The best of ripe, red British in summer and late summer can be excellent.

Nothing, however, approaches the flavour of Mediterranean imports in high summer, especially the Provençal, Italian and Spanish varieties. The large beef or marmande tomatoes, with their dense flesh and comparatively few seeds can be tasty in summer from these same places (ignore

Dutch ones). So can their intensely red plum ones, which are the best for cooking with.

Cherry tomatoes are sweetest from June to September. Check that you buy the distincticly flavoursome proper cherry tomato rather than runts from ordinary varieties (the label should make this clear).

Given the often anaemic opposition, tinned tomatoes sometimes seem the best alternative for full-flavoured cooking. Purée needs careful handling not to taste raw and uninteresting (fry it off in a little olive oil until it darkens a few shades before using). Dried tomatoes are an intensely flavoured, if expensive, treat.

See also pp. 167-8; pp. 195-6 (recipes).

TOPS: see Cabbages

TRUFFLES: see Funghi/Truffles

TURNIPS

J F M A M J J A S O N D
★ ★ ★ ○ ★ ★ ☆ ☆ ★ ★ ★ ★
☆ ● ●

British and imported (especially very small new season varieties from France).

See also p. 217 (recipe suggestion).

TURNIP TOPS: see Cabbages

VEGETABLE OYSTER: see Salsify

WATER CHESTNUTS: see Eastern Exotics

WATERCRESS

J F M A M J J A S O N D
☆ ☆ ☆ ★ ★ ★ ★ ☆ ☆ ☆ ☆ ☆

British grown. Supplies can drop off in very cold weather.

See also pp. 50-1 (recipe suggestion).

WESTERN EXOTICS (AFRICAN, CARIBBEAN AND AMERICAN)

See also Chilli Peppers; Herbs/Coriander; Okra.

Increasingly available in supermarkets. A more splendid range is to be found in markets and shops serving ethnic communities.

J F M A M J J A S O N D
Chayote   ○ ○ ○ ○ ○ ○ ○ ○ ○ ○ ○ ○

Called christophene in the West Indies. Deepy furrowed, pear-shaped member of squash family, popular in Mexico. The younger and paler the better. Both skin and seed can be eaten from more tender specimens. The flesh is crisp and juicy, good for stir-fries, blanched in salads, cooked like courgettes or stuffed and baked.

J F M A M J J A S O N D
o o o o o o o o o o o o

Dudi

African representative of the large family of gourds, which has both bitter and mild other members. This mild one, sometimes called calabash, is generally smooth and bottle shaped. Cook like a large courgette.

J F M A M J J A S O N D
o o o o o o o o o o o o

Plantain

Large, floury, unsweet bananas, always eaten cooked. Staple to the Caribbean, South and Central America and Central Africa. Can be boiled in their skins for about 30 minutes; ripe ones, black-skinned, can also be peeled and fried in lengthways slices. Also good roasted or barbecued (slit the skin first).

J F M A M J J A S O N D

Sweet Potatoes

Elongated red, beige or brown-skinned tuber. Comes in sizes from not much larger than a large baking potato to ten times as big. Glorious orangey sweetish flesh. Cook like a potato; either peel and boil or steam, then mash with butter or bake.

See also p. 241 (recipe suggestion).

J F M A M J J A S O N D
o o o o o o o o o o o o

Yams

There are many varieties of starchy root vegetable that fall under this heading, including the sweet potato above). They come variously from Africa, the Caribbean, South America and Asia. The biggest are the white, common and yellow yams – most with dark matted skins and creamy or white flesh, some as large as an obese cat. Varieties of taro, such as Dasheen and Eddoe, are smaller but used in the same way. All are boiled, baked or roasted like potatoes. Most have rather waxy stodgy consistencies, which are an acquired taste.

WHITE CABBAGE: see Cabbages

WHITE RADISH: see Eastern Exotics/Mooli

WHITE SPROUTING BROCCOLI: see Broccoli

WHITE TRUFFLE: see Funghi

WITLOOF: see Belgian Chicory

YAMS: see Western Exotics

ZUCCHINI: see Courgettes

FRUIT

As with vegetables, fruit is often no cheaper in supermarkets than at high street greengrocers. Markets often offer the best value.

ALMONDS

J F M A M J J A S O N D
● · · · · · · · · · ● ●

Of course pre-packed almonds – shelled, blanched, split, ground and so on – are available all year as a cookery ingredient. But the sweetest imports, in the shell for cracking and eating as a dessert nut, come in around the Christmas period.

See also p. 33 (recipe suggestion).

APPLES

J F M A M J J A S O N D
★ ☆ ☆ ○ · · · ☆ ★ ★ ★ ★
    ○ ○ ○

Less than half our total consumption of apples is now British-grown. Of the imports, French and Italian Golden Delicious taste fine at the beginning of their season in early autumn, Granny Smiths from Europe and the southern hemisphere have a certain relentless crunch and tang, and North American reds can be good here at the beginning of the year.

The British season is basically September to January, with a few earlies in August (notably Discovery – best eaten very young and fresh) and a few stragglers from cold store available through until April. Of the hundreds of varieties that have been cultivated in Britain over the centuries, the largest sector of the retail market concentrates on half a dozen or so, of which

Cox's Orange Pippin and Egremont Russet are immediately the most attractive in flavour.

Through specialist greengrocers, farm-gate sales, markets and dedicated fruit farms, make your own voyage of discovery through any other varieties you can find, especially the older ones.

See also pp. 232-3 (recipe).

APRICOTS   J F M A M J J A S O N D
                                          · · ★ ★

Mediterranean imports and British-grown. When ripe, this small single-stoned fruit's velvety yellow skin blushes orange and red. The flesh should be sweet and juicy.

Dried apricots are at their soft, tangy best imported from the Mediterranean between December to February, when many stores sell them loose.

ASIAN PEARS (Nashi)   J F M A M J J A S O N D
                                      ● ● ○ ●   ○   ★ ★ ● ● ●
                                                            ☆

Small British crop; imports from China, Japan, North Korea, Taiwan and New Zealand. Round fruit with a skin resembling a russet apple, very crisp white flesh and a mild sweet flavour. Best eaten peeled.

BANANAS   J F M A M J J A S O N D
                                          · · · ○ ○ ○ · · · · · ·

Imported from Africa, the Caribbean, Central and South America. The trade reckons the best come in late spring, especially from the Windward Isles and Jamaica.

BILBERRIES   J F M A M J J A S O N D
                                                  ★ ★
                                                  ○ ○

Also called whortleberries (*myrtilles* in France), these small dark blue berries with a slight bloom have an unassertive tang. Good for tarts, pies and sauces.

BLACKBERRIES   J F M A M J J A S O N D
                                                  ★ ★ ★ ★

Commercially grown varieties of the common hedgerow bramble are soft, less pippy and very perishable. Buy to eat on the same day. Teams well with apple in many a rustic crumble. The mild, winey flavour also complements game well. Makes excellent jam.

See also pp. 197-8 (recipe).

BLACKCURRANTS   J F M A M J J A S O N D
                                                        ★ ★
                                                         ○ ○

The most widely used and robustly flavoured of the currants – sharp and
fruity. The distinctive character shows itself off well in tarts, pies, jams, jellies, sweet and savoury coulis and sauces, ices and so on. Flavours the
French liqueur *creme de cassis*, which is a useful ingredient in its own right
for adding punch to meat sauces as well as scenting white wine (especially
from the Aligoté grape) to make the famous aperitif, *kir*.

BLUEBERRIES   J F M A M J J A S O N D
                                                      ★ ★ ★
                                                       ○ ○ ○

Plump, mild, blue-black berry with slight bloom. Good for pies and tarts as
well as cooking in various batters to make American-style breakfast foods
such as blueberry muffins and blueberry pancakes.
    See also p. 160 (recipe).

BRAZIL NUTS   J F M A M J J A S O N D
                                                 ● · · · · · · · · · ● ●

Imported in shells for cracking and eating as a dessert nut mostly around
Christmas. Available shelled, as a cookery ingredient and in packs of mixed
nuts throughout the year. One of the nastiest nuts when stale or off.

CAPE GOOSEBERRIES   J F M A M J J A S O N D
                                                 ● ● ● · ·   ●

Also called Physalis. A papery beige 'Chinese lantern' enclosing a spherical
orange berry with a fabulous tart, sweet, musty, aromatic flavour. The
restaurant trade dips them in fondant icing and serves them with the petits
fours after meals. Addicts eat them as they are. Relatively expensive.

CARAMBOLA: see Starfruit

CHERIMOYA: see Custard Apples

CHERRIES   J F M A M J J A S O N D
                                                      ○ ★ ★ ★ ·
                                                           ○

British-grown with American and European import to supplement and extend the season. Dessert varieties can be any colour from pale yellow to
blackest red. Perhaps the most well-known way of cooking them is in a
Yorkshire-pudding-style batter to make *clafoutis*. As a non-purist, I find

them toothsome with other red fruit in summer puddings. The sour cooking varieties such as Morello – available only for a very short summer season centring on August – are dark red and make delicious jams, pies, sauces, ices and so on.

See also pp. 160-1 (recipe).

CHESTNUTS

Softest and most delicate of nuts, generally eaten roasted, when the pliable casing and bitter, furry, inner skin is easier to remove, the texture softens further and the flavour is mild and earthy. To remove the skins for cooking, either pierce then roast or grill until the shell is blackened and hard, or blanch as follows. Cut a cross shape in the base, bring to the boil (from cold) in a saucepan of water, take off the heat and let them stand for a couple of minutes, then take out two or three at a time and peel them with gloved fingers. If the temperature of the water falls below hand-hot, put it back over a low flame for a while.

Tins of chestnut purée are useful standbys – sweetened for puddings, unsweetened for savoury stuffings and the like. Crystallised chestnuts – *marrons glacé* – are an expensive treat if you like their mealy texture and subtle flavour.

CLEMENTINES: see Easy-Peel Citrus

COCONUT

Supplies are kept up year-round from South-East Asia, from July to January, and Sri Lanka and the West Indies (especially Santo Domingo) for the rest of the time.

See also pp. 32-3 (recipe suggestion).

CRAB APPLES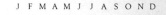

Small, sharp ancestor of large modern cultivated apples. Not commonly available. If you don't have your own tree, beg from someone who has or scout around Women's Institute market stalls. Good for making jelly.

CRANBERRIES

See p. 242 (recipe).

CUSTARD APPLES

J F M A M J J A S O N D
o o o ● ●

Dense, easily damageable globular or slightly heart-shaped fruit with green indented skin, slightly soft to a firm squeeze when ripe. Cut in half and eat the sweet, fragrant flesh with a spoon, spitting out the black seeds (from which the fruit gets its originally Peruvian other name, cherimoya) as you go. Beige, gritty and juiceless inside when frost-damaged or over-ripe.

DAMSONS

J F M A M J J A S O N D
★ ★

The best in England are sold at farm-gates in Cumbria's Lyth Valley in season. Makes excellent pies, crumbles, jellies, jams.

See p. 205 (recipe).

DATES

J F M A M J J A S O N D
● ● · · · · · · ● ● ●

Middle Eastern and North African staple. The fresh ones have a strange, fibrous texture and are less sweet than the dried, which I personally prefer.

EASY-PEEL CITRUS

J F M A M J J A S O N D

Clementines   ● ●   ● ●
Mineolas   ● ●
Ortaniques   ● ● ● ●   ●
Satsumas   ●   ● ● ●

Ortaniques, imported from Spain and Jamaica, are a sweet, juicy cross between an orange and a tangerine. As well as the most popular mandarin/tangerine crosses – such as the small, seedless clementines, and mild-tasting satsumas – look for varieties such as Kara, Mandora and Wilkings (spread through from late October to March), with their slight differences in balance of acidity and fragrance, and the late season Israeli Temple Jafferine (February to March) and Topaz (April)

FIGS

J F M A M J J A S O N D
● ● ● o

Fresh black figs should be bought when dense and yielding to a gentle squeeze. They should be sweet as nectar.

From November to February or so, the best of each Mediterranean autumn's soft, succulent, freshly-dried figs are imported from countries such as Turkey (Izmir are the best). These are in a different league to the hard, pippy blocks of dried fig that put many people off the fruit for life.

See also p. 201.

GOOSEBERRIES   J F M A M J J A S O N D
       ★ ★ ★

Love 'em or hate 'em.
   See also pp. 143-4 (recipe).

GRANADILLA: see Passion Fruit

GRAPEFRUIT   J F M A M J J A S O N D
       ○ ○ ○ ○ ○ ○ ○ • • ○ ○ ○

Pink grapefruits, a fruit for which Marks & Spencer claim to have created
the British market, are imported sporadically from Israel (winter/early
spring), Florida and California. Winter imports from Jaffa include the less
tart variety, sweetie.

GRAPES   J F M A M J J A S O N D
       • • • • • • • • • • • •

The sweetest and most distinctively fragrant are the late-season Muscats,
which should be eaten as dark and yellow as possible before they actually
start rotting. Other good varieties include Almeria, Alphonse, Italia,
Napoleon and Sultana.

GREENGAGES   J F M A M J J A S O N D
       • • ☆
       •

Small plums with a special fragrance and sweetness. The ripest should be
eaten unadorned; make tarts, pies, crumbles, jams and so on with the rest.

GUAVAS   J F M A M J J A S O N D
       • • • • • • • • • • • •

In Jane Grigson's words, 'smells better than it tastes', but the cubed flesh
adds an interesting musty note to exotic fruit salads. Also good for jams
and preserves.

HAZELNUTS   J F M A M J J A S O N D
       • • • • • • • • • ★ ★ ○
       ○ ○

Although available more or less all year as a cooking ingredient (imported
from countries such as Italy and Turkey), the best in-shell dessert nuts are
imported in the run up to Christmas. English crops of Kentish Cobs
(October) and the related filberts (November) top the lot for fresh, creamy
flavour.
   See also pp. 84-5 and 242-3 (recipes).

KARA: see Easy-Peel Citrus

KIWI FRUIT

J F M A M J J A S O N D
○ ○ ○ ○ ○ ○ ○ ○ ○ ○ ○ ○

This fluffy-skinned egg-shaped fruit with its startling translucent green flesh, tiny black seeds and white core, is the now decidedly passé emblem of *nouvelle cuisine's* bottom line. But don't underrate it; when perfectly ripe and well kept, it can have a delightfully balanced fragrance and fresh flavour.

KUMQUATS

J F M A M J J A S O N D
● ● ● · ·   ● ●

Tiny grape-shaped, orange, citrus fruit, of which the peel is often sweeter than the mouth-drawing flesh. Eat the whole thing.

See also pp. 73 and 236 (recipe suggestions).

LEMONS

J F M A M J J A S O N D
○ ○ ○ ○ ○ ○ ○ ○ ○ ○ ○ ○

See p. 73 (recipe suggestion); pp. 67-8 and 87 (recipes).

LIMES

J F M A M J J A S O N D
○ ○ ○ ○ ○ ○ ○ ○ ○ ○ ○ ○

LOGANBERRIES

J F M A M J J A S O N D
                    ★ ★

Large, bland blackberry/raspberry cross.

LOQUATS

J F M A M J J A S O N D
                ○ ●

Egg-sized soft japonica fruit with apricot-coloured, velvety skin and pale orange flesh concealing large, smooth pits. Sweetest when the skin is covered in brown patches and looks damaged, almost rotten. Very elusive flavour which disappears completely if the fruit is cooked.

See also p. 109.

LYCHEES

J F M A M J J A S O N D
● ●   ●

Imported from China and the Far East, the best varieties such as Dragon Eye can be bought on the branch from specialist oriental emporia for a dramatic dessert display. More usually, lychees are sold just as the waxy, slippery, pearly-white fruit with its two or three large, smooth pits

See also p. 52 (recipe suggestion).

MANGOES J F M A M J J A S O N D

○ ○ ○ ○ ○ ○ ● ● ● ● ● ●

Different varieties, of varying size and colour, from green tinged with yellow to a deep mottled red, are flown in from all over the world. As common in tropical zones as the apple is in temperate. The best are sweet and smooth-fleshed, the worst stringy and tasting of turpentine.

Judge ripeness from the fragrance, softness and healthy appearance – colour is not necessarily a guide.

See also pp. 247-8 (recipe).

MEDLARS J F M A M J J A S O N D

★

Hardly available at all through retail outlets. If you have access to a tree, eat the fruit when dark and almost rotten in appearance. Make excellent jelly.

MELONS J F M A M J J A S O N D

· · · · ○ ● ● ● ● ○ ○ ·

French, Spanish and Mediterranean imports with the season stretched and supplemented from further afield, especially the Amnericas. The varieties most commonly sold here are: cantaloup (best August to November) – a group of rough-skinned greeny-yellow melons with pinky orange flesh; charentais (best July to September) – green with fragant orange flesh; Gallia (best May to September) – a variety of 'netted' or 'musk' melon with yellow skin when ripe and pale green flesh; ogen (best July to November) – a type of cantaloup with smooth speckled green skin and pale green or golden flesh; watermelon (best July to October) – often very large, especially in the latter half of the season, and sold in slices with green skin and red, very juicy mild flesh shot through with big black pips; honeydew (best July to September) – yellow or green ribbed skin and pale flesh with a sweet, bland flavour when ripe.

If a melon is properly ripe, the area immediately around the stem smells good and yields to pressure.

See also pp. 164 and 184 (recipe suggestions).

MANDORA: see Easy-Peel Citrus

MINEOLAS: see Easy-Peel Citrus

MORELLO CHERRIES: see Cherries

MYRTILLES: see Bilberries

NASHI: see Asian Pears

NECTARINES   J F M A M J J A S O N D
                                              o ● ● ● o

Smooth-skinned peach with a full-flavoured edge of fine sweet plum. The
dark-red skinned ones are good enough, the white-fleshed ones even
better.

See also p. 164 (recipe suggestion).

ORANGES   J F M A M J J A S O N D
                                              ● ● o o · · · · · · ● ●

Imports available in some condition or other all year. Most commonly retailed varieties here are Spanish Navellinas (from November), over-taken
by Spanish and North African Navels (from December), with Israeli varieties such as Shamouti (from late December/January) running through
with Valencia lates until March or so. The sour Seville oranges, so good for
marmalade and duck sauces, have a short season during the first two
months of the year. Mild-tasting blood oranges are a mid-season treat.

See also p. 40 (recipe suggestion); pp. 47-8 (recipe).

ORTANIQUES: see
Easy-Peel Citrus

PAPAYA   J F M A M J J A S O N D
                                              · · · · · · · · · · · ·

Also called pawpaws, these look like large, hard-skinned, yellowy-green
pears. The fragrance will permeate the skin quite strongly when the fruit is
ripe. Cut in half, discard seeds, sprinkle with fresh lime juice and eat with a
spoon.

PASSION FRUIT   J F M A M J J A S O N D
                                              · · · · · · · · · · · ·

The commonest sort available here are slightly larger than a golf ball and
have a wrinkled dark auberginey-brown shell when ripe. Inside is a mucoid
knot of pale green seeds covered in delicious tangy yellow slime. Cut fruit
in half and eat with a teaspoon, swallowing pips and all. Very good pro-
cessed with fresh mango flesh to a purée and then sieved for an exotic fruit
sauce.

A larger, smooth, milder-tasting relation is the grenadilla.

PAWPAW: see Papaya

PEACHES

J F M A M J J A S O N D
○ ● ● ● ○

A delicate fruit, rarely found in tip-top condition after the rigours of import, although you have more chance with the white-fleshed varieties.

See also p. 164 (recipe suggestion); pp. 197-8 (recipe).

PEARS

J F M A M J J A S O N D
★ ★ ★ ○ · · · · ○ ★ ★ ★
○ ○   ○

As with apples, less than half of our supplies are grown in this country. The commonest British-grown varieties are long, tapering Conference, which has a yellowy-green skin with russeting and firm, bland, juicy flesh, and Comice – more perfumed, intense flavour, rounder in appearance and larger, with greeny-yellow, speckled skin and some russeting. Imported Williams take some beating.

See also pp. 230-1 (recipe).

PERSIMMONS

J F M A M J J A S O N D
○   ● ●

Apple-shaped but an even, deep orange colour all over, persimmons are incredibly astringent if slightly under-ripe, numbing your salivary glands until you think you have done irreperable damage. They turn inedibly watery if over-ripe. When perfect, they should have their tops cut off like eggs and be eaten with a spoon.

PHYSALIS: see Chinese Gooseberry

PINEAPPLES

J F M A M J J A S O N D
● ● ● ● ● · · · · · ● ●

Ripe pineapples feel heavy for their size with the scent of the flesh drifting appetisingly through the skin. The area immediately around the stem should yield to pressure. To peel efficiently, cut off base and top and stand it upright. Then cut down all round with a sharp knife to take the majority of the skin off. Now, holding the fruit in one hand, score deeply and at an angle under a spiral of 'eyes' from top to bottom. Repeat the other side of the same spiral of 'eyes' so that you have cut a 'V'-shaped groove removing that whole spiral. Repeat with the next spiral and continue until all have been removed and the fruit is grooved like a screw. Now cut across in thick slices. The harder core is sweet and crunchily edible in the ripest pineapples.

See also p. 73 (recipe suggestion); pp. 84-5 (recipe).

PLUMS   J F M A M J J A S O N D
                                         · · · · · · ○ ● ● · · ·

Favourite dessert varieties include Cambridgeshire and Oulin's Gage and
the famous purple Victoria. Good cookers include Early Prolific, Pershore
Yellow Egg and Warwickshire Drooper.

   See also p. 164; p. 198 (recipe).

POMEGRANATES   J F M A M J J A S O N D
                                         ●   ● ● ● ●

Look for specimens with hard, almost wizened skin streaked with red for
the sweetest contents.

   See also p. 201; pp. 214-15 (recipe).

POMELO   J F M A M J J A S O N D
                                         ● ●   ●

Coarse-textured, rather dry, bland citrus fruit. The enormous size, intem-
perate proportion of pith to flesh and yellowy-green colour of the skin,
make it, frankly, rather unappealing.

PRUNES   J F M A M J J A S O N D
                                         ● ● · · · · · · · · ● ●

The freshest are good eaten in the same way as dates.

QUINCES   J F M A M J J A S O N D
                                         ·   ★ ★ ·

Large, hard fruit like a misshapen pear with fuzzy skin. Wonderfully fragrant. The flesh is coarse and grainy. Usually used for preserves.

   See also p. 218 (recipe suggestion); p. 229 (recipe).

RASPBERRIES   J F M A M J J A S O N D
                                                 · ★ ★ ★ · ·

See also p. 147 (recipe suggestion).

REDCURRANTS   J F M A M J J A S O N D
                                                   ★ ★

The essential tang in summer pudding. Makes excellent tarts and preserves.

RHUBARB   J F M A M J J A S O N D
                                         ★ ★ ★ ★ ★   ★

The earliest Yorkshire forced, with its pale yellow leaves and thin, succulent, baby-pink stems, appears in December and runs through until March, by which time the outdoor crop is also on sale, finishing mid-May.

See also p. 52 (recipe suggestion); pp. 59-60 (recipe).

SATSUMAS: see Easy-Peel Citrus

SEVILLE ORANGES: see Oranges

SHARON FRUIT   J F M A M J J A S O N D
                                 • •   • •

A user-friendly variety of persimmon. Looks like a large, waxy, orange tomato and can be eaten whole, like an apple. They have dense orange flesh and, at their best (still quite firm), a taste as sweet as honey.

STAR FRUIT   J F M A M J J A S O N D
                                 • • • • • • • • • • • •

Also called carambola. Long, deeply-ridged yellow fruit, star-shaped in cross section. Unobjectionable watery tart flavour when ripe, quite sour when not.

STRAWBERRIES   J F M A M J J A S O N D
                                 • • • ○ ○ ★ ★ ★ ★ • • •

TAMARILLO   J F M A M J J A S O N D
                                 • • • • • • • • • • • •

Plum-shaped fruit from the Antipodes, sometimes called tree tomato. When ripe, the smooth skin is very dark purple/red, almost black, the flesh is soft and suppurating with blood-red juice, and the flavour is strong, tart and fragrant.

TEMPLE: see Easy-Peel Citrus

TOPAZ: see Easy-Peel Citrus

TREE TOMATO: see Tamarillo

UGLI   J F M A M J J A S O N D
                                 • • ○ ○

Looks like a rough, green grapefruit. Reasonably good flavour.

WALNUTS   J F M A M J J A S O N D
                                 ★ • • • • • • • • ★ ★ ★
                                 •   • • •

Available all year as a cookery ingredient and as a dessert nut sold in its shell around Christmas, but the fresh or 'wet' ones at the beginning of the season have an incomparable creamy flavour.

See also p. 201; pp. 213, 223 and 232-3 (recipes).

WHITECURRANTS　　　　　　　　　　J F M A M J J A S O N D
　　　　　　　　　　　　　　　　　　　　　　★ ★

The subtlest-flavoured of the currants. A rare treat for French-style open tarts. Also makes excellent jelly.

WHORTLEBERRIES: see Bilberries

WILKINGS: see Easy-Peel Citrus

FISH

A couple of autumns ago, after a week in Spain where excellent fish and shellfish are considered an everyday necessity, I all but lost interest in buying fish here. The Spanish fishmonger's regard and care for his produce was evident on every iced tray. In a Madrid market, the Saturday I left, there were 10 sorts of fresh prawn – most sold alive (rising to the equivalent of £65 kilo for the very best). In a comparable London market three days later, there were two – shell on or shell off – both frozen.

Drew Smith, editor of *The Good Food Guide*, was the first to sound a popularist alarm bell in his *Guardian* column. Most people in Britain do not have access to a good fishmonger, the small proportion of supermarkets that have a wet fish counter seem at best often merely to be selling thawed fish instead of rock-hard frozen, and Billingsgate is going to have to work awfully hard to restore its reputation with many of the best restaurant kitchens, who now use small suppliers in preference.

It's all very well printing a chart of fish in season, but pretty useless if almost nobody can buy them. If you are lucky enough to be in striking distance of a conscientious fishmonger's, feel smug and treasure it.

As supplies are brought here from further and further afield, with few exceptions, and weather permitting, most fish are available almost all year. Even the received wisdom about bivalves only being safe to eat when there's an 'r' in the month proves not to be strictly true as anyone who's been to Belgium in mid-summer and eaten a bowl of mussels will know.

The established bible of fish from the waters around Britain is Alan Davidson's *North Atlantic Seafood*.

BRILL   J F M A M J J A S O N D
          ★ ★ ★ ☆ ☆ ☆ ☆ ☆ ☆ ☆ ☆ ☆

Second only to turbot as a fine-fleshed, large, meaty flat-fish. Usually filleted before cooking.

 See also p. 165 (recipe suggestion).

CARP   J F M A M J J A S O N D
          ●   ● ● ●

Chiefly available imported from Israel around the end of the year. Roast or bake, perhaps with a stuffing.

CLAMS   J F M A M J J A S O N D
          ☆ ☆ ☆ ☆ ☆ ☆ ☆ ☆ ☆ ☆ ☆ ☆
          ○ ○ ○ ○ ○ ○ ○ ○ ○ ○ ○ ○

The small varieties are scrubbed then either shucked and eaten raw or cooked to open in the same way as mussels. They have a rich flavour and good, slightly chewy texture. The large brutes need 15 minutes in a medium-hot oven to open.

 See also p. 204 (recipe).

COCKLES   J F M A M J J A S O N D
          ☆ ☆ ☆ ☆ ☆ ☆ ☆ ☆ ☆ ☆ ☆ ☆

Bought live and treated like tiny clams, these are perhaps the most underrated of our shellfish. As they cook and open, they give out a delicious liquor.

COD   J F M A M J J A S O N D
          ★ ★ ☆ ☆ ☆ ☆ ☆ ☆ ★ ★ ★ ★

See also pp. 52 and 175 (recipe suggestions).

COLEY   J F M A M J J A S O N D
          ★ ★ ☆ ☆ ☆ ☆ ☆ ☆ ★ ★ ★ ★

Also called saithe. Less coarse when young. Treat like cod or haddock.

CONGER EEL   J F M A M J J A S O N D
          ★ ★ ★ ★ ☆ ☆ ☆ ☆ ☆ ★ ★ ★

Firm-fleshed, meaty white fish.
 See also p. 79 (recipe).

CRAB   J F M A M J J A S O N D
                                        · · · ★ ★ ★ ☆ ☆ ☆ ☆ ☆ ☆

See also p. 131 (recipe).

CRAWFISH   J F M A M J J A S O N D
                                            ★ ★ ★ ☆ ☆ ☆

Also called spiny lobster. Sweeter, denser and fuller-fleshed than ordinary
lobster, although it has no claws.

CRAYFISH   J F M A M J J A S O N D
                                        · · · · · · · · · · · ·

Small freshwater crustacean. Tender, sweet flesh.

DAB   J F M A M J J A S O N D
                                        ☆ ☆ ☆ ☆ ☆ ☆ ☆ ☆ ☆ ☆ ☆ ☆

Thin flat fish. Treat as plaice.

DOGFISH: see Huss

DOVER SOLE   J F M A M J J A S O N D
                                        ★ ★   ☆ ★ ★ ★ ★ ★ ★

King of the thin flat fish. The flesh is incomparably toothsome and silky.
The best need no more than to be cooked for several minutes on each side
under a pre-heated hot grill until the skin is well-charred and the flesh
cooked through but still just pink along the bone. Be careful, it is easy to
underestimate the cooking time (in this case, I think marginally over-
cooked is better than marginally under-cooked).
Serve with just a mean squeeze of lemon.

DUBLIN BAY PRAWNS: see Langoustines

EEL   J F M A M J J A S O N D
                                        ☆ ☆ ☆ ☆   · ☆ ★ ★ ★

Weird creature of fens and tidal rivers. Do they really all swim thousands
of miles only to debauch in the Sargasso Sea? A slightly strong, meaty flavour. Excellent smoked.
See also p. 237.

FLAKE: see Huss

FLOUNDER   J F M A M J J A S O N D
                                        ★ ★ ★   ☆ ☆ ☆ ☆ ☆ ☆

Thin flat fish. Much inferior to plaice.

GREENLAND HALIBUT: see Mock Halibut

GREY MULLET   J F M A M J J A S O N D
★ ★ · · · · ★ ★ ★ ★ ★ ★

Round, white fish resembling sea bass. Fry, grill or bake, perhaps with a stuffing.

GRILSE   J F M A M J J A S O N D
★ ★

Juvenile salmon. Treat as sea trout.

GURNARD   J F M A M J J A S O N D
★ ★ ★ ★ · · ★ ★ ★ ★ ★ ★

Firm-fleshed white fish with strange armoured head. Good for stews, bakes and fish pies.

HADDOCK   J F M A M J J A S O N D
★ ★ · · ★ ★ ★ ★ ★ ★ ★ ★

See also pp. 96 and 175 (recipe suggestions).

HAKE   J F M A M J J A S O N D
★ ★ · · · ★ ★ ★ ★ ★ ★ ★

Rich-flavoured, firm white fish.
See also pp. 175-6 (recipe).

HALIBUT   J F M A M J J A S O N D
★ ★ ★ ★   ★ ★ ★ ★ ★ ★

One of the firmest-fleshed of the large flat white fish. The cold-smoked Flemish version, thinly sliced with a squeeze of lemon and brown bread and butter, is a rarer treat than smoked salmon.
See also p. 97; pp. 165 and 175 (recipe suggestions).

HERRING   J F M A M J J A S O N D
★ ★ ☆   ☆ ★ ★ ★ ★ ★ ★ ★

Oily fish, now common and cheap again after a period of embargo following over-fishing. Grill, fry or bake, perhaps with a stuffing. Excellent pickled and smoked.

HUSS   J F M A M J J A S O N D
★ ★ ★ ☆ ☆   ☆ ★ ★ ★

Also called flake, rigg and dogfish. A soft, delicate-fleshed cartilaginous fish. Good fried.

See also p. 219 (recipe suggestion).

JOHN DORY   J F M A M J J A S O N D
★ ★ ★ · · · · · · · · ·

The bones and debris make a good stock. The fillets can be treated as plaice or sole.

LANGOUSTINES   J F M A M J J A S O N D
☆ ☆ ☆ ☆ ☆ ☆ ☆ ☆ ☆ ☆ ☆ ☆

Also called Dublin Bay prawns and scampi. Sea-living crustacean resembling a tiny lobster with attenuated claws. Good sweet flesh. Hard, finger-pricking shell.

See also p. 237 (recipe suggestion).

LEMON SOLE   J F M A M J J A S O N D
★ ★ ★ ★   ☆ ☆ ☆ ☆ ★

Good thin flat fish. Grill as for Dover sole.

LING   J F M A M J J A S O N D
★ ★ · · · · · · ★ ★ ★ ★

Unexciting cod relative.

LOBSTER   J F M A M J J A S O N D
· · · ★ ★ ★ ★ ★ ★ ☆ ☆ ☆

King crustacean. For the best flavour, buy live, then either bring slowly to the boil (from cold) in water, to soothe it to sleep before it dies; plunge straight into boiling water, which kills it in seconds; or bang the point of a large, sharp cook's knife straight down into the centre of the cross-shape on the top of its head, which kills it instantaneously.

See also pp. 187-8 (recipe).

MACKEREL   J F M A M J J A S O N D
★ ★ ★ ★ ★ ★ ☆ ☆ ☆ ☆ ★ ★

Plump, oily fish. Grill, fry or bake, perhaps with a stuffing.
See also pp. 139-40 (recipe).

MOCK HALIBUT   J F M A M J J A S O N D
· · · · ☆ ☆ · · · ☆ ☆ ☆

Stronger-flavoured than real halibut but not as firm.

MONKFISH   J F M A M J J A S O N D
                          ☆ ☆ ☆ ☆ ☆ ☆ ☆ ☆ ☆ ☆ ☆ ☆

Excellent, close-textured, pearly-white-fleshed fish. One of the few fish that works well on kebabs.

See also pp. 40 and 74 (recipe suggestions); pp. 137-8 and 155 (recipes).

MUSSELS   J F M A M J J A S O N D
                          ☆ ★ ★ ★   ☆ ★ ★ ★

Live mussels should be bought from cool, moist conditions and can be stored overnight in the bottom of the fridge wrapped in damp newspaper. For basic cleaning, scrub the mussels well under cold running water. Remove all barnacles by scraping with a small blunt knife. Pull off the 'beards' – knots of coarse, dark filaments, sticking out from between the shells. Throw away any mussels that float in a bowl of water, that do not close tightly when tapped firmly a couple of times, or that feel very heavy for their size and might prove to be full of mud. When clean, they will keep for a day or so in a bucket of fresh cold water. To assist the cleaning further, sprinkle a handful of oats into the bucket. The mussels ingest this and it apparently helps to purify their systems.

See also pp. 53 and 202 (recipe suggestions); pp. 55-7 and 220-1 (recipes).

OYSTERS   J F M A M J J A S O N D
                          ★ ★ ★ ★ · · · ☆ ★ ★ ★ ★

The Portuguese and Pacific varieties are available all year.

See also pp. 184-5; pp. 190-1 (recipe).

PILCHARDS   J F M A M J J A S O N D
                                     ★ ★ ★

This delicate, highly perishable oily fish has a short, exclusive season.

PLAICE   J F M A M J J A S O N D
                ★   ☆ ☆ ★ ★ ★ ★ ★ ★

Britain's most popular flat fish.

See also p. 165 (recipe suggestion).

PRAWNS   J F M A M J J A S O N D
                         · · ☆ ☆ ★ ★ ★ ★ ★ ★ ☆ ·
                                  ○ ○

See also pp. 102 and 111-2 (recipes).

RED MULLET   J F M A M J J A S O N D
                                         ○ ○ ● ● ●

Excellent small red Mediterranean fish with a fine earthy flavour and a toothsome liver. Grill, barbecue or bake.

RIGG: see Huss

SAITHE: see Coley

SALMON   J F M A M J J A S O N D
                                     ☆ ☆ ☆ ★ ★ ★ ★ ★ ☆ ☆ ☆ ☆

A perennial subject for debate is farmed salmon, which is available all year, discernably inferior to wild, which can only be caught from February to August. The farming-lobby point to consistent standards and prices that have actually fallen over the last 10 years. Others say that this can't begin to make up for wild's firmer, leaner texture and more complex flavour.

For the classic method to cook medium-sized whole salmon to serve cold, bring it to the boil from cold in a fish kettle, immersed in court bouillon (water with white wine, herbs and seasoning) or well-salted water (some advocate the degree of salinity of seawater, although this makes it difficult to use the stock for anything but an emetic afterwards). Turn the heat off immediately the liquid boils and leave the fish completely covered in the stock until quite cold.

See also pp. 52-3 and 237; pp. 98-9, 136-7 and 246-8 (recipes).

SALMON TROUT: see Sea Trout

SARDINES   J F M A M J J A S O N D
                                         ☆ ☆ ☆ ● ● ●

The whole fresh fish are excellent grilled or barbecued.

SCALLOPS   J F M A M J J A S O N D
                                     ★ ★ ★ · · · · · · ☆ ☆ ★

To clean scallops if you buy large scallops complete in their double shell, hold the round top in a towel and cut through the hinge and round the joint with a sharp knife while twisting the shell open. Rinse under running water and discard the greeny-black sac and the frilly 'garter'. Most fishmongers now sell them just on the one flat shell with these initial stages already accomplished. Queenies are small scallops – a Manx speciality.

See also pp. 40-1 (preparation); pp. 40-1 and 59-60 (recipes).

SCAMPI: see Langoustines

SEA BASS · · · · · · ★ ★ ★ ★ ★ ★

Excellent white fish with perhaps the most delicate flavour of all.
See also p. 165 (recipe suggestion); pp. 97 and 177 (recipes).

SEA BREAM ★ ★ ★ ★ ★ ★ ★

Delicate white flesh. Grill or bake.

SEA TROUT ★ ★ ★ ★ ★ ·

Also called salmon trout. Similar to salmon but has infinitely more delicate
pink flesh. Cook as grilse or medium-sized salmon.
See also p. 120 (recipe).

SHRIMPS · ☆ ★ ★ ★ ★ ★ ★ ★ · ·

SKATE ★ ★ ☆ · · · · · ★ ★ ★ ★

Silky soft-fleshed cartilagenous flat fish.

SMELT ★ ★ ★   ★ ★ ★ ★

Small, slim, semi-oily silver fish. Fry.

SPINY LOBSTER: see Crawfish

SPRATS ★ ★ ★   ★ ★ ★

Small, oily fish. Grill. The excellent smoked sprat is around from November until the spring.

SQUID · · · · ★ ★ ★ ★ ★ ★ ○ ○

Squid are easy to clean. Cut off the head and tentacles in one piece. Discard the eyes, being careful that their ink does not squirt everywhere.
Squeeze out the guts and gunge from the body sheath (you can pick out
the ink sac and keep for Spanish dishes such as black rice). Pull out the
transparent 'collar-stiffener' quill from the wall of the sheath. The mottled
skin on the outside scrapes off readily. You are left with the edible white

sheath and tentacles to slice and fry, chop and use in many different preparations, or stuff and bake or grill.

TUNA	J	F	M	A	M	J	J	A	S	O	N	D
	○	○	○	○	○	○	○	○	○	○	○	○

A firm, meaty, oily fish, well suited to grills and barbecues.

TURBOT	J	F	M	A	M	J	J	A	S	O	N	D
	★	★	·	☆	☆	☆	☆	★	★	★	★	★

The most highly-prized of the firm-fleshed, white, meaty flat-fish. The whole fish can be vast – usually sold filleted.

See also p. 165 (recipe suggestion); p. 98 (recipe).

WHELKS	J	F	M	A	M	J	J	A	S	O	N	D
	·	·	·	☆	☆	★	★	★	★	☆	☆	·

Large predatory mollusc. Best when young and briefly cooked. Tends toward the rubbery.

WHITEBAIT	J	F	M	A	M	J	J	A	S	O	N	D
		★	★	★	★	★	★					

The tiny fry of several species of fish. Usually prepared by tossing in flour and frying. Most often now sold from frozen.

WHITING	J	F	M	A	M	J	J	A	S	O	N	D
	★	★	·	·	·	·	☆	☆	☆	☆	★	★

Unassuming white fish. Treat as inferior haddock.

WINKLES	J	F	M	A	M	J	J	A	S	O	N	D
	☆	☆	☆	☆					☆	☆	☆	☆

Tiny, tasty black sea snails. Eat by winkling them out with a pin. Once a popular Sunday tea-time delicacy served with brown bread and butter.

WITCH	J	F	M	A	M	J	J	A	S	O	N	D
	★	★	★					★	★	★	★	★

Treat as inferior sole.

MEAT, POULTRY AND GAME

At its best, butchery is still an everyday high street craft. You cannot ask a supermarket chilled cabinet to throw in the trimmings for your cat!

BEEF   J F M A M J J A S O N D
★ ★ ★ ★ ★ ★ ★ ★ ★ ★ ★ ★

UK with some Irish and European imports. From breeds such as the Aberdeen Angus and Hereford, Britain produces some of the best beef in the world. The best cuts benefit from hanging for about two weeks, when the meat becomes quite dark and plum-coloured. Even some supermarkets have now recognised the advantages in eating quality and offer what they call 'traditionally matured beef'. A good veining and marbling of creamy fat imparts succulence and flavour, although as the market has become more obsessed about animal fat and squeamish, farmers have responded with leaner and consequently less toothsome breeds. On the other hand, the move towards organically produced 'real' beef can only be applauded.

Apart from traditional British cuts, American and continental butchery techniques are now supplying the top end of the market with some interesting new cuts.

See also p. 74 (recipe suggestion); pp. 157-8 (recipe).

CHICKEN   J F M A M J J A S O N D
★ ★ ★ ★ ★ ★ ★ ★ ★ ★ ★ ★

UK supplemented with European imports and speciality imports, especially from France. You get what you pay for: cheap ordinary fresh chicken will come from crowded conditions, be pumped up with water to massage the texture, and taste of either nothing or fish meal (some are now marked to inform you that no water has been added). Most frozen broiler birds are infected with salmonella, which is only killed off by thorough cooking. Free-range are sometimes, but not necessarily, better. The conditions in which corn-fed chickens (with their yellow flesh), and the small and succulent poussins and spring chickens are raised are sometimes as industrial as those for ordinary broilers. Some are good, some not so.

Properly free-range fresh birds from farms and specialist producers, hung for a few days (some purists go up to two weeks) are a revelation, but, of course, more expensive. Poulet Noir (a particular breed) often taste very good. The best bird of all, from high quality specialist importers, is the French Poulet de Bresse.

Most birds sold now are for roasting or cutting into joints and grilling, braising, frying or using in a wealth of recipe dishes. Older, tougher boiling fowl have excellent flavour for stocks, soups, stews and pies. Capons are castrated cocks which make good large roasting birds.

See also pp. 53 and 128 (recipe sugestions); pp. 62-4, 133-4, 188-90 and 223 (recipes).

DUCK   J F M A M J J A S O N D

☆ ☆ ☆ ☆ ☆ ☆ ★ ★ ★ ★ ★

UK and Irish and European imports. Farmed ducks of mediocre-to-plain dull quality and their joints are available all year. Traditionally-raised fresh farm birds are at their best in the latter half of the year.

The fancier end of the market has made much of imported vacuum-packed duck *magrets* (sometimes, most would say mistakenly, seen as *mai-gret*), for the last few years. Debate rages about whether a proper *magret* must come from a force-fed duck raised for its foie gras. Correctly, a *magret* is only the larger muscles of the duck's breast, the smaller, sweeter bit being called the *supreme* (as with a chicken). Most of the *magrets* you can buy here are the whole breast, just hunks of red meat to be cooked in the same way as a steak but rather less interesting.

Wild duck – such as mallard and teal – is a totally different thing.

GOOSE   J F M A M J J A S O N D

★ ★ ★ ★

Farmed. A heavy-boned bird with substantial fat coverage. Until you are used to them, buy much larger ones than you suppose you'll need. Roasted properly, the flesh is full-flavoured and smooth in texture. Old birds can be inedibly stringy. Collect the fat for cassoulet and roasting potatoes.

See also p. 238; pp. 239-40 (recipe).

GROUSE   J F M A M J J A S O N D

★ ★ ★ ☆ ☆

The best of game birds, either young and roasted or older and casseroled. Check with your supplier whether it has hung for the desirable couple of days first.

GUINEA-FOWL   J F M A M J J A S O N D

★ ☆ ☆ ☆ · · ★ ★ ★ ★ ★ ★

Farmed. In flavour, half-way between chicken and a game bird. Season well all over, inside and out, stuff with half an orange, then roast on a rack over a roasting tin at Gas 6/200°C/400°F for about an hour. If possible, and your butcher hasn't done so already, hang for a few days first.

HARE   J F M A M J J A S O N D

★ ★ ★ ☆ ☆ ★ ★ ★

Hang for a week or so, depending on conditions, before gutting. Young hares – levrets – can be roasted whole. Usually only the saddle is roasted of older animals, with the rest being casseroled.

See also pp. 42-3 (preparation); pp. 225-6 (recipe).

LAMB   J F M A M J J A S O N D
☆ ★ ☆ ★ ★ ★ ★ ★ ☆ ☆ ☆ ☆

Don't ignore the qualities of mature lamb, or hogget, in the first few months of the year. Although some British lambs are brought forward for the Easter season, the majority are born in early summer and eaten, still at their absolute prime, until the end of August.

See also p. 53; p. 92 (recipe suggestion); pp. 65-6, 66-7, 140-1 and 179-80 (recipes).

MALLARD   J F M A M J J A S O N D
☆ ☆   ☆ ☆ ★ ★

Large wild duck with lean gamey flesh. Doesn't require more than a day's hanging.

PARTRIDGE   J F M A M J J A S O N D
☆   ☆ ★ ★ ☆

Hang for a few days if possible, if your supplier hasn't already attended to this. Roast.

PHEASANT   J F M A M J J A S O N D
☆   ☆ ★ ★

The largest game bird – cocks more so than the supposedly more toothsome hens.

See also p. 203; p. 219 (recipe suggestion).

PIGEON   J F M A M J J A S O N D
★ ★   ☆ ★ ★ ★ ★

For the tenderest meat, choose plump-breasted birds with pinky, rather than dark red, flesh. Most sorts of pigeon can be eaten but, of those commonly available here, the wood pigeon has the best flavour.

PORK   J F M A M J J A S O N D
★ ★ ★ ★ ☆ ☆ ☆ ☆ ★ ★ ★ ★

Britain is virtually self-sufficient in pork, with just a few joints creeping in from Denmark.

See also pp. 74 and 185-6 (recipe suggestions); pp. 80-1, 178-9, 192-3 and 208 (recipes).

QUAIL   J F M A M J J A S O N D
                                           · · · ☆ ☆ ☆ ☆ ★ · · · ·

Farmed in Britain and so available all the year round, but only really worth
searching out when there is no other game around.

RABBIT   J F M A M J J A S O N D
                                           ★ ★ ☆ ☆ ☆ ☆ ☆ ★ ★ ★ ★ ★

Farmed rabbit is reared in Britain and imported from China. Wild has a
mild gamey flavour.

See also pp. 196-7, 206-8 and 226-7 (recipes).

SNIPE   J F M A M J J A S O N D
                                           ☆   ☆ ☆ ☆ ★ ☆

Long-billed game bird best served roasted. One of the creatures one is supposed to cook with its guts in.

TEAL   J F M A M J J A S O N D
                                           ☆ ☆   ☆ ☆ ★ ★

Small wild duck. Roast or grill, no hanging required.

TURKEY   J F M A M J J A S O N D
                                           ★ ☆ ☆ ☆ ☆ · · · ☆ ☆ ★ ★

See p. 219 (recipe suggestion).

VEAL   J F M A M J J A S O N D
                                           ☆ ☆ ☆ ☆ ☆ ☆ ☆ ☆ ☆ ☆ ☆ ☆

Calf-rearing for veal is now supposed to be more respectable than its recent reputation. Wrestle with your own conscience.

VENISON   J F M A M J J A S O N D
                                           ★ ☆ ☆   · · ★ ★ ★ ★

Farmed animals are beginning to make venison an everday meat. The flavour of wild usually has more character.

See also pp. 81-2 (recipe).

WOODCOCK   J F M A M J J A S O N D
                                           ☆   ☆ ★ ★

Small long-billed game bird, slightly larger than snipe. Hang for a couple of
days and roast with its guts still in.

CHEESE

A certain well-known cheesemonger's in Jermyn Street, which looks and smells like everybody's ideal of a high-class London cheese-shop, recently told me that there is 'no such thing as seasonality in cheese, sir. It is all the same, all year round'. Admittedly, the quality of the product has to be high before differences begin to show. Many supermarkets and delis keep the stuff in such unsuitable conditions – too cold or tightly suffocating in plastic – that, sure enough, everything they stock tastes pretty uniformly of mild, pure, baby soap. At the other end of the spectrum, the best cheese shop in London is Jeroboam's.

The staff there realise that, of course, cheese is seasonal; the milk's qualities depends on the pasture, which has as distinct a growing period as any crop; the climatic conditions at the time of processing affect the final character of the cheese, and cheeses take different lengths of time to mature.

With the exception of cheese made from goat's milk, most production takes a dip in high summer. Goat's milk cheese is not available at its best in winter. The most comprehensive catalogue of cheese presently available is Androuet's *Guide du Fromage*, on which the seasonal information for the very personal selection of cheeses below is based. As it is impossible to give specific months for most cheeses, the best periods are given in seasons. French cheeses from the strictly controlled *appellation d'origine* areas are shown below as Ad'O.

APPENZELLER   *all year, dip in spring*

Switzerland's best answer to Cheddar. Eat at least 18 months old.

BANON   *spring, summer*

Bomb-shaped, mild, dense, soft cheese, wrapped in leaves and tied with raffia.

BEAUFORT (Ad'O)   *winter, spring, summer*

Rich, hard cheese. Eat a year old made from the winter milk if possible.

BEAUMONT   *summer, autumn*

Mild, disk made from unpasteurised cow's milk.

BLEU D'AUVERGNE (Ad'O)   *all year*

Firm, sharp, strong blue cheese made from cow's milk.

BLEU DES CAUSSES (Ad'O) *summer, autumn*

Medium-flavoured blue cheese made from cow's milk made close to the Roquefort region.

BOULETTE D'AVESNES *summer, autumn, winter*

Soft, red washed-rind flavoured with herbs.

BRESSE BLEU *all year*

Popular, commercially produced soft blue.

BRIE DE MEAUX (Ad'O) *summer, autumn, winter*

The brie that comes in large wheels. Always best made from unpasteurised milk.

See also pp. 186-7.

BRIE DE MELUN (Ad'O) *summer, autumn, winter*

Smaller cheeses than Brie de Meaux, also more solid, saltier and more liable to dry up.

BONCHESTER *all year*

The British answer to Roquefort. Inconsistent.

CAERPHILLY *all year*

A cheese best eaten fresh rather than kept for any time.

See also p. 111.

CAMEMBERT (Ad'O) *end spring, summer, autumn*

The *fermier* made from unpasteurised milk always has more depth of flavour and a greater likelihood of acheiving a good soft texture than pasteurised brands.

See also p. 239.

CANTAL (Ad'O) *summer, autumn*

Good French farmhouse equivalent of Cheddar.

CARRÉ DE L'EST *all year*

Commercially produced, mild square relative of Coulommiers.

CASHEL BLUE *sporadic throughout year*

A truly fine soft Irish blue cheese, best eaten when it is sagging and weeping and the rind is dusted with red mould.

CHAOURCE (Ad'O)   *summer, autumn*

Soft, mild cow's milk cheese with a bloomy rind.

CHAROLAIS   *summer, autumn*

One of the best goat's milk cheeses produced in France. Dense and white, in the form of a truncated cone, with a pronounced nuttiness.

CHEDDAR   *all year, made from spring and summer milk*

The only ones with real depth of character are farmhouse labels such as Montgomery. Best eaten a year old, when the flavour is full and nutty without being aggressively tangy.

   See also pp. 54, 129, 166.

CHESHIRE   *all year*

The best is the nutty Appleby, many experts' favourite British cheese.
   See also p. 186.

CHEVROTINS   *summer, autumn*

Various varieties of mild, pleasant, French goat's milk cheese.

COMTE (Ad'O)   *summer, autumn, winter*

French relative of Gruyère.

COTHERSTONE   *summer, autumn, winter*

Supple cheese from the Yorkshire Dales. Inclined toward soapy texture and bland flavour but occasionally very pleasant.

COULOMMIERS   *summer, autumn, winter*

Tangy soft cheese with bloomy rind speckled with rusty mould.

CROTTIN DE CHAVIGNOL (Ad'O)   *dried for winter*

Small, hard, strong pellets of dried, mature goat's milk cheese.

DOUBLE BERKLEY   *rare*

Made only by Charles Martell in Gloucestershire.
   See also p. 93.

EPOISSES   *summer, autumn, winter*

Pungent soft cheese with shiny brick-coloured rind, washed with local spirit (*marc*).

EXPLORATEUR   *all year*
Commercially produced very full-fat cheese.

FOURME D'AMBERT (Ad'O)   *summer, autumn*
Exquisite, creamy, well-balanced blue cheese.

GORGONZOLA   *all year*
Commercially produced soft, full-flavoured Italian blue cheese.
  See also p. 54.

GRATTE PAILLE   *summer, autumn, winter*
Fine, soft, well-balanced cheese.

GRUYÈRE   *late summer to late winter*
The classic Swiss cheese.

LAGUIOLE (Ad'O)   *summer, autumn, winter*
Tangy mountain cheese similar to Cantal.

LANGRES   *late spring, summer, autumn*
Pungent soft cheese with light brown washed rind. Good eaten with *marc*.

LEZAY   *summer*
Good commercially produced goat's milk cheese.

MAROILLES (Ad'O)   *summer, autumn, winter*
Flat, square, soft cheese with shiny orange-brown rind, a horribly persis-
tant odour and a remarkable full flavour.

MIMOLETTE   *all year*
Commercially produced northern French and Dutch spheres, resembling
orange-brown Gouda and, if mature, with a gentle, nutty flavour.

MONTRACHET   *late spring, summer, autumn*
Good, mild goat's milk cheese wrapped in leaves.

NEUFCHATEL (Ad'O)   *all year*
A range of soft, white, smooth, salty, bloomy-rinded cow's milk cheeses
from the north of France. Around Valentine's Day, they are produced in a
somewhat tacky heart-shape. An excellent variety is the log-shaped Boudard de Neufchâtel.

PITHIVIERS AU FOIN   *summer, autumn*

Flat, square, soft cheese wrapped sparcely in hay and tasting of fresh meadows.

PONT L'EVÊQUE (Ad'O)   *summer, autumn, winter*

Tangy soft cheese with smooth apricot rind. One of the most important cheeses of Normandy
    See also p. 129.

REBLOCHON (Ad'O)   *summer, autumn*

Mild-tasting supple cow's milk cheese, with a faint smell of fresh earth.

RIBBLESDALE   *summer, autumn, winter*

Fine supple cheese from the Yorkshire Dales.

RIGOTTE   *all year*

Pleasant, bland, commercially produced cheese, sometimes with a rind dusted with paprika.

ROQUEFORT (Ad'O)   *all year*

Salty, piquant ewe's milk blue cheese. The *Societé* label is a sign of fair quality but for real excellence, look instead for the names *Gabriel Coulet* or *Papillon* on the foil wrappers.

SARIETTE   *rare*

Beautiful white, soft, chalky cheese coated with the herb savory. The same people make another variety containing olives.

SAINT-FLORENTIN   *summer, autumn, early winter*

Good, pungent soft cheese from Burgundy, with a shiny washed rind.

SAINT-MARCELLIN   *all year*

Mild, soft cheese with delicate grey natural rind

SAINTE-MAURE   *summer, autumn*

One of France's best goat's milk cheeses.

SAINT-NECTAIRE   *summer, autumn*

Semi-hard cheese with a mild edge of old cellars. The best has lozenge-shapes imprinted into the rind.

SHARPHAM   *late spring, summer, autumn*

Excellent English answer to Brie.

SINGLE GLOUCESTER   *all year*

Another excellent rarity from Charles Martell.

STILTON   *all year with a dip after Christmas*

King of British blue cheeses.
   See also pp. 45-6 and 238-9.

TOMME DE SAVOIE   *late spring, summer, autumn*

Mildly nutty.

VACHERIN MONT D'OR (Ad'O)   *late autumn, winter, spring*

Fabulous, rich, runny cheese. A Christmas and winter favourite all over
Europe.
   See also pp. 203 and 239.

WHEATLANDS   *spring, summer, autumn*

Soft, rich, British cheese with a fine edge of fresh hay.

RESTAURANTS

Addresses for chefs mentioned in text.

In spite of having worked on it, I still say that *The Good Food Guide* is the
best guide to restaurants in this country, in that – whether you agree with
the selection and ratings or not – it is the only comprehensive one to give
fully written reviews rather than bland advertising copy or rows of
symbols.

JEREMY ASHPOOL, *Jeremy's at the King's Head*, South Street, Cuckfield,
   West Sussex
RAYMOND BLANC, *Le Manoir aux Quat'Saisons*, Church Road, Great
   Milton, Oxfordshire
JOHN BURTON-RACE, *L'Ortolan*, The Old Vicarage, Church Lane, Shin-
   field, near Reading, Berkshire
DAVID CHAMBERS, *Oak Room*, *Le Meridien*, Piccadilly, London W1

DAVID DORRICOTT, *Truffles*, *Portman Inter-Continental*, 22 Portman Square, London W1

SIMON HOPKINSON, *Bibendum*, Michelin House, 81 Fulham Road, London DW3

ED KEELING, *Hyatt Regency New Orleans*, Poydtas Plaza and Loyola Avenue, New Orleans, Louisiana, USA

ROS HUNTER, *Village Restaurant*, Market Place, Ramsbottom, Lancashire

KEVIN KENNEDY, *Boulestin*, 1A Henrietta Street, London, WC2

JOHN KING, *Ritz Club*, Piccadilly, London W1

PETER KROMBERG, *Le Soufflé*, *Inter-Continental*, 1 Hamilton Place, London W1

ROWLEY LEIGH, *Kensington Place*, 201-205 Kensington Church Street, London W8

PRU LEITH, *Leith's*, 92 Kensington Park Road, London W11

JOHN LOUNTON (sous chef), *The Dorchester*, Park Lane, London W1 (closing for 14 months' refurbishment from late 1988)

IAN MCANDREW (formerly of Restaurant 74, Canterbury), plans to open in Queens Gate, London, in late 1988

ANTON MOSIMANN, *Mosimann's* (formerly the Belfry Club), West Halkin Street, London SW1

JOHN MURRAY, at the time of writing, working with Roger Vergé in France. A name to watch for the future.

PEDRO SUBIJANA, *Akelarre*, Paseo Igueldo s/n, San Sebastian, Spain

FRANCO TARUSCHIO, *Walnut Tree Inn*, Llandewi Skirrid, near Abergavenny, Gwent

PRODUCERS AND RETAILERS

Addresses for those mentioned in text

The most useful trade directory of specialist producers nationwide is Henrietta Green's *British Food Finds*.

Pasta
Lina's, 18 Brewer Street, London W1

Cheese
Mrs Gwynfor Adams (Caerphilly), Fferm Glyneithinog, Pontselei, near Boncarth, Dyfed

A. L. and F. I. Appleby (farmhouse Cheshire), Hawkstone Abbey Farm, Weston-under-Redcastle, Shrewsbury, Salop

Michael Day (wholesale), The Huge Cheese Company Ltd. The Old School House, Upper Dickler, Hailsham, East Sussex

Charles Martell (Double Berkley, Single and Double Gloucester), Laurel Farm, Dymock, Gloucestershire; stall in Cirencester market on Mondays and Fridays

Jeroboams (best retail in London), 24 Bute Street, London SW7

Manor Farm (Montgomery farmhouse Cheddar), North Cadbury Court, near Yeovil, Somerset

Amanda and George Streatfeild (Streatfeild Hood farmhouse Cheddar), Denhay Farm, Broadoak, Bridport, Dorset

Hugh Rance (retail and wholesale), Wells Stores, Reading Road, Streatley, Berkshire

Fish

Mike Buchanan (fine Scottish smoked salmon), Wood Cottage, Otter Ferry, Argyll.

Ken Condon (best smoked salmon in London, also wet fish), 363 Wandsworth Road, London SW8

Mr Crispin (wet fish), West End Supplies, 10 Mill Street, Kingsbridge, Devon

J & W Griggs (fine smoked salmon, also wet fish), 130 High Street, Hythe, Kent; also a shed on the Landing Beach, Hythe

Meat

Edward Hamer (Welsh lamb), Plynlimon House, Llanidloes, Powys; also shops in Machynlleth and Rhayader

---

BIBLIOGRAPHY
as mentioned in text

The best cookery book shop in London is Heidi Lascelles's, Books for Cooks, 4 Blenheim Crescent, London W11.

J. ANDERSON, *The Food of Portugal*, Robert Hale, London, 1987

P. ANDROUET, *Guide du Fromage*, Aidan Ellis Publishing Ltd, Henley-on-Thames, 1983

S. BECK, L. BERTHOLLE AND J. CHILD, *Mastering the Art of French*

Cooking, Volume 1, Cassell & Co, London, 1963; paperback, Penguin 1966

S. BECK AND J. CHILD, *Mastering the Art of French Cooking, Volume 2*, Michael Joseph, London, 1977; paperback, Penguin 1978

M. BERRIEDALE-JOHNSON, *The British Museum Cookbook*, British Museum Publications, London, 1987

S. CAMPBELL, *English Cookery New & Old*, Consumers' Association and Hodder & Stoughton, London, 1981

P. CASAS, *The Foods and Wines of Spain*, Alfred A Knopf Inc, New York, 1982; paperback, Penguin 1985

M. COSTA, *Four Seasons Cookery Book*, Thomas Nelson & Sons Ltd, London, 1970; paperback, Papermac 1981

E. DAVID, *An Omelette and a Glass of Wine*, Robert Hale, London, 1984; paperback, Penguin 1986

E. DAVID, *French Provincial Cooking*, Michael Joseph, London 1960; paperback, Penguin 1964

A. DAVIDSON, *North Atlantic Seafood*, Macmillan, London, 1979; paperback, Penguin 1980

A. DEL CONTE, *Gastronomy of Italy*, Bantam Press, London, 1987

E. DE POMIANE, *Cooking with Pomiane*, Bruno Cassirer (Publishers) Ltd, London, 1962

J. DIMBLEBY, *The Josceline Dimbleby Christmas Book*, Martin Books, London, 1987

N. DOUGLAS, *Venus in the Kitchen*, William Heinemann Ltd, London, 1952; paperback as *Lovers' Cookbook*, New English Library, London, 1971

J. EGERTON, *Southern Food*, Alfred A Knopf Inc, New York, 1987

H. FAWCETT, *The Good Food Guide Second Dinner Party Book*, Consumers' Association and Hodder & Stoughton, London, 1979

H. GREEN, *British Food Finds*, Rich & Green, London, 1987

J. GRIGSON, *Jane Grigson's Vegetable Book*, Michael Joseph, London, 1978; paperback, Penguin 1980

M. HAZAN, *Classic Italian Cookbook*, Macmillan, London, 1980; paperback, Papermac 1981

M. HAZAN, *The Second Classic Italian Cookbook*, Macmillan, London, 1978; paperback, Papermac 1983

M. HAZAN, *Marcella's Italian Kitchen*, Macmillan, London, 1987

E. LAMBERT ORTIZ, *The Book of Latin American Cooking*, Robert Hale, London, 1984; paperback, Penguin 1985

I. MCANDREW, *A Feast of Fish*, Macdonald Orbis, London, 1987

B. MAHER, *Classic Cakes*, Walker Books, London, 1986

J. F. MARIANNI, *The Dictionary of American Food and Drink*, Ticknor & Fields, New York, 1983

B. NEAL, *Bill Neal's Southern Cooking*, University of North Carolina Press, Chapel Hill, 1985

C. RODEN, *A Book of Middle Eastern Food*, Thomas Nelson, London, 1968; paperback, Penguin 1970; reissue as *A New Book of Middle Eastern Food*, Viking, London, 1985; paperback, Penguin 1986

C. RODEN, *Mediterranean Cookery*, BBC Books, London, 1987

I. S. ROMBAUER AND M. ROMBAUER BECHER, *The Joy of Cooking*, enlarged for 5th edition, Dent, London, 1975

H. SABERI, *Noshe Djan: Afghan Food and Cookery*, Prospect Books, London, 1986

D. SMITH (ed), *The Good Food Guide*, Consumers' Association and Hodder & Stoughton, London, annual

J. STERN AND M. STERN, *Real American Food*, Alfred A Knopf Inc, New York, 1986

E. VIEIRA, *The Taste of Portugal*, Robert Hale, London, 1988

A. WILLAN, *French Regional Cooking*, Hutchinson, London, 1981; paperback, Hutchinson 1983

A. WILLAN, *Observer French Cookery School*, Macdonald, London, 1980; paperback Macdonald 1983.

INDEX

Page numbers in **bold** type indicate entries in the Glossary. The Glossary generally gives a description of ingredient and indicates the best times to buy. Where in addition to this, ideas for preparing, cooking and eating are given, these are indexed separately.

chicken 26, **307**; buying 35, 53, 54, 75, 93, 111, 128, 148, 166, 186, 203, 220, 238; cooking ideas 53, 128, 273, 307, in Recipes 46, 133, 153, 171, (giblets) 196; used 45-6, 75-7, 178-9, 196-7, 206-8
  Blackened chicken sandwich 133-4
  Chicken and salsify phyllo pie 62-4
  Circassian chicken 223
  Sweetcorn and chicken chowder 188-90
chicken livers: cooking ideas 21, in Recipe 135; used 209
chickpeas 16; used 140-1, 214-5
  Toasted chickpeas 35-6
chicory *see* Belgian chicory
chilli oil 16
chilli peppers 19-20, **259**; buying 32, 51, 72, 88-9, 108, 126-7, 146, 163-4, 183, 201, 217, 235-6; cooking, eating ideas 20, (dried and powder) 167-8, in Recipes 224; used 157-8
  Oriental beef pot-roast 157-8
  Roasting peppers 150-2
Chinese cooking 19, 19-20, 253, **261-3**, 268, 269, 272, 275, 282; Recipes 131, 137-9, 157-8; Steaming dough 101
Chinese artichokes **264**; buying 32, 51, 217, 236; cooking ideas 264
Chinese flowering cabbage 263
Chinese keys (galangale) **262**
Chinese leaves **259-60**; buying 32, 51, 72, 88-9, 108, 126-7, 146, 163, 163-4, 183, 201, 217; Recipe ideas 157
  Prawn filling 102
Chinese mustard greens **263**
Chinese parsley *see* coriander
Chinese split buns 101-2
chip butties 133
chips (parsnips) 72
chips (potatoes) 279; Recipe idea 55
chitterlings: cooking ideas 75
chives **271**; buying 146, 163-4, 183; cooking, eating ideas 171, 174, 181
chocolate, for cooking 17
  Linda Sue's chocolate cheesecake 86-7
choi-sum **263**
chowder: Sweetcorn and chicken chowder 188-90
christophene **284-5**
chutney, mango: sandwiches 133
cider 16

cilantro *see* coriander
cinnamon 20; Recipe ideas 224, 226-7
Circassian chicken 223
citrus fruits, easy-peel **290**; *see also* individual fruits
clams **299**; buying 34, 53, 74, 92, 110, 128, 148, 165, 185, 202, 219, 237; cooking 299
  Spanish clams 204
Clapham peasant stew 226-7
Classic béarnaise 171-3
Classic mayonnaise 168-71
claytonia: in salads 135
clementines **290**; buying 33, 51, 52, 218, 236-7
cob nuts, Kentish **291**; buying 202
cobbler: fruit cobbler 197-8
cockles **299**; buying 34, 53, 74, 92, 110, 128, 148, 165, 185, 202, 218, 219, 237
cocoa powder 17
coconuts **289**; buying 33, 52, 73, 89, 127, 147, 165, 184, 202, 218, 236-7; Recipe ideas 32-3
cod 19 (salt cod), **299**; buying 52, 53, 148, 165, 185, 202, 219, 237; cooking ideas 52, in Recipe 171 (salt cod), 175
  Salt cod with leeks and truffles 37-8
Cold baked hake 175-6
Cold olive-oily broad beans in their pods 114-5
coley **299**; buying 53, 185, 202, 219, 237; cooking ideas 34, 299
'collards' 257; *see also* greens
Common or garden corn bread 192
conger eel **299**; buying 34, 53, 74, 89, 92, 110, 185, 202, 219, 237
  Conger eel bake 79
coriander leaves 20, **271-2**; Recipe idea 77-8
coriander seeds: spice **272**
  Okra and new potato salad 77-8
corn, and corn on the cob *see* sweetcorn
corn meal: bread Recipes 191-2
corn salad (lamb's lettuce) 146, **275**
corn syrup *see* golden syrup
courgette flowers 260
courgettes **260**; buying 32, 51, 72, 88-9, 108, 126, 126-7, 146, 163-4, 183, 201, 217, (baby courgettes) 164; cooking ideas 183, in Recipes 154, 224
  Courgette and mushroom salade tiède 135-6